ENGLISH G Grammatik

Test- und Übungsbuch

Cornelsen

Dieses Test- und Übungsbuch wurde verfaßt von

Prof. Franz Vettel, Heppenheim
Prof. Hellmut Schwarz, Mannheim

in Zusammenarbeit mit

David W. Bygott, Oxford
Helen Weiss, Heidelberg

und der Verlagsredaktion:

Martin Rosenthal (Redaktionsleitung) unter Mitarbeit von
Margaret Kersten

Zeichnungen:

Robert Broomfield (Exercise-Teil), Tunbridge Wells
Gabriele Heinisch (S. 138), Berlin
Erich Rauschenbach (Test yourself-Teil), Berlin

Erläuterung der im Test- und Übungsbuch verwendeten Symbole:

* bezeichnet Testsätze, in denen grammatikalische Erscheinungen behandelt werden, die man nur zu verstehen, aber nicht selbst zu verwenden braucht.

□ bezeichnet Testsätze, in denen es um grammatikalische Erscheinungen geht, die in der Regel erst in der Sekundarstufe II behandelt werden.

• bezeichnet Übungen mit höherem Schwierigkeitsgrad.

Die dem Test- und Übungsbuch zugrundeliegende ENGLISH G Grammatik hat die Bestellnummer 3728.

1. Auflage – 10. Druck 1992
Alle Drucke dieser Auflage können, weil untereinander unverändert, im Unterricht nebeneinander verwendet werden.

Druck: Cornelsen Druck, Berlin

ISBN 3-464-00319-1
Vertrieb: Cornelsen Verlagsgesellschaft, Bielefeld
Bestellnummer 3191

ENGLISH G Grammatik
Test- und Übungsbuch

Key to the exercises

Cornelsen

ENGLISH G Grammatik

Test- und Übungsbuch · Key to the exercises

1. Auflage – 10. Druck 1992
Alle Drucke dieser Auflage können, weil untereinander unverändert, im Unterricht nebeneinander verwendet werden.

Druck: Druckhaus Langenscheidt, Berlin

ISBN 3-464-00319-1
Vertrieb: Cornelsen Verlagsgesellschaft, Bielefeld
Bestellnummer 3191 (Key)

INHALT

Seite

1. The noun and the article · Das Nomen und der Artikel 3
2. The adjective and the adverb · Das Adjektiv und das Adverb 4
3. Quantifiers, the pronoun, question words, word order Mengenbezeichnungen, das Pronomen, Fragewörter, Wortstellung 7
4. Modals - Modale Hilfsverben 9
5. The main verb: forms and tenses · Das Vollverb: Formen und Zeiten 13
6. The main verb: the simple form and the progressive form in different tenses · Das Vollverb: Die simple form und die progressive form in verschiedenen Tempora 15
7. The passive · Das Passiv 20
8. The infinitive · Der Infinitiv 22
9. The gerund and gerund or infinitive · Das Gerundium und Gerundium oder Infinitiv 24
10. The participle · Das Partizip 26
11. Reported Speech · Indirekte Rede 29
12. Clauses · Gliedsätze 36

1. The noun and the article · Das Nomen und der Artikel

1

1. shelves	5. potatoes	9. sheep	13. beaches
2. aircraft	6. surveys	10. feet	14. heroes
3. roofs	7. children	11. countries	
4. studios	8. sportsmen	12. sexes	

2

1. Belgians	3. Israelis	5. Frenchmen	7. Americans
2. Swiss	4. Danes	6. Japanese	8. Englishmen

3 editions, explosions, leaflets, losses, populations, prizes, receivers, schedules, sources, thirds

4 countable (sing.): spice, apprentice, telex, lioness
countable (pl.): mice, pros, lights, slices
uncountable (sing.): advice, electricity, progress, happiness, chaos, homework, news, politeness, radiation, discrimination, U.S.A.
uncountable (pl.): outskirts, thanks, clothes, pliers, tights, police

5

1. a lot of/no/little	5. a little	9. a bit of
2. much more/further	6. a few	10. very
3. much	7. a fine	
4. a lot of/much	8. are the	

6

1. further information
2. good news
3. a very good knowledge of English
4. little evidence/proof
5. a lot of damage
6. little good advice
7. No news is good news.
8. This homework is too difficult.
9. I'm sure (that) this furniture is (made of) plastic.

•7

1. much	6. a little	11. countries	16. decorators
2. news	7. luck	12. few	17. a lot of
3. a lot of	8. a lot	13. much	18. progress
4. a/some	9. radios	14. damage	19. a little
5. knowledge	10. these	15. conveyor-belts	20. information

8

1. them
2. Were they; ones
3. are; them
4. ones; pair of
5. have; them; pairs

•9 1. pollution; 2. society; 3. the knowledge; 4. discrimination; 5. permission; 6. life; 7. the pride; 8. Spain; 9. electricity; 10. happiness; 11. politics; 12. defence; the modernization

10 1. petrol; 2. Parliament; 3. the textbooks; 4. nature; 5. young people; 6. American society; 7. the bread; 8. the life; 9. Grandad/Grandfather; 10. the Kellers'; 11. women

11 1. -; 2. -; 3. the; 4. -; 5. -; 6. -; 7. the; 8. -; 9. the

12 1. an; 2. -; 3. a; 4. -; 5. a; 6. an; 7. a; 8. a; 9. a; 10. an

13 1. -; 2. the; 3. an; 4. -; 5. a; 6. -; 7. -; 8. -; 9. -; 10. -; 11. the; 12. -; 13. the; 14. -; 15. -; 16. the; 17. a; 18. -; 19. the; 20. -; 21. a; 22. a; 23. the; 24. -; 25. an; 26. -

2. The adjective and the adverb - Das Adjektiv und das Adverb

1 1. - ; -; 2. man; 3. men/women; man/woman; 4. - ; -; 5. man; -; 6. -

2 1. the most sensible thing; 2. the new; 3. the important; the unimportant; 4. The best thing; 5. the possible

3 1. ones; 2. ones; 3. side/aspect/problem; 4. one; 5. -; 6. one; 7. -

4
1. smaller
2. models
3. lighter
4. series
5. calculators
6. heavier
7. more powerful
8. -
9. more attractive
10. machines
11. larger
12. models
13. easier
14. calculators
15. more convenient
16. machines
17. more useful
18. less expensive
19. series
20. -

5
1. more convenient
2. bigger
3. (the) saddest
4. (the) worst
5. further/farther
6. fitter
7. filthier
8. better
9. (the) most intelligent
10. (the) nicest
11. (the) least
12. (the) most

6
1. nearest
2. oldest
3. latest
4. further
5. oldest
6. next
7. last
8. furthest/farthest

7
1. an alarm clock of her own
2. his own car
3. five children of her own
4. clothes of their own
5. a bedroom of her own/her own bedroom
6. their lives
7. his own money
8. in their own home
9. a house of their own
10. their deaths; their hands; their pockets

•8
1. was seriously damaged
2. is unusually tall for a 13-year-old
3. didn't defend effectively enough
4. the headmaster hadn't come into the room unexpectedly
5. privately educated
6. compared all the documents carefully
7. at such an unbelievably low price
8. their answers are amazingly similar

9
1. democratically elected
2. happily married
3. simply made
4. fully discussed
5. well organized
6. probably chosen
7. wonderfully looked after
8. recently discovered

10
1. hardly
2. pretty/fairly
3. closely
4. fairly/pretty
5. mostly
6. lately
7. high/wide
8. freely
9. high
10. close/near
11. highly
12. just

11

1. different
2. regularly
3. roughly
4. generally
5. finally
6. heavily
7. enthusiastically
8. nearly
9. unacceptably
10. naughty
11. in a silly way
12. rude
13. surprisingly
14. differently
15. just
16. funny
17. really
18. seriously
19. real
20. similarly
21. violent
22. negatively
23. necessarily
24. certainly
25. carefully

12

1. seemed nervous
2. sound very good
3. becomes/gets angry/annoyed
4. tastes really fantastic
5. (carefully) tasted the wine carefully
6. smell very well/properly
7. sounded very excited
8. was/became very popular
9. feel very soft
10. felt ... carefully
11. (gently) felt the wounded dog's leg gently
12. sounds good
13. the sea looked calm
14. became very sad

13

1. historically
2. badly
3. funnily
4. worst
5. more sensibly
6. in a friendly way
7. fastest
8. least
9. better
10. bad
11. effectively
12. fully

14

1. sooner
2. more popular
3. bigger
4. harder
5. more secure
6. higher
7. more
8. fatter
9. longer
10. earlier
11. later
12. exactly
13. less serious
14. more intelligent
15. less famous
16. more ordinary
17. less difficult
18. higher
19. more expensive
20. more boring

15

1. Most of the people in the crowd clapped enthusiastically.
2. Who is going to the anti-apartheid demonstration tomorrow?
3. Have the police come across a case like this before?
4. Unfortunately, the office was closed that day (unfortunately).
5. Lucy usually visits her aunt once a month.
6. Luckily, Peter's car wasn't often at the garage last year.
7. David went to a conference in Hamburg twice two years ago.
8. Generally speaking, Rosemary thoroughly enjoyed her camping holiday in France last year.
9. She has probably already been there.
10. Vanessa plays the violin extremely well.

•16 1. Why does California so often appear ...?
2. This is a topic that writers discuss a lot - perhaps because so many of them choose to live there.
3. A few years ago Christopher Isherwood .../Christopher Isherwood ... said about California a few years ago, "This ... means that we get to the answer soonest."
4. ... the way California's farmers and scientists frequently rush ... .
5. ... Californians never give up searching ... .
6. You definitely can't escape ... he points out that (each year) one in three moves house each year.
7. ... what is going to happen to it tomorrow.
8. ... before he went to the White House in 1981.
9. ... a lot of tourists particularly enjoy .../enjoy about California particularly is ... .

3. Quantifiers, the pronoun, question words, word order
Mengenbezeichnungen, das Pronomen, Fragewörter, Wortstellung

1

1. any	4. any	7. any	10. some
2. some	5. some	8. some	11. some
3. some	6. any	9. any	12. some

2 1/C; 2/D; 3/H; 4/G; 5/I; 6/B; 7/E; 8/F; 9/A

3

1. something terrible	5. somewhere near Bordeaux
2. anywhere in Asia	6. somebody to deliver
3. anything newer	7. something cold
4. anybody from Germany	8. anybody carrying

4

1. All	4. every	7. any	10. each (every)
2. anywhere	5. all	8. each	11. every
3. every (each)	6. every	9. each	12. each

5

1. nobody	4. no	7. Nobody	10. nothing
2. no	5. nowhere	8. none	11. Nothing
3. nothing	6. nothing	9. Nothing	12. nowhere

6

1. nobody to meet	3. nothing to see	5. nothing worth watching
2. nobody to discuss	4. nowhere to park	6. nowhere to put

7

1. neither of them has
2. neither of them
3. both of them like
4. neither of them
5. be either of
6. they both work at the same place
7. none of their friends
8. either of
9. either of the
10. the counters both looked the same

8

1. responsibility; mine
2. choice; ours
3. ability; hers
4. behaviour; theirs
5. suggestion; ours
6. plan; yours

9

1. old schoolmate of ours
2. relation/relative of yours
3. pupil of Inge's
4. books of mine
5. A neighbour of Mrs Kirkley's
6. friend of hers
7. remark of the President's
8. marriage than theirs

10

1. cut herself
2. opened
3. looked after themselves
4. relaxed
5. surprised ourselves
6. imagined
7. heard herself
8. changed
9. introduced themselves
10. remembered
11. hurt themselves
12. wondered
13. did; decide

•11

1. happened
2. remembered
3. had imagined
4. had realized
5. hadn't bought
6. allowed themselves
7. to move/moving
8. said to herself
9. felt
10. concentrating
11. cut her hand
12. hurt myself
13. worry
14. take care of yourself
15. changed

12

1. bought themselves
2. meet
3. buy each other
4. convinced themselves
5. are looking forward
6. stand each other
7. write to each other
8. hurt themselves; kill themselves (injure themselves fatally)

13

1. Who do you mean?
2. What town does she live in?
3. How long has she lived/been living there?
4. And what does she do?
5. What sort of pictures does she paint?
6. Who does she sell her pictures to?
7. How much/What does an Angela Pickering picture cost?
8. And can she sell enough pictures to pay the rent?
9. Would it be possible (Could we) visit her on Saturday?
10. Who has invited us?
11. What is he looking forward to? Meeting me?
12. And who gave him the impression that I could help you?

14

1. What
2. Which
3. What
4. What
5. What
6. What/Which
7. what/which
8. what/which

15

1. told his wife that he wouldn't/ wasn't going to buy his son
2. tell him; told him it
3. said to her; "Show me it/ it to me."
4. he gave it back to her
5. their new coach to the players
6. all his plans to them
7. something to him
8. the machine to me
9. bringing me a few stamps from town
10. asked her them

16

1. does a fashion last
2. do they want
3. must their customers lose
4. do the people in the industry introduce
5. do you see
6. has my next-door neighbour worn
7. she wears
8. the fashion experts will make
9. she'll consider
10. will she discover

4. Modals · Modale Hilfsverben

1

1. must
2. must
3. must
4. mustn't
5. must
6. needn't
7. mustn't
8. needn't
9. needn't
10. mustn't

2
1. managed to/was able to
2. could
3. can't
4. 's managed to/'s been able to
5. won't be able to/can't
6. could
7. being able to
8. can
9. 'll be able to/can
10. couldn't/wasn't able to
11. can
12. can
13. could
14. was able to

3
1. was supposed to; should/ought to
2. Shall
3. should/ought to
4. is to
5. should/ought to, 're ... supposed to
6. is to
7. is supposed to
8. should/ought to; 're to

4
1. will/'ll be buying
2. will/'ll want
3. will/'ll be fetching
4. will/'ll be
5. will/'ll be giving
6. will/'ll be keeping
7. will/'ll be doing
8. will/'ll be helping
9. won't get/'ll not get
10. will/'ll make

5
(may or might is possible in each case)
1. He may be ill.
2. He may have gone to the doctor's first.
3. He may have decided to drive to work when he missed the bus.
4. He may have had a breakdown.
5. He may not have been able to get a taxi.
6. He may have had an accident.
7. He may not have heard the alarm clock.
8. He may not be coming to work at all today.
9. He may have been told to see the boss first.
10. He may be looking for a new job.

6
1. have gone
2. have stayed up
3. ask; have had; be; have had to
4. have gone out
5. have asked
6. have broken in; have climbed in
7. have given
8. have left; be; have gone
9. have bought; do
10. have remembered; hold

7
1. know
2. post
3. be; be working
4. read; speak; go
5. go (be going); be waiting
6. be working
7. be doing; bite
8. be having
9. have
10. be playing

8

1. can't
2. should/ought to
3. can; must
4. 'll
5. may/might
6. can
7. can't/mustn't
8. needn't
9. couldn't
10. Shall
11. Would
12. can't/mustn't; mustn't

9

1. needn't wait
2. must have been
3. mustn't say
4. may/might have been
5. 'll have read
6. managed to/was able to convince
7. 's to be
8. can't have come/arrived
9. should be
10. was (supposed) to come; had to fly
11. couldn't wait
12. 'll ring/phone

10

1. should/ought to be doing
2. will be waiting
3. have to go
4. may/might be looking
5. needn't go
6. couldn't understand
7. will know
8. Shall ... come
9. can't hear
10. won't like

11

1. ... you must have left it at school.
2. ... I had to put the parcel on the window-sill.
3. It must have been lying there all morning.
4. ... I must have left it on the bus.
5. We mustn't forget to take Tom the video cassette.
6. ... so I needn't have made all this cake.
7. ... so I had to take a taxi.
8. You're to phone the boss right away.
9. My American cousins might be coming for Christmas this year.
10. It shouldn't be too difficult.
11. I think you should take the green one.

12

1. 1 + a); 2 + b)
2. 1 + b); 2 + a)
3. 1 + b); 2 + a)
4. 1 + a); 2 + b)
5. 1 + b); 2 + a)
6. 1 + b); 2 + a)
7. 1 + a); 2 + b)
8. 1 + a); 2 + c); 3 + b)
9. 1 + c); 2 + b); 3 + a)

13

Mary: Well, what (1) shall we do tonight/this evening - on our first Saturday in the new flat? Have/Give a party perhaps?

Sally: But (2) shouldn't we/oughtn't we to finish painting the kitchen first? (3) We can't cook anything for a party anyway with such a mess in there.

Diana: (4) We needn't cook at all. (5) There must be a shop somewhere around here where (6) you can buy pizzas, surely?

Mary: Well, there's a little shop that sells frozen food round the corner - so (7) we should/ought to be able to get frozen pizzas at least. But (8) we should/ought to have thought of a party earlier, then (9) I could have gone to the food department at Marks & Spencer's on the way home yesterday.

Sally: (10) We can't afford a party at all, not even if we shop at Marks & Spencer's. Don't forget, (11) we've got to/have to buy more paint for the kitchen.

Diana: Don't be such a spoil-sport!

Mary: Hey, you two! (12) We mustn't start shouting at each other. Let me make a suggestion. (13) Couldn't we just make a few sandwiches? (14) That shouldn't/oughtn't to be too expensive. And (15) we can get up early tomorrow and paint all day.

Diana: What! (16) I wasn't allowed to stay in bed on Sunday mornings in my parents' house, and now (17) you won't let me sleep either! But (18) I must admit the suggestion is fair. - Oh heavens! It's ten o'clock already. (19) Peter'll be waiting for me at the bus-stop. (20) We're supposed to be meeting/to meet Tim in the High Street at quarter past. (21) Will you two wash up? Don't be angry with me. (22) I'll bring back buckets of paint from town - I promise!

•**14**

1. 'll
2. may/might
3. 'd
4. Can
5. can
6. should/ought to
7. Would
8. will/should
9. May
10. Will/Would/Could
11. needn't

•**15**

1. should
2. will
3. can
4. can
5. will be able to
6. need not/should not/ought not to
7. can
8. must
9. must not/should not
10. may/might
11. should/ought to
12. will/would
13. will not
14. cannot
15. must
16. is said to/may/might
17. must
18. need not
19. must
20. must
21. will

5. The main verb: forms and tenses - Das Vollverb: Formen und Zeiten

1
1. washes
2. tidies
3. doesn't walk
4. takes; walks
5. does
6. doesn't eat; eats
7. interrupts
8. doesn't play; practises
9. watches
10. likes/loves

2
1. 's had; for
2. 've written; since
3. has ... helped; since
4. 've lived; for
5. have seen; since
6. haven't played for
7. have applied; since
8. 's worked; since
9. 's been; since
10. has phoned; for
11. haven't heard; for
12. 've made; since
13. 've lost; since
14. 's ... had; for
15. have gone/been; for
16. hasn't rained since
17. haven't washed; for
18. 's knitted; since
19. 've kept/had; for

3 ... was washing her hair. And she had an awful lot of homework to do later. She planned to finish her history essay, too. Peter was playing his guitar and was making a terrible noise so she didn't know how she was supposed to manage. She couldn't even hear herself think! She didn't expect to be able to finish until very late, so she couldn't go out with anyone that night. She thought she was getting a headache, too, with all the noise, so she wanted to go to bed early if she could finish her essay before supper.

4
1. wrote
2. hasn't received
3. asked
4. hasn't been able to
5. 's applied
6. 's had
7. answered
8. told
9. hasn't given up
10. 's borrowed
11. 's made up his mind
12. emigrated
13. left
14. was able to
15. offered
16. refused
17. has offered
18. hasn't accepted
19. enjoyed
20. left
21. has found
22. has suggested

5 1. So far I have had two office jobs in the school holidays.
2. I used a computer at school, but I have not used one since (I left school).
3. I went to France for six weeks on an exchange visit last summer, but I have never been to a German-speaking country.
4. I learned some Arabic when my father worked in Cairo.
5. I have used Arabic/it once or twice to interpret for Arab visitors to the town.
6. I learned typing and shorthand at evening classes last winter.
7. I have done voluntary work at our local children's home every week since last Christmas.
8. I organized a concert given by our school choir this spring.

6 1. 's gone
2. did she go
3. has repaired
4. 've heard
5. wrote; hasn't corrected
6. 've brought; bought
7. did Shakespeare die
8. has stolen; did you notice

7 1. haven't seen
2. were
3. worked
4. Did you see
5. 've known; got
6. 's had; hasn't been/gone out
7. have you known; 've been; went
8. has been; saw

8 1. arrived; 'd left
2. went; hadn't had; went
4. 'd (had) burned
3. hadn't lived; became
5. had; 'd forgotten
6. were; 'd had
7. arrested; 'd broken
8. 'd worked; became
9. introduced; 'd met

•9 1. left
2. had been
3. had ordered
4. saw
5. felt
6. had arrived
7. had put
8. went
9. appeared
10. had come
11. killed
12. had joined
13. had told
14. had become
15. had ever known
16. was hit
17. walked
18. had walked
19. noticed
20. was
21. found
22. had fallen
23. carried
24. asked
25. had covered
26. had done
27. had wounded
28. could
29. died
30. learned
31. had beaten
32. meant

10 1. 1 + b); 2 + a)
2. 1 + b); 2 + c); 3 + a)
3. 1 + c); 2 + a); 3 + b)
4. 1 + a); 2 + c); 3 + b)

11
1. 're going to; 'll
2. 'll
3. 'll
4. 're going to
5. 'll
6. 're going to
7. 'll
8. 'll
9. 'll

12
1. 'll
2. is ... going to
3. 's going to
4. 'll
5. 'll
6. 's going to
7. 's going to
8. will be

13
1. 'll
2. is going to
3. 'm going to
4. 'll
5. 're going to
6. 'll
7. 'll

•14
1. had known
2. knocked
3. has happened
4. has been shot
5. shot
6. drove
7. 's set off
8. 's going to wait
9. 'll find out
10. gets
11. 'll do
12. does everyone think
13. went out
14. heard
15. has/had asked
16. 're/were going to get married
17. wasn't
18. was found
19. had examined
20. (had) spoken
21. looked after
22. walked
23. had made
24. has walked
25. rained
26. walked
27. 'll see
28. 've found
29. will be needed
30. found
31. did it get
32. was anyone
33. has taken
34. 'll have guessed
35. killed
36. will discover

6. The main verb: the simple form and the progressive form in different tenses - Das Vollverb: Die simple form und die progressive form in verschiedenen Tempora

1
1. go; 're spending
2. are you reading; read
3. Does Tim go
4. 's typing
5. buy
6. are coming; come
7. visits; takes
8. 's playing

2
1. 1 + b); 2 + a)
2. 1 + a); 2 + b)
3. 1 + a); 2 + b)
4. 1 + b); 2 + a)
5. 1 + a); 2 + b)
6. 1 + b); 2 + b)
7. 1 + b); 2 + a)

3

1. is walking; goes
2. 'm cooking; comes
3. 'm; 'm cleaning up; is coming
4. are you running; 'm going; 're reading
5. does he say?
6. lives; 's staying
7. go; watch; gives
8. wants; grows; expect
9. tastes; is tasting
10. 're having; stays
11. Are you doing; try; hate
12. says; 's looking forward
13. are helping; thinks
14. is playing ; sounds
15. take; change
16. hope; like
17. don't know; Are you taking; looks; 'm taking
18. belongs; 'm looking; 's
19. shuts; promise; get
20. 's coming; wants; arrives

4

1. 's staying
2. 's enjoying
3. likes
4. 's thinking
5. leaves
6. goes
7. feel
8. think
9. are doing
10. 're meeting
11. says
12. arrive
13. 'm looking forward
14. 'm spending
15. have
16. go
17. interest
18. see
19. 'm taking
20. 'm getting
21. look
22. thinks
23. 's writing
24. publish
25. suggests
26. get
27. leave/'re leaving
28. aren't driving
29. lives
30. is getting
31. like
32. 's marrying
33. treats
34. 're staying
35. has
36. is calling

5

1. 's been working since
2. haven't seen; for
3. 's been playing; for
4. 's been watching; since
5. 've had; since
6. haven't heard; for
7. 've been looking; for
8. has gone; since

6

1. has always wanted
2. has been saving
3. has put
4. has been making
5. has saved
6. has already prepared
7. has bought
8. has been learning
9. has been practising
10. has improved
11. has been listening
12. has been getting
13. has been looking forward
14. has come

7 1. 've been waiting; since
2. 've known for
3. have been working for
4. has been; since
5. has been looking; since
6. has been cleaning; for
7. haven't been; for
8. 's written; since
9. Since; 've had; haven't had to work
10. has rung; since; heard

8 1. Have you ever drunk
2. How long have you been working
3. 've made
4. has always wanted
5. 've been feeding; for; now
6. 've been discussing; since; haven't found; so far/yet
7. 've made; 've been decorating; all afternoon
8. has been looking; for hours; 's just found

9 1. was
2. was crossing
3. was cleaning
4. noticed
5. supposed
6. was washing
7. looked
8. was steering
9. put away
10. called
11. was sleeping
12. came
13. were watching
14. were getting
15. shouted
16. replied
17. sent
18. was reading
19. was cooking
20. was repairing
21. looked
22. were spending
23. happened/had happened

10 1. 1 + a); 2 + b)
2. 1 + a); 2 + b)
3. 1 + b); 2 + a)
4. 1 + b); 2 + a)
5. 1 + a); 2 + b)
6. 1 + b); 2 + a)

11 1. has already done it
2. did he buy it
3. have you been doing
4. went to see her yesterday
5. was lying/sitting in a chair in the garden
6. 's been ill recently
7. 's been hanging them/working all day
8. hasn't finished it yet
9. did she apply for it

12 1. Have you seen; saw; was leaving
2. moved
3. Did you see; did; was looking; put; was serving; has just gone
4. left; was raining; took; Did you leave; have you been; got
5. 've noticed; worked; took; opened
6. got; 've been going out
7. 've bought; got; has just opened; didn't cost; haven't sold; 've already bought
8. saw; was fishing; 's completely disappeared (completely); 've been helping; haven't seen

9. were having; started; Did the school burn; has been giving
10. 've been learning; didn't understand; were
11. have just seen; did it say
12. have you been staying; saw; was waiting; was reading
13. was; wasn't; didn't hear; watched/were watching; had; has become; 's been working

13
1. 've brought; made
2. have been boiling
3. phoned/rang (up); were already packing
4. has been working; planted; cut; 's been painting
5. came; were talking/chatting (to each other)
6. left; was having lunch; has seen
7. 've been; didn't like
8. has sunk; has been reporting

•14
1. rang
2. was making
3. was clearing
4. had he rung/was he ringing
5. hadn't he come/ didn't he come
6. went
7. had carefully turned off
8. saw
9. called out
10. was sitting
11. 've hurt
12. slipped
13. 've been
14. realized
15. had only sprained
16. noticed
17. have you done
18. dropped
19. was working
20. suggested
21. 've been coughing
22. 've been getting
23. had given
24. decided
25. was waiting
26. has been lost
27. gave
28. was searching
29. found
30. had
31. had disappeared
32. had left
33. turned
34. opened
35. was sitting
36. had been
37. have you been sitting
38. 've been trying
39. 've managed
40. had found
41. had helped
42. spotted
43. had fallen

15
1. seem
2. miss
3. be watching
4. be going
5. be pouring
6. be wondering
7. stop
8. be raining
9. be waiting
10. recognize
11. be making
12. be helping
13. rush
14. be standing
15. say
16. feel

16

1. 'll have mended
2. will have been
3. will have told
4. 'll have finished (papering)
5. 'll have read it
6. will have been painted
7. 'll have got
8. 'll have bought
9. 'll have started
10. will have been built

•17

1. 're getting married/'re going to get married
2. is sending/is going to send
3. won't allow
4. don't get married
5. fly
6. 'll discover
7. 'll just have/'m just going to have
8. 'm going to make
9. 'm going to learn
10. won't know
11. get
12. 'll hate
13. Are you going to do
14. 'll be
15. 'll be able
16. leave
17. will be waiting
18. will improve
19. 'm not going to be
20. 'm going to become
21. won't mind
22. 'm meeting
23. 're going to find
24. is
25. 'll come
26. Will I manage
27. get
28. will help

18

1. 1 + a); 2 + b)
2. 1 + a); 2 + b)
3. 1 + b); 2 + a)
4. 1 + b); 2 + a)
5. 1 + a); 2 + b)

•19

1. was blowing
2. were walking
3. had had
4. realized
5. had forgotten
6. 've left
7. 'll go
8. will I find
9. put
10. got
11. don't/can't remember
12. haven't seen
13. took
14. were standing
15. chased
16. noticed
17. turned
18. was still lying
19. comes
20. 'll miss
21. don't hurry
22. 've been standing
23. 're looking forward/'ve been looking forward
24. arrives
25. 'll take
26. heard
27. was coming
28. was still gliding
29. 's going to hit
30. were waiting
31. 'll try
32. 've heard
33. Have you decided
34. 'll wait
35. brings

36. do/can you see
37. is sitting
38. looks
39. have I seen
40. 's staying
41. was wandering
42. were climbing
43. does it taste
44. doesn't taste
45. 've ever drunk
46. 're spilling/'ve spilled
47. doesn't matter
48. 'm going to
49. 'll wash
50. is looking
51. 's been watching
52. sat down
53. 's getting up
54. 's going to come over
55. did you do
56. 've been counting
57. 've ordered
58. 're going to serve
59. 'll be sitting
60. 'll put on
61. got
62. made
63. had disappeared
64. won't tell
65. won't spoil
66. 's planned

7. The passive · Das Passiv

1

1. is known
2. predicted
3. was born
4. were practised
5. stole
6. followed
7. got married
8. was sent
9. had been built
10. was impressed
11. returned
12. was invited
13. was thrown
14. gave
15. was arrested
16. was solved
17. was encouraged
18. left
19. had grown
20. was shot
21. were based
22. was made
23. won
24. died

2

1. haven't been fed
2. have been closed
3. was published
4. are broken into
5. are committed
6. had to be used
7. had been left open
8. are entered
9. be done
10. can be locked
11. is being held
12. can be fixed
13. is being started

3

1. are the envelopes kept
2. was being beaten up
3. was it found
4. she'll be elected
5. were beaten
6. we're being followed
7. 'm being considered
8. was still being built

4

1. was scored
2. have been stolen
3. was won by a contestant
4. had been borrowed
5. have been driven by a Grand Prix racing driver
6. was taken
7. 's disliked by some of the girls
8. was blown off
9. were delivered
10. were forced

5

1. Your problems won't be laughed at.
2. Our retired people will be taken care of.
3. Your views will be taken notice of.
4. The problems of the homeless will be dealt with.
5. Our ethnic minorities won't be discriminated against.
6. People will be helped to find jobs.
7. The problems of the unemployment will be listened to.
8. Pudley will be talked about wherever I go.
9. You'll always be told the facts.
10. Pudley won't be made fun of in future.

•6

1. When were you given this news?
2. The Mayor was thanked for his support.
3. She was asked a few difficult questions.
4. The meal will probably be paid for by the firm.
5. That will be taken care of later.
6. He was asked for his advice three times, but he never had time.
7. The film will be followed by a short discussion.
8. That was already promised to the workers a year ago.
9. If you had predicted a hundred years ago that Man would be able to fly one day you would have been laughed at.
10. The manager was offered a lot of money, but he didn't want to move to London.

•7

1. is believed to have come
2. is thought to have worked
3. is said to have been wearing
4. is understood to have (had)
5. is known to have been carrying
6. is believed to have hidden
7. are expected to try
8. is understood to have referred to
9. are believed to have spoken
10. is said to have
11. is thought to have rejected
12. isn't believed to have had

8

1. can't be cancelled
2. must have been given
3. can't be repaired
4. should be complimented
5. must have been delayed
6. must have been put on

7. should be evacuated
8. mustn't have been invited
9. should be taken
10. must have been designed

9
1. timetable (to be) changed
2. troublemaker (to be) expelled
3. tax expert (to be) invited
4. attention (to be) paid
5. integration (to be) encouraged
6. time (to be) given
7. pupils (to be) kept

10
1. slides and swings were taken down
2. old trees were cut down
3. expensive car park has been built on the site (there)
4. have been put up saying NO PARKING
5. of money was spent on the car park (it); people must be encouraged to use it
6. is said to be doing something
7. of the town is being spoilt completely
8. latest plans to be changed before it's too late

8. The infinitive - Der Infinitiv

1
1. be typing
2. to have been built
3. be delivered
4. have taken
5. to be making
6. to be done
7. leave
8. to use
9. be working
10. have been misled
11. to be heard

•2
1. to be paid
2. to develop
3. have been working/have worked
4. have completed
5. point to
6. to be studying
7. to have been used
8. be built
9. to be provided
10. be

3
1. best place for surfing
2. last person to be told
3. first solar power station to be built
4. best/quickest way to get
5. only/first Australian to have won
6. best/quickest/cheapest way to go

4
1. somebody/someone to give me legal advice
2. a thing to put/stand your camera on
3. somebody/someone to carry my luggage
4. somebody/someone to repair the roof

5. something to be discovered in the future
6. somewhere to spend the night
7. somebody/someone to design it
8. him to return/come back

5
1. doesn't know how to cash it
2. isn't sure where to park her car
3. doesn't seem to understand when to pay attention to others
4. who told me who(m) to invite to the celebration the day after tomorrow
5. he has no idea how to start a conversation with her
6. she's got to/has to decide which to accept
7. have (got) to recognize quickly whether to leave out details
8. isn't sure how long to wait for her new boy-friend
9. wondered how to get rid of his old motor-bike
10. decide whether to accept the offer

6
1. a surprise for you to discover
2. can't wait for the next one to reach
3. wasn't easy for the boys to arrange
4. wasn't time for the group to go sight-seeing
5. possible for them to visit
6. stayed there long enough for Michael to see
7. makes sense for me to think
8. is too soon for us to be
9. be difficult for the five boys to concentrate
10. be strange for their classmates to sit

7
1. wants his parents to give him more money
2. would like/'d like him to spend less on cigarettes and visits to the cinema
3. told him to work harder
4. wish him to become a lawyer
5. would like/'d like them to understand
6. should/ought to allow him to go to South America
7. told him to concentrate on
8. expect him to pass his exam(ination)

8
1. the strangers to leave
2. the Prime Minister doubt
3. the relationship to continue
4. the council to reject
5. the blacks share
6. the lorry driver to lose
7. the viewers rush into
8. the sales assistant to examine

9 1. Diana's unconventional clothes often make people in the street stop and stare at her.
2. The judge's neighbour was grateful to him for letting her use his telephone.
3. The police ordered the families living near the factory to evacuate their homes at once.
4. A laboratory technician let the journalist enter the building before the experiment started.
5. According to Julia it was the pressure of work that finally made her actress friend take a holiday.

•10 1. the person to ask
2. the first Dane to stay
3. you to stay with us
4. the place to visit
5. you go to Beaulieu
6. how to get there
7. busy to come with you
8. me borrow your map
9. to have been made
10. me come here
11. my English to improve
12. me to stay with her

9. The gerund and gerund or infinitive - Das Gerundium und Gerundium oder Infinitiv

1 1. for not passing her French exam(ination)
2. Instead of learning French at home
3. on arriving
4. by writing them on a piece of paper and sticking it
5. In learning the new language
6. for helping me to get this job as au pair

2 1. decided against going with
2. spend time and money on doing
3. coped with buying a ticket
4. was arrested for damaging
5. was ... being considered
6. of being told
7. blamed ... for not reading
8. was accused of committing
9. apologized for spoiling
10. could be ... of explaining

3 1. for suggesting
2. of reducing
3. of developing
4. of taking
5. from eating
6. of knowing
7. about introducing
8. about having
9. for organizing
10. to taking

4
1. new film is worth seeing
2. old lamp isn't worth keeping
3. aren't worth picking
4. He's worth knowing
5. is worth doing ... it's worth doing

5
1. going to/visiting the exhibition of local history at the town hall
2. go to/spend the day at/visit the new indoor swimming pool
3. go/have a trip to the coast - to Bournemouth, say
4. knowing/saying/telling when the weather will be
5. going on a boat trip on the Thames
6. we invite Mum and Dad to come with us
7. asking/inviting them
8. asking them at least
9. feeling it'll be a waste of time

6
1. taking
2. making
3. complaining about
4. to change
5. watching
6. helping
7. cleaning
8. telling
9. living
10. growing

•7
1. to feed
2. scoring
3. moving
4. to hurt
5. to ring
6. advertising
7. to give
8. thinking
9. writing
10. treating
11. applying
12. to become
13. working

8
1. complained about me (my) giving
2. expected me to teach
3. are worried about her failing
4. isn't happy about the number of German lessons being reduced
5. isn't keen on him (his) studying
6. would ('d) like him to become
7. justified being given
8. was no use talking to him/her/the head now
9. appreciated me (my) organizing it/the trip
10. would ('d) like them (the pupils) to visit Berlin
11. are tired of being asked for
12. wouldn't allow him (Robert) to come
13. don't like the idea of him (his) missing

•9 1. taking part in
2. having hurt
3. in causing
4. have happened
5. to walk
6. of getting
7. in helping
8. searching
9. looking
10. of finding
11. setting off
12. feeling
13. to spot
14. falling
15. from hitting
16. for allowing
17. to go up
18. of taking
19. against letting
20. set off
21. making
22. for coping with
23. of cancelling
24. for helping
25. in accepting

10. The participle - Das Partizip

1 1. Lucy's aunt runs an old-fashioned guesthouse offering bed and breakfast.
2. Lucy has got a part-time job there serving breakfast.
3. She's just taken some toast to a man reading a daily newspaper.
4. A woman wearing a low-cut summer dress has just ordered some more coffee.
5. The little black dog sitting near her feet is barking aggressively.

2 Gopal: I worked for a company making automatic barriers for car parks.

Philippa: I visited old people needing help with things such as shopping and washing.

Simon: I had a job in the personnel department of a firm producing frozen food.

Howard: I interviewed unemployed people hoping to work on my uncle's farm for a few weeks.

Shirley: I had a job programming computers with a big American electronics company.

Roy: I'd like to be a vet and I had a job on a sheep farm in Wales helping to check the condition of the animals.

3 1. new law allowing lorries to have
2. routes leading through
3. the older, lighter vehicles moving along
4. old bridges already finding it hard
5. people living in the country

4 1. people travelling on municipal buses and Underground trains
2. passengers using public transport
3. a report presenting/describing the results of the increased fares
4. number of passengers travelling by Underground
5. numbers of traffic accidents occurring/happening daily/every day

5 1. a firm producing home computers and video equipment
2. a fast-growing industry
3. a money making idea
4. a daughter studying French
5. the man talking to our hostess
6. the attractive-looking man
7. that girl sitting on her own in the corner near the window
8. a prize-winning concert pianist

•6 1. felt the aircraft rolling
2. saw the plane spin
3. go
4. to see (when I saw) the parachute open
5. heard something crash
6. heard the poor fellow shouting for

•7 1. hear a bus coming now
2. saw smoke/smelled gas coming
3. saw her write
4. 've seen her riding it
5. saw him break it
6. hear her heart beating
7. saw her pick up the goods and put them in her (shopping) bag
8. saw/heard everybody/somebody wishing him a happy birthday
9. used to go and see/watch him play
10. 've never seen him drinking it/any

8 1. lay on the beach watching
2. sat beside her reading
3. went to the hotel to fetch
4. came running
5. stood in front of her breathing
6. is sitting in the hotel waiting for you
7. you to come and have
8. got up smiling

9 1. have it re-decorated
2. and/to have it repaired
3. have it extended
4. have it re-planted
5. have a new one/another one designed

10 1. the "ON/OFF" switch usually found at the back or the side of the machine
2. a button labelled "EJECT"
3. The numbers shown in this "window" ... unused space left on the cassette
4. the required TV channel
5. a chosen time/a time chosen by you
6. a programme transmitted on a second channel
7. a borrowed cassette ... a recording made on somebody else's machine
8. a safety control not seen on a lot of VCRs

11 1. not wanting
2. Having failed
3. Hoping
4. Never having been
5. Being
6. Not having realized
7. Having expected
8. Having discussed
9. Having enjoyed
10. Having improved

12 1. if kept
2. Whenever using
3. before taking a break
4. whether intending
5. Unless switched off
6. Whenever operating
7. as if cleaning
8. If pulled
9. Before starting
10. if started
11. if put
12. until convinced

13 1. With the sun shining
2. With petrol going up
3. With blood pouring
4. With the banks closed
5. With the area of high pressure moving away
6. With most of the tickets for tomorrow's big concert sold
7. With the race won
8. With a large group of strikers standing

14 1. introduced
2. completing
3. running
4. pointing out
5. reaching
6. run
7. kept
8. intending
9. replaced
10. flying
11. happening
12. trying
13. getting ready
14. shaking
15. providing
16. published
17. offering
18. buying

15 1. riding
2. record-breaking
3. not having taken
4. riding down/along the road
5. testing a friend's machine
6. admitting
7. lawyer defending Haslam
8. behaving
9. (being) done
10. pointing out
11. being
12. representing the British team

11. Reported speech · Indirekte Rede

** Note: In informal or spoken English there is often no back-shift in reported speech. This applies especially to exercises 4, 10, 13 and 14.

1 Mrs Woodward told them that she wasn't interested in politics.
Mr Ferguon said that he was definitely voting Liberal.
Mrs Parkinson told them that she was considering voting for the Socialists this/that time.
Mr McAllister told them that their party had never helped the working class.
Mrs Sherwood told Shirley that she had just joined the Conservative party.
Mrs Holliday told them that she'd voted Labour since 1945 and she wasn't going to change now/then.
Mr Woodward told them that he'd been looking forward to asking them some questions about their policies.
Mr Pym told them that he'd been thinking about voting for their party for some time.
Mrs Lawson told them that she'd voted for the SDP at the last election.
Mrs Hitchcock asked what election they meant/were talking about. She asked if there was going to be one.
Mr Ainsworth told them that he'd voted for their party the time before, but the Conservative candidate had won.
Mr Hoolihan told them that he'd read their leaflet not long before and (that) he agreed with their policies.
Mr Jenkinson told Shirley that he'd known her grandfather.
Mrs Patterson told them that she was going to vote Conservative.
Mr Armstrong told them that his wife and he were going to vote Labour.

Mrs Townsend told them that the Conservative candidate would win.
Mr Bradbury told them that he'd vote for their candidate.
Mrs Thompson told them that she was sure their candidate would be elected.

2
1. was delighted at Sir Richard's change of heart.
2. Dr Essop Jassai ... said he was pleased about his/Sir Richard's decision.
3. Dr Jassai pointed out/said that they had been trying to claim that apartheid was no longer so bad, but the/this discussion had made it clear that all the hurtful things still existed in South Africa.
4. Mr S. Kotze ... said that his Government was against people trying to gain political advantage from the way the film was shown.
5. Mr Kotze went on to say/added/said that they had not stopped people from seeing the film and (he stressed that), in general, there were adequate facilities in each separate community.
6. Sir Richard Attenborough said/announced that he had decided not to go to South Africa unless his film was allowed to be shown to mixed audiences in every cinema.
7. Sir Richard said/added that all his personal profits from showings of the film in South Africa would be given to multi-racial organizations in South Africa.
8. Mr Cassin Salonjee ... said he was very, very happy to hear about Sir Richard's attitude.
9. Mr Salonjee added/explained that his/Sir Richard's decision made sense when you considered Gandhi's principles and values.
10. The group ... said they were sorry that Sir Richard wouldn't be coming/going to their country, but they hoped he'd visit them in the future ... .

3
1. Colin asked Sue how long she had owned her motor-bike.
2. He wondered if she would let him ride it.
3. Sue asked Colin when he had bought his machine.
4. She wanted to know who his repairs were done by.
5. She asked him how many miles his bike did per gallon.

4 hadn't seen a bike like that before, and he told us he was probably the first person in the country to buy one.

Then Kathy asked him how it worked, and he explained that it had got a small motor that was driven by a battery and (at the same time) it had also got ordinary bike pedals. He said it was up to the rider how he or she operated it. It was possible to use either just the pedals or just the battery-drive motor, he told us, and it was possible to use both at the same time, too.

When I asked him if it could go very fast, he admitted it couldn't, but he said it travelled at up to 15 mph. Then Kathy asked Andrew how he'd found out about it. He said he'd read an article in a Sunday newspaper, he'd liked the idea and had decided to buy it at once.

Well, I still wanted to know why he'd decided to buy it and Kathy asked the same question. So he explained that it was just what he needed. He told us he'd managed to get a job at last, Dad, you see. But it was in the hospital at the top of Jordan Hill and he said if you rode a normal bike, you had to get off and push. Well, of course, I agreed it was a steep hill. But I still wanted to know why he didn't take a bus to work.

That's when he told us he enjoyed the exercise. He just needed something to help him to get up that hill, that was all. He didn't want to be late to work every day.

Kathy asked him what was wrong with ordinary motor-bikes or proper mopeds, so Andrew explained that this was better, because he didn't have to have insurance or pay road tax and he didn't even have to wear a crash helmet. He said his/this bike wouldn't cause any pollution, either. That's when I told him/them this would interest you, Dad.

5

1. The head explained that the school needed a place where teachers and students could meet.
2. Councillor Walker said he thought that the car park was too small already.
3. He told Mrs Jones that the school needed all the space in the car park for cars.
4. Councillor Bell told Mrs Jones that the neighbours had already complained that the students' cars were causing problems in the street outside the school.
5. He stressed that the council had received a large number of protests about the school.
6. The head pointed out that the corner of the car park which the school wanted to use was inconvenient for cars.
7. She explained that the school used this corner for bicycles not cars.
8. She emphasized that the same number of cars could park in the car park after the clubroom had been built.

9. Councillor Walker repeated that the car park wouldn't have enough space if the school was allowed to build a clubroom.
10. The head asked the councillor if all the members of the council would visit the school the following week to look at the corner of the car park which the school wanted to use.

6
1. how old these machines were
2. if/whether you sold a lot of carpets abroad
3. whether you'd got more male or female employees
4. asked you if/whether we'd get a chance to talk to some of your employees
5. asked you if your employees got a company pension when they retired
6. wondered how long you yourself had worked here
7. asked you whether we'd be able to buy some of your company's products at a special price at the end of the tour
8. asked you if I should close this door
9. wanted to know if I might touch this wool
10. asked you if we could go to a quieter room now

•7 him why that was, he said it was because we were starting to allow our customers to take money out of their accounts via ATMs. Of course, I told him that most customers found the ATMs a useful service. But he told me last week he'd read about a court case in Japan. He explained that an employee of the national telephone company had used his knowledge of communications systems to steal money from accounts at three different banks. Mr Kowalski pointed out that the police could listen to private telephone conversations and, similarly, it was possible for crooks to "listen" to an electronic message sent from an ATM outside a bank to the bank's central computer.

I asked him how this could help a crook. He said that if he used an ATM to get some money out of his account one day, a crook might be using a cassette recorder at that moment to record the message that the ATM was sending to the central computer. He said that then, after he'd been given his money and had gone away, the crook could re-play the message he had recorded - and the central computer would think he'd asked it to pay out the same sum of money again. He said this/that worried him, so I told him I'd find out more about it.

•8 was open to attack if someone tried hard enough. And Boris Melnikoff pointed out that for every three or four hours they put into designing a system, there was someone who would stay up an extra hour to defeat it. However, Michael Strada, a technical specialist at PLUS SYSTEM Corp stressed that it would have to be an educated crook, though it could be done. And he pointed out that they were introducing special codes now that would help to protect ATM systems. Another expert predicted it would be five years before all the nation's ATM networks were adequately protected from crimes of this kind. But a banker in New York doubted that there was a very great risk. He/She emphasized that if a crook wanted to do this he'd need very expensive equipment. But he/she pointed out that an ATM usually only paid out small sums, say \$ 50 or \$ 100. And for \$ 50 or \$ 100, he/she said, it would probably be easier just to mug people after they'd used an ATM.

So perhaps you needn't worry too much, Mr Kowalski, though there are problems, you're right.

9
1. asked the old lady if he could help her.
2. She asked him if/whether he'd mind
3. asked her how much she wanted to pay
4. wasn't so important, she explained, but the room had to be
5. told her she looked tired
6. told him that she'd had to leave her home in Salzgitter at 5 o'clock that morning
7. She told him that she was taking part in
8. 'd just come from the airport

10 her son and her mother-in-law when Hagar had escaped. She added that it was strange - there had been no panic, no screams. Everyone had been very calm, she said.

I talked to a man called Philip Cox next. He told me that he had been in Norry's Road with his friend, Dave Stacey at the time. He said that they had been in the middle of discussing the state of his (Philip Cox's) car. Suddenly they had looked up, he went on, and had seen a great lioness standing 20 yards away looking at them.

Mr Stacey explained to me that they had been more shocked than frightened because it was the last thing they had expected to see.

Mr Cox went on to say that the lioness had disappeared down the garden path of Number 58 and that they had followed her. He said that they had had a look to see where she'd gone. He told me that they had seen her in the garage, so they had gone to call the police.

The next person I talked to was a circus employee. He explained that he had arrived on the scene before the police and that he had managed to shut the garage door. He said that he had seen the lioness inside the garage, sitting on top of an old fridge.

I then interviewed Mr Norman Boast who told me that he lived at Number 58, but that he had only learned about the drama from a neighbour. He said that he (himself) had stayed indoors.

Another circus worker told me that they had put up a huge cage around the mouth of the garage and that Dick Chipperfield, a lion tamer, had then arrived.

Mr Chipperfield explained to me that he had crept into the garage and (had) made some special lion sounds. He said that Hagar had felt lost and she had made some aggressive noises. But he added that he had shown her the way to the cage and after that she had been okay. He said that after a good night's sleep he was sure that she would be fine.

11
1. suggested he should put it in the garage
2. told him he had better wash them
3. asked him if he would mind helping her to lay it
4. told him he had better not take too much
5. asked him if he would mind passing it
6. asked him if he would like to have another cup
7. asked him if he wanted to have a second (another) piece
8. suggested he should help her to do it

12
1. My assistant advised me to read an article in the 'Financial Times'.
2. The Managing Director told me to show/bring him the new plans as soon as possible.
3. The Sales Manager suggested discussing (we should discuss) the new advertising campaign over lunch.
4. The Marketing Director asked me to attend an exhibition in Detroit next month.
5. The Export Manager asked me if I'd mind visiting our Chicago office while I'm in the States.
6. The Personnel Manager offered me a bigger desk.
7. My secretary advised me that I'd better ring up the architect at once.
8. My doctor ordered me to get more exercise.
9. He told me not to work such long hours.

13 a) if she wanted/would like to go to the Odeon with me this evening she said that she did/would, but that she had an orchestra practice after school today. She said she had them every week. When I asked her how long it would last, she said she didn't know, but that it usually lasted about an hour. But she told me that they'd had one the day before and it had gone on for over two hours. She said that they were giving a concert at the town hall tomorrow. Of course, I explained to her that I didn't really want to miss the start of the film. Sandra asked me what time it started and I told her that it started at 7.15. So she insisted that she'd be here by then, even if she had to miss her tea.

b) had ordered the books the Thursday before and they hadn't arrived. Mr Lind said he could remember me doing that because I had gone there personally. So I naturally asked where they (the books) were. And do you know what he replied? He said he didn't know, but that they weren't there. He added that he'd sent them to me the next day. Of course, I asked him if he was sure and he should go to the bookshop and have a look. I was really furious by then and told him not to be silly. Then he pointed out that he'd taken the parcel to the post-office himself and added that he hadn't any idea why it hadn't got here. He insisted that it wasn't his fault.

14 him/her about the lovely 15-foot-high hedge that had separated my back garden and your back garden from the railway line - until 10 o'clock yesterday/that morning. He/She told me he/she didn't know what I meant. But when I said a new road was going to be built in this part of town to link the new housing project at Fairfield Farm with the main road, he/she said he/she knew that. And he/she asked me to tell him/her what my problem was.

I explained that the new road was (is) to run between the end of my back garden, where the hedge had been, and the railway line. And between your back garden and the railway line, too, of course, Mrs Silver. Then he/she asked me if I'd known (whether I hadn't known) for two months that this road would be built.

Of course, I told him/her I had known that and that you'd known it, too. But I said some workers had arrived here with a bulldozer half an hour earlier and the whole hedge had been torn up. I said it was terrible. And I complained that we'd been given no warning. It had been a complete surprise, so we could do nothing to stop it. I asked him/her if he/she realized that we'd been promised only two days before/only three days ago that the hedge would be saved. And do you know what the councillor said?

He/She said it was terrible, it was most unfortunate, and that he/she was very sorry this had happened. So I asked him/her about the conditions the council had made when they'd given the building company permission to develop the site. He/She said as far as he/she could remember, they'd told them/the building people/the building company the hedge should be kept if possible. He/She said it seemed it hadn't been possible. He/She then went on to say he/she imagined the hedge had been too wide.

Well, I told him/her I thought you and I had been misled. And I said I'd like him/her to do two things for me. When he/she asked me what the first thing was, I told him/her to make the building company plant a new hedge immediately. He/She said he/she could try. Then he/she asked me what else I'd like him/her to do. And that, Mrs Silver, is when I told him/her not to ask me to vote for him/her in the next council elections!

12. Clauses · Gliedsätze

1
1. will be
2. have; won't be able to
3. won't want to; find out
4. won't buy; are looking for
5. goes down; will have to
6. have made/make up; won't be able to
7. choose; 'll have to
8. 'll have; don't change
9. decide; will be
10. put; 'll provide

2
1. prices continue to ... customers will buy cheaper
2. you're writing ... 'll come back
3. of living goes up ... go up
4. don't need a passport ... visit a country ... is
5. 'll ring you up immediately/at once ... I get
6. haven't applied for ... you should do so now

3
1. 'd continue to buy them ... they cost
2. 'd ... have to stop buying them ... they went up
3. would complain ... he didn't get
4. they became too expensive, I might buy
5. was asked to pay ... 'd refuse
6. cost more than ... 'd stop buying them
7. needed a lettuce ... 'd pay ... they asked/were asking

4 1. I knew any of the other guests/people who are going
2. I would if I could (but I can't)
3. I'd be happy to give you a lift if I had my car here.
4. I'd love to come with you if I could afford it.
5. She'd pass it if she worked harder.
6. He might (pass it) if he wasn't/weren't so nervous.
7. I might do/leave if they didn't offer me higher wages.
8. If it was/were up to me, /If she said yes, we'd get married tomorrow.

5 1. I'd probably have written to you if I hadn't been so busy recently./ If I hadn't been so busy recently, I might have written to you.
2. Mr Fowler probably wouldn't have had the accident if he'd realized how wet the roads were./If Mr Fowler had realized how wet the roads were, the accident mightn't have happened.
3. Diana would probably have got tickets for the concert if she hadn't got to the box-office too late./If Diana hadn't got to the box-office too late, she might have got tickets for the concert./Diana would probably have been able to go to the concert if she'd got to the box-office in time./If Diana had got to the box-office in time, she might have been able to go to the concert.
4. Carol and Wayne probably wouldn't have gone to the cinema if it hadn't suddenly started to rain when they got to the tennis court./ If it hadn't suddenly started to rain when they got to the tennis court, Carol and Wayne mightn't have gone to the cinema.
5. Mrs Margaret Thatcher probably wouldn't have become Britain's first female Prime Minister if the Conservatives hadn't won the election in 1979./If the Conservatives hadn't won the election in 1979, Mrs Margaret Thatcher mightn't have become Britain's first female Prime Minister.
6. Wayne probably wouldn't have walked home last night if he hadn't missed the last bus./If Wayne hadn't missed the last bus, he mightn't have walked home last night.
7. The strike would probably have been prevented if the management had given the workers the full facts./If the management had given the workers the full facts, the strike might have been prevented.
8. Jane would probably have got the job she applied for if one of the directors hadn't thought it was a job for a man./If one of the directors hadn't thought the job was for a man, Jane might have got it.

9. Victoria probably wouldn't have lost/would probably have won the match if she'd tried harder./If she'd tried harder, Victoria mightn't have lost/might have won the match.
10. Mrs Davies would probably have bought the shoes if the shop had had her size./If the shop had had her size, Mrs Davies might have bought the shoes.

•6
1. if she hadn't seen
2. hadn't seen ... she wouldn't have been able to impress her boy-friend/Marty
3. wouldn't have escaped ... if he hadn't been
4. hadn't flown through ... it wouldn't have broken
5. wouldn't have started working/to work ... if he hadn't crashed ... wouldn't have become
6. had lost his interest ... he wouldn't have taken part in
7. might have overtaken ... if he'd driven
8. had managed to overtake ... he would have won
9. wouldn't have known ... if she hadn't worked it out
10. wouldn't have shown ... if Sneva hadn't won

7
1. the pound had stayed/remained ... would have earned a lot
2. The firm wouldn't have made any workers redundant if they had made
3. wouldn't have been made redundant if the firm hadn't got
4. hadn't lost ... wouldn't have felt so
5. Barbara hadn't felt so bad, she'd have paid
6. 'd paid attention ... she wouldn't have caused
7. she hadn't caused an accident, she wouldn't have appeared/arrived/come so late
8. 'd probably have got ... if she hadn't appeared/arrived/come for the interview so late

8
1. had ended
2. had taken place
3. wouldn't have been able to
4. 'd won
5. would have become
6. 'd have been given
7. would win
8. would be
9. would think about
10. was/were
11. 'd introduce
12. were
13. would be
14. had
15. would have to
16. would be

9 1. A ferry is a boat/hovercraft that (which) carries people and goods across a river, channel etc.
2. A foreigner is a person/somebody who/that lives in/was born in another country.
3. Apartheid is the policy of racial segregation that (which) is practised in South Africa.
4. A commuter is a person/somebody who/that travels from his/her/their home in the suburbs or the country to his/her/their job in the city.
5. A Greyhound is a bus that (which) travels from city to city in the U.S.A.
6. A customs duty is something that (which) you have to pay the Government for certain goods you import or export.
7. A cheerleader is a person/somebody who/that encourages a crowd to cheer for a team, e.g. at a game of American football.
8. A deaf person is somebody who/that cannot hear.
9. A limerick is a funny or nonsense poem that (which) has five lines and rhymes.
10. A lecturer is a person/somebody who/that teaches at a college or university.
11. A link is something that (which) joins/connects two separate things.
12. A trade union is something that (which) protects workers' interests.
13. A target is something that (which) you aim at.
14. A pension is a sum of money that (which) you get/receive from the Government when you retire.
15. Rent is the money that (which) you have to pay your landlord or landlady for your house or flat.
16. A musician is a person/somebody who/that plays or writes music.
17. Beef is a kind of meat that (which) comes from an ox, bull or cow.
18. A hairdresser is a person/somebody who/that cuts hair.
19. A cheque is something that (which) you can use instead of money to pay for things.
20. A pessimist is a person/somebody who/that always thinks something bad/terrible is going to happen.

10 1. anybody whose support/contribution has been
2. the ones/documents that I wanted
3. to marry somebody whose likes and dislikes aren't at all similar to yours
4. that isn't working
5. two people whose names you've/have been forgotten
6. a TV/set that can receive/a TV/set that can provide you with

11

1. that (which)	11. which	21. that (which)
2. that (which)	12. who/that	22. that (which)
3. that (which)	13. who/that	23. that (which)
4. which	14. which	24. that (which)
5. that (which)	15. that (which)	25. that
6. which	16. that (which)	26. that
7. that	17. that (which)	27. that (which)
8. which	18. that	28. which
9. that (which)	19. who/that	29. which
10. that (which)	20. that (which)	30. which

12

1. will keep his hands warm in winter
2. some spices she has never tried in a recipe before
3. a machine that will answer the phone automatically
4. a telescope that is powerful enough to let him study Neptune
5. some clothes that she can wear when she appears in court
6. an algebra book she read about in an educational magazine
7. a map that shows details of the waters around Corsica
8. a sleeping-bag that is small enough to fit in her rucksack
9. a TV set that can receive all the new channels
10. a racket he can beat all his opponents with
11. a record she heard on the radio recently
12. an engine he could put in to try and make it fly

•13

1. want to share an office with somebody I couldn't get along with, either
2. 'd find it hard to get over the loss of a pet I'd loved
3. wouldn't support a plan I wasn't in favour of, either
4. 'd be sorry to miss a trip I'd been looking forward to, too/I wouldn't like to miss a trip I'd been looking forward to, either
5. buy raw materials from a firm I couldn't depend on, either
6. I wouldn't agree to do a job I thought I couldn't cope with, either/ I'd turn down work I thought I couldn't cope with, too

14

1. get	7. since/because	13. 'll feel	19. hear
2. see	8. however	14. 've pushed	20. has
3. use	9. though	15. since	21. while
4. since	10. As/Since	16. 've done	22. wherever
5. as	11. arrive	17. when	
6. 're	12. 're	18. is/has been	

Inhaltsverzeichnis

Vorwort 4

1. The noun and the article · Das Nomen und der Artikel
Test yourself 8
Exercises 12

2. The adjective and the adverb · Das Adjektiv und das Adverb
Test yourself 18
Exercises 22

3. Quantifiers, the pronoun, question words, word order · Mengenbezeichnungen, das Pronomen, Fragewörter, Wortstellung
Test yourself 30
Exercises 34

4. Modals · Modale Hilfsverben
Test yourself 42
Exercises 46

5. The main verb: forms and tenses · Das Vollverb: Formen und Zeiten
Test yourself 56
Exercises 62

6. The main verb: the simple form and the progressive form in different tenses · Das Vollverb: Die simple form und die progressive form in verschiedenen Tempora
Test yourself 70
Exercises 74

7. The passive · Das Passiv
Test yourself 88
Exercises 92

8. The infinitive · Der Infinitiv
Test yourself 98
Exercises 102

9. The gerund and gerund or infinitive · Das Gerundium und Gerundium oder Infinitiv
Test yourself 108
Exercises 112

10. The participle · Das Partizip
Test yourself 118
Exercises 122

11. Reported speech · Indirekte Rede
Test yourself 130
Exercises 134

12. Clauses · Gliedsätze
Test yourself 144
Exercises 148

Vorwort

1. Zielsetzung und Funktionen

Wie der Titel ausweist, wurde dieses Test- und Übungsbuch in engem Bezug zur ENGLISH G Grammatik entworfen. Es kann aber auch durchaus mit einer anderen Grammatik bzw. völlig losgelöst von irgendeiner Grammatik verwendet werden.
Das ENGLISH G Grammatik Test- und Übungsbuch (in der Folge: TÜB) ist für fortgeschrittene Englischlernende bestimmt und sowohl lehrbuchbegleitend als auch lehrbuchunabhängig einzusetzen. Es kann in Verbindung mit jedem Lehrwerk etwa ab dem 5. Lernjahr (bei Englisch als erster Fremdsprache) bzw. ab dem 3. Lernjahr (bei Englisch als zweiter Fremdsprache) benutzt werden. Aufgrund seiner besonderen Gestaltung (→ 3.) liegt ein weiterer Schwerpunkt seiner Verwendung in der Oberstufe, so daß es bis zum Abitur herangezogen werden kann.
Das TÜB besitzt zwei zentrale Funktionen: Es ermöglicht dem Lernenden
a) seine Grammatikkenntnisse exakt zu überprüfen und
b) bestehende Wissenslücken mit Hilfe genau zugeordneter Übungen zu schließen.
Daneben trägt es durch die systematisch gegebenen Verweise auf die ENGLISH G Grammatik (in der Folge: EGG) dazu bei, mit einer Schulgrammatik vertraut zu werden und sie zeitsparend und sinnvoll zu gebrauchen.
Aufgrund dieser Anlage eignet sich das TÜB einerseits für die vom Lehrer gesteuerte Arbeit im Klassenzimmer, wobei es beispielsweise als Basis für besondere Wiederholungsstunden (etwa vor oder nach Klassenarbeiten) dient. Andererseits kann es die Grundlage für die selbständige häusliche Tätigkeit des Schülers bilden, der z.B. Lernrückstände beseitigen oder sich auf Prüfungen vorbereiten möchte.

2. Auswahlprinzipien

Das TÜB soll den Schüler zur eigenständigen Arbeit ermutigen und ihn nicht durch die Überfülle grammatikalischer Themen abschrecken. Deshalb wurde das in der EGG enthaltene Strukturenangebot (das ohnehin keine Vollständigkeit anstrebt) im TÜB auf einige Schwerpunkte begrenzt. Vorrangig wurden diejenigen grammatikalischen Bereiche ausgewählt, die deutschsprachigen Schülern erhöhte Schwierigkeiten bereiten und sich bei Unterrichtsbeobachtungen und der Auswertung von Schülerarbeiten als besonders fehlerträchtig erwiesen. Die Aufnahme einer grammatikalischen (Teil-) Struktur wird damit in erster Linie durch die Bedürfnisse des Lernenden gerechtfertigt und ist folglich eher pädagogisch als vom linguistischen System her begründbar. Diese Leitlinie gilt auch für die Verwendung spezifischer Test- und Übungsformen: sie sind vor allem am Lernerfolg des Schülers und nicht an der Einhaltung gewisser methodisch-didaktischer Grundsätze (z.B. der Einsprachigkeit) orientiert.

3. Aufbau und Konzeption

Das TÜB besteht aus 12 Kapiteln, die chronologisch dem Aufbau der EGG folgen, ihn aber nicht genau widerspiegeln. Die Kapitel bauen nicht aufeinander auf, sondern sind in sich abgeschlossen und können unabhängig voneinander behandelt werden.
Jedes Kapitel gliedert sich in einen Test yourself-Abschnitt und darauf folgende Übungsseiten. Beide Teile sind eng aufeinander bezogen, lassen sich allerdings auch ohne den jeweils anderen Teil bearbeiten (→ 4.).

3.1 Die Test yourself-Abschnitte

Alle Test yourself-Abschnitte bestehen aus drei Teilen:
a) dem eigentlichen Test-Teil, b) dem Key, c) dem Exercise finder.

a) Der Test-Teil
Jeder der 12 Test-Teile bietet in den meisten Fällen mehrere Testsätze zu einer grammatikalischen Erscheinung an; damit wird die Aussagekraft der Lösungsergebnisse erhöht. Die Test-Teile sind unterschiedlich strukturiert, da ihre Gestaltung von den jeweils zu überprüfenden Grammatikphänomenen abhängig gemacht wurde. Es gibt jedoch drei zentrale Testbatterien, die in fast jedem Kapitel erscheinen:

- einen *(English-English) Fill in*-Test, bei dem vorangestellte oder in Klammern hinzugefügte englische Wörter oder Teilsätze nach den entsprechenden Umformungen in vorgegebene Sätze eingesetzt werden müssen.
- einen *(German-English) Fill in*-Test, bei dem deutsche Wörter oder Teilsätze ins Englische übersetzt und in vorgegebene englische Sätze eingesetzt bzw. an sie angeschlossen werden müssen. (Vereinzelt sind auch komplette Sätze zu übersetzen.) Diese zweisprachige Testform wurde vor allem bei denjenigen grammatikalischen Erscheinungen angewandt, deren Fehlerträchtigkeit aus dem Einfluß der Muttersprache resultiert. Durch ihre spezifische Gestaltung und die weitgehende Ausschaltung lexikalischer Fehlermöglichkeiten wird deutlich, daß sie nicht an „Übersetzung“, sondern ausschließlich an grammatikalischen Interferenzproblemen orientiert ist.
- einen *Spot the mistakes*-Test, bei dem Sätze präsentiert werden, die fast alle einen grammatikalischen Fehler enthalten, den es zu finden und verbessern gilt. Dieser Test-Teil hat sich in den Erprobungen als besonders wirkungsvoll und motivierend erwiesen. Er führt dem Lernenden noch eindringlicher als die anderen vor Augen, ob er ein Strukturmuster wirklich sicher beherrscht oder von verlockend kontextualisierten, wenn auch falschen Lösungen in die Irre geführt werden kann. Um den Reiz und damit den Lerneffekt noch zu erhöhen, entstammen gelegentlich einige der angebotenen Fehler anderen als den im jeweiligen Kapitel behandelten Fehlerbereichen. Wie von der Testtheorie gefordert, steht den Schülern die richtige Version unmittelbar anschließend zur Verfügung (→ 3.1 b), so daß sich falsche Lösungen nicht einprägen können.

b) Der Key
Der Key präsentiert die (fettgedruckten) Lösungen zu allen vorausgegangenen *test items.* Er enthält meistens auch denjenigen Teil des Satzes (in normalem Druck), durch den die richtige Lösung begründet wird. Zusätzlich gibt der Key bei jeder Lösung die jeweils zutreffenden Paragraphen der EGG an, so daß der Lernende ggf. gezielt in der Grammatik nachschlagen kann. (Verweise in eckigen Klammern beziehen sich auf Grammatikparagraphen, die außerhalb des zentralen Kapitelthemas zur Erklärung nützlich sein können.)
Durch die drucktechnische Anordnung bleibt der Key bei der Bearbeitung der Testsätze verdeckt; er steht dem Schüler durch Umblättern der Seite aber jederzeit zur Verfügung (→ 4.3).

c) Der Exercise finder
Der Exercise finder ist dreispaltig angelegt. Die linke Spalte führt alle Testsätze in numerischer Reihenfolge auf und ordnet sie den entsprechenden Paragraphen der EGG (mittlere Spalte) zu. (Die numerische Reihenfolge der Testsätze wird durch die

Grammatikparagraphen gesteuert.) Die rechte Spalte umfaßt die Nummern der Exercises, die sich auf die jeweiligen Testsätze beziehen. Steht den Nummern der Exercises eine herausgerückte fette Ziffer voran, so verweist sie auf ein fremdes Kapitel, in dem Übungen zu dem getesteten grammatikalischen Stoff angeboten werden. Nummern, die nach dem Semikolon folgen, beziehen sich hingegen auf Übungen des eigentlichen Kapitels. (Beispiel: Im Exercise finder des Kapitels 2 [S. 21] steht für die Testsätze 16, 19, 21 und 25 in Kapitel 1 die Übung 8, im „eigentlichen" Kapitel 2 die Übung 3 zur Verfügung.) Es liegt in der Natur der Sache, daß es im zweigeteilten Vollverb-Kapitel (Kapitel 5 und 6) besonders viele Querzuweisungen bei den Exercises gibt. – Mit Hilfe des Exercise finder kann der Lernende, der eine oder mehrere Testaufgaben zu einem bestimmten grammatikalischen Phänomen falsch gelöst hat, auf einen Blick feststellen, welchen Grammatikparagraphen und welche Übungen er durcharbeiten sollte (→ 4.).
Als Ausnahme sind im Exercise finder des Kapitels 4 – Modale Hilfsverben – einige wenige Testsätze nicht erfaßt, weil ihnen keine Übungen zugeordnet werden.

3.2 Der Übungsteil

Das TÜB enthält insgesamt ca. 170 Exercises. Je nach Übungsgegenstand wurden sie auf der Wort-, *phrase*-, Satz- oder Textebene gestaltet. Die Mehrzahl ist voll kontextualisiert; viele bieten auch vom Inhaltlichen her einen Anreiz zur Bearbeitung. Großer Wert wurde auf ein Angebot unterschiedlicher Übungstypen gelegt. So gibt es etwa Klassifizierungsübungen, in denen der Lernende Beschreibungskategorien der Grammatik besser erfassen und transferieren lernt. Daneben finden sich kommunikativ angelegte Übungen und außerdem zweisprachige Übungen, in denen Fehlerbereiche in den Mittelpunkt gerückt werden, die ihre Ursache in der Interferenz der Muttersprache haben. Diese kontrastiven Übungen stellen jedoch keine „Übersetzungen" dar, da der Schüler jeweils nur die grammatikalisch wichtigen Teilsätze in der Fremdsprache wiederzugeben braucht.
Um den ungleichen Lernvoraussetzungen der Schüler Rechnung zu tragen, werden zu einem grammatikalischen Phänomen häufig zwei oder mehrere Exercises mit unterschiedlichem Schwierigkeitsgrad angeboten. Deutlich schwerere Übungen werden dabei durch das Symbol • gekennzeichnet.
Unter jeder Übung findet sich noch einmal die Angabe derjenigen Paragraphen der EGG, die dem Exercise zugrundeliegen und auf die der Lernende bei der Lösung der Übung zurückgreifen kann. (Im Kapitel 4 – Modale Hilfsverben – wird der Lernende von Exercise 8 an auf das entsprechende Gesamtkapitel der EGG verwiesen.)
Da ein wesentlicher Anwendungsbereich des TÜB – vor allem in der Oberstufe – in der selbständigen Arbeit der Lernenden liegt, wurde der Schlüssel zu den Exercises ins Buch eingelegt. Er steht damit den Schülern zur Verfügung, kann aber vom Lehrer auch leicht entfernt werden, wenn pädagogisch-didaktische Erwägungen dies erfordern.

4. Arbeitsformen

Der Aufbau des TÜB gestattet eine äußerst flexible Benutzung. Im folgenden werden eine als „Normalmodell" bezeichnete Arbeitsform und darüberhinaus einige Varianten dargestellt.

4.1 Das „Normalmodell“

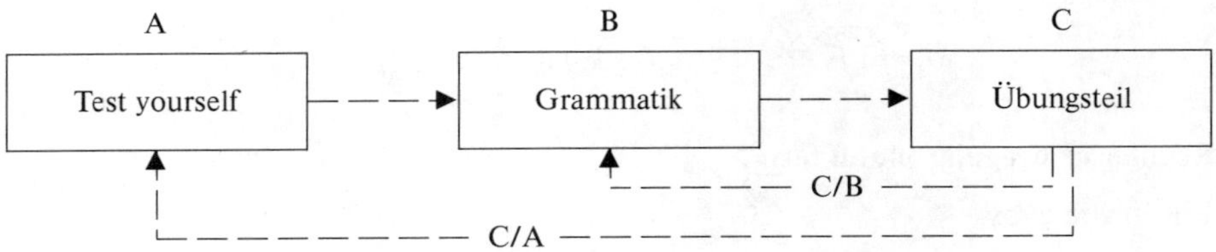

Aus der Graphik geht der Weg hervor, den der Schüler beim Durchgang durch ein Kapitel einschlagen kann:
- die Test yourself-Abschnitte (A) bilden den Ausgangspunkt;
- bei falsch gelösten Testsätzen werden die entsprechenden Paragraphen in der EGG (B) rekapituliert;
- im Übungsteil (C) werden die den falsch gelösten Testsätzen zugeordneten Exercises absolviert;
- tauchen bei der Bearbeitung der Übungen Schwierigkeiten auf, wird erneut die Grammatik herangezogen (C/B);
- zum Abschluß können zur Kontrolle noch einmal diejenigen Testsätze gelöst werden, bei denen zu Beginn der Arbeit Fehler auftraten (C/A).

4.2 Alternative Modelle

Das „Normalmodell“ bedient sich aller angebotenen Werkteile und bewirkt dadurch den größten Lerneffekt. Das TÜB ermöglicht aber auch andere Vorgehensweisen, die sich etwa aus zeitökonomischen Gründen als sinnvoll erweisen können:
a) die Schüler lassen C unmittelbar auf A folgen;
b) sie beginnen mit B und bearbeiten dann erst A und evtl. C;
c) sie bearbeiten C in Verbindung mit B und lösen A zum Abschluß.

4.3 Praktische Hinweise zur Arbeit mit den Test yourself-Abschnitten

Zu den Testsätzen: Die Schüler lösen die Testaufgaben der Reihe nach – vorzugsweise in Stillarbeit. Sie schreiben ihre Lösungen auf ein Blatt Papier (sofern ihnen das TÜB nicht selbst gehört). Bei Unklarheiten und Zweifeln, vor allem im *Spot the mistakes*-Teil, blättern sie sofort um und vergewissern sich im Key der richtigen Lösung.
Zum Key: Nachdem alle Testsätze bearbeitet sind, vergleichen die Schüler ihre Lösungen mit den im Key gegebenen und korrigieren ihre Fehler. Die Nummern der falsch gelösten Aufgaben werden kenntlich gemacht bzw. gesondert notiert. Kann sich der Schüler eine Lösung nicht erklären, sollte sofort der angegebene Grammatikparagraph (→ B) herangezogen werden.
Zum Exercise finder: Die Schüler vergleichen die Nummern ihrer falsch gelösten Testsätze mit der Aufstellung im Exercise finder. Haben sie bei allen einem Grammatikparagraphen zugeordneten Sätzen Fehler gemacht, sollten im Regelfall sowohl der aufgeführte Paragraph (→ B) als auch alle für diese betreffende Testaufgabe vorgesehenen Exercises (→ C) durchgearbeitet werden. Wurde jedoch nur einer von mehreren Testsätzen zu einem Grammatikproblem fehlerhaft gelöst, sollten die Schüler von der Schwere des Fehlers her selbst entscheiden, ob sie die Lektüre der Grammatik und die Bearbeitung der Übungen für nötig erachten.

The noun and the article

Test yourself

A **Regular or irregular plural form?**

Fill in the gaps.

1.	guy:	guys	=	monkey:	...?
2.	radio:	radios	=	Negro:	...?
3.	mass:	masses	=	brush:	...?
4.	leaf:	leaves	=	belief:	...?
5.	tooth:	teeth	=	foot:	...?
6.	giraffe:	giraffes	=	sheep:	...?
7.	helicopter:	helicopters	=	aircraft:	...?
8.	house:	houses	=	mouse:	...?

B Put in the right article, determiner, pronoun and form of the verb "be". Sometimes it would be wrong to fill in anything.

9. What ... nice day! – Yes, it's ... lovely weather. Much better than yesterday.
10. You can't wear your white jeans. ... still in the washing-machine.
11. This is your captain speaking. I have ... good news and ... bad news. ... bad news ... that we are lost.
12. There's always a difference between an experiment and ... real life.
13. ... Parliament will not sit again till the autumn.
14. Some people are afraid that some day ... computers will replace ... teachers.
15. After ... school Carol's boy-friend was waiting for her at the bus-stop opposite ... church.
16. The little boy walked up the hill to ... prison and stared up at its tall gates.
17. ☐ You had better buy ... both books.
18. No matter how hard they tried, ... most immigrants could not escape from poverty.
19. ☐ He wants to be ... waiter like his father.
20. ☐ Mr Nelson became ... MP at 26.
21. We warned them not to go skating on such ... thin ice.
22. You say Jane's father is dead? What ... terrible news!
23. I'm in ... hurry now. Could you ring me up tonight?

C Fill in the gaps with English equivalents for the German words given in brackets.

24. When Derek's aunt died, he tried to get rid of ... . (die alten Möbel)
25. I can't find the scissors. – ... in the top drawer? (Ist sie nicht)
26. ... one race is superior to another. (Es gibt keine Beweise dafür, daß)
27. That terrible Miss Ward always makes us do ... . (viele Hausaufgaben)
28. ... given in the newspapers ... always right. (Informationen; sind nicht)
29. * You had better wait until ... . (die Polizei kommt)
30. How ... flies. Susan left school last year and little Tom is nearly 14. (die Zeit)
31. Sometimes ... can be even more dangerous than ... . (das Wasser; das Feuer)
32. ... keep going up and people just have to put up with it. (Die Preise)

33. ... Peter Shaw used to believe that the Germans worked harder than the English. (Der neunzehnjährige)
☐ 34. He poured ... into the bath. (die halbe Flasche)
☐ 35. ... Petra didn't enjoy music at all. (Als Kind)
36. Something of ... may help to decide an election. (einer solchen Wichtigkeit)

D Spot the mistakes.

There is one mistake in each of the following sentences or groups of sentences. But this may mean that more than one word is wrong. Spot the mistakes and write down what you think is the correct version.

37. He drank several glasses whisky to escape from reality.
38. My trouser is getting too small. I really need a new one.
39. I talked to Shirley about it and she gave me a good advice.
40. I hope that anyone who uses this book will have good knowledges of the basic grammatical terms.
41. No, John. You can't go out tonight. Work before the pleasure, you know.
42. Five hours later the plane crossed the border which separated the civilization from the jungle.
43. In Britain the women are paid, on average, lower wages than the men.
44. Which British queen often visited Germany? Was it the Queen Victoria?
45. After the school Anne went straight home because there was a lot of homework to do.
☐ 46. Dick was offered the double salary by the new firm.
☐ 47. His mother is housewife, and his father works as engineer for a computer firm.
48. What a fun school would be if you didn't have to think about your report.
49. As result of the strike the management promised better working conditions.
50. Irene is a typist, but she's out of work, so she helps out two nights the week.
☐ 51. A Frenchman, two Swisses and two germans were arrested for smuggling last night.
☐ 52. In 1649 the Scottish declared Charles II to be their King.
53. I've heard that Coventry is quite a nice town, but what is its surroundings like?

"We're seven dwarfs, but not The Seven Dwarfs."

Key

A

1. monkeys .... § 8 a
2. Negroes .... § 8 c
3. brushes .... § 7
4. beliefs .... § 8 b
5. **feet** .... § 10 a
6. **sheep** .... § 10 b
7. **aircraft** .... § 10 b
8. **mice** .... § 10 a

B

9. What **a** nice day! Yes, it's **lovely weather**... . ... §§ 14 a; 14 b; 34 b
10. ...**They're** still... . ... § 15
11. ...**some** good news and **some** bad news. **The** bad news **is**... . ... § 16 a
12. ...an experiment and **real life**. .... § 24 a
13. **Parliament** will not sit... . ... § 24 c
14. ...some day **computers** will replace **teachers**. .... § 24 c
15. After **school**...opposite **the** church. .... § 27
16. ...up the hill to **the** prison... . ... § 27
- □ 17. ...buy **both books**. .... § 29
18. No matter how hard they tried, **most immigrants** could not escape... . ... § 30 b
- □ 19. He wants to be **a** waiter... . ... § 32
- □ 20. Mr Nelson became **an** MP... . ... § 32
21. ...on **such thin ice**. .... § 24 b
22. What **terrible news**! .... § 34 b
23. ...in **a** hurry... . ... § 35

C

24. ...get rid of **the old furniture**. .... § 14 b
25. **Aren't they**... ? .... § 15
26. **There is no evidence that**... . ... § 16 a
27. ...**a lot of/lots of homework**. .... § 16 a
28. **Information**...**isn't** always right. .... § 16 a
- * 29. ...**the police come**. .... § 16 d
30. How **time** flies. .... § 24 a
31. Sometimes **water** can be even more dangerous than **fire**. .... § 24 b
32. **Prices** keep going up... . ... § 24 c
33. **Nineteen-year-old** Peter Shaw... . ... § 25 b
- □ 34. ...**half the bottle**... . ... § 29
- □ 35. **As a child**... . ... § 32
36. Something of **such importance**... . ... § 34 a

D

37. ...several **glasses of whisky**... . ... § 14 c
38. My **trousers are**... . I really need **(some) new ones**. .. § 15
39. ...she gave me **some good advice**. .... § 16 a
40. ...**a good knowledge** of the basic grammatical terms. § 16 a

	41. ...work before **pleasure**.	§ 24 a
	42. ...the border which separated **civilization** from the jungle.	§ 24 a
	43. In Britain **women** are paid... lower wages than **men**.	§ 24 c
	44. ...Was it **Queen Victoria**?	§ 25 a
	45. After **school**...	§ 27
☐	46. He was offered **double the salary**...	§ 29
☐	47. His mother is **a housewife**, and his father works as **an engineer**...	§ 32
	48. **What fun** school would be...	§ 34 b
	49. **As a result**...	§ 35
	50. ...she helps out two nights **a week**.	§ 33
☐	51. ...**two Swiss** and two **Germans**...	§§ 11 a; 11 c
☐	52. ...**the Scots**...	§ 11 b
	53. ...what **are its surroundings** like?	§ 16 b

Exercise finder

Test yourself	ENGLISH G Grammatik	Exercises
1, 2, 4	§ 8 a/b/c	1
3	§ 7	1
5, 6, 7, 8	§ 10 a/b	1
9	§ 14 a	3, 4, 5, •7, 13
9, 22, 48	§ 34 b	13
9, 24	§ 14 b	3, 4, 5, 6, •7, 13
10, 25, 38	§ 15	4, 8
11, 26, 27, 28, 40	§ 16 a	3, 4, 5, 6, •7, 13
12, 21, 30, 31, 39, 41, 42	§ 24 a/b	•9, 10, 13
13	§ 24	10
14, 32, 43	§ 24 c	10, 13
15, 16, 45	§ 27	11, 13
17, 34, 46	§ 29	13
18	§ 30 b	13
19, 20, 35, 47	§ 32	12
23, 49	§ 35	13
29, 53	§ 16 b/d	4, 5
33	§ 25 b	•9, 10, 13
36	§ 34 a	13
37	§ 14 c	5, 6, 13
44	§ 25 a	10
50	§ 33	13
51, 52	§ 11 a/b/c	2

For instructions on how to use this Exercise finder see pages 5-6.

Exercises

The plural of nouns

1 Put the following nouns into the plural. Then choose the correct noun to finish each sentence.

aircraft, beach, child, country, foot, hero, potato, roof, sex, sheep, shelf, sportsman, studio, survey

1. It's quite common to see Japanese video equipment on the ... of Britain's big department stores.
2. People who live near Heathrow Airport are often woken up by the sound of ... taking off or landing.
3. The ... of hundreds of houses were torn off during the storm.
4. The election results will be broadcast live from special radio and TV ... in Westminster.
5. "Would you prefer chips or boiled ... , sir?" the waitress asked.
6. According to all the ... published in recent years, only a minority of the population would like the U.K. to be turned into a republic.
7. The sales assistant claims that this game is suitable for ... of all ages.
8. Perhaps the nicest thing about the Olympic Games is that ... from all over the world get a chance to meet each other and make friends.
9. The headmistress criticized the teenager who'd organized the vandalism, but she also blamed the other members of the gang for following him like ... .
10. When Ann first started her new company, her father-in-law helped her. But she's able to stand on her own two ... now.
11. In 1983 the Queen of England, Elizabeth II, was the head of fifteen independent ... , all of which were members of the Commonwealth.
12. The majority of jobs can be done by people of both ... .
13. As a result of the latest tanker disaster, an enormous oil-slick is moving towards the ... of southern California.
14. The firemen, who had worked through the night to save as many lives as possible, were described by reporters at the scene of the accident as ... .

§§ 7; 8 a/b/c; 10 a/b

2 Find the right noun for the nationality, then write down its plural form.

Example: Kevin discussed business with three Germans. (people from Germany)

Kevin O'Hara, the sales chief of an Oxford computer company, had a busy time at an electronics exhibition in Cologne last month. He met a group of ... (1. people from Belgium), whom he'd sold equipment to before, two ... (2. people from Switzerland) who were looking for some special equipment for their private hospital, a delegation of ... (3. people from Israel) who wanted to buy several computers for a university science laboratory and two ... (4. people from Denmark) who immediately ordered a large machine for their factory in Esbjerg. He also spoke to a team of ... (5. people from France) who needed a machine to co-ordinate their research programme and a group of ... (6. people from Japan) who arranged to visit his company in Oxford later in the year. In addition, Kevin met several ... (7. people from the U.S.A.) and ... (8. people from England) whom he already knew.

§§ 11 a/b/c

Countables and uncountables, singular and plural nouns

3 Decide which nouns are countable. Then write them down in the plural form.

advice, chemistry, damage, edition, equipment, evidence, explosion, furniture, homework, information, knowledge, leaflet, loss, news, pollution, population, prize, progress, receiver, schedule, segregation, source, third, unemployment, weather

§§ 14 a/b; 16 a

4 Put the following nouns into four groups.

advice, apprentice, chaos, clothes, discrimination, electricity, happiness, homework, lights, lioness, mice, outskirts, news, pliers, police, progress, pros, politeness, radiation, slices, spice, telex, thanks, tights, U.S.A.

countable (sing.)	countable (pl.)	uncountable (sing.)	uncountable (pl.)
...	...	...	...

§§ 14 a/b; 15; 16 a/b/d

5 Look carefully at the words and phrases in brackets. Then write down all the words and phrases that can be used to finish each sentence.

Example: John's daughter dislikes her new maths teacher because he gives the pupils ..too much / lots of.. homework. (many/a lot/too much/lots of)

1. John Anderson, a London detective, finds that his job gives him ... satisfaction. (a lot of/no/fewer/little)
2. He's a member of a team trying to catch a gang of drug smugglers, but they need ... information. (another/a new/much more/further)
3. An MP has just phoned to complain, because they don't seem to have made ... progress yet. (lots of/many/much/a lot)
4. "Perhaps you think that a bit of heroin won't cause ... damage?" the MP said. (many serious/many/a lot of/much)
5. "Listen," the MP said, "I think I ought to give you ... advice." (a few/a little/a bit/an)
6. "I don't think you'll ever solve this case unless you have ... police officers working on it." (much/a lot/a few/a little)
7. This particular MP happens to have ... knowledge of London's night clubs. (many/little/few/a fine)
8. "Why ... police watching that club in Hook Street?" he asked. "It's a waste of time. I know the owner." (is a/are a/is the/are the)
9. "Because we've just been given ... interesting news," John told him. (a few/a piece/an/a bit of)
10. "One of the waiters at the club has just bought an expensive new sports car, although he doesn't get ... high wages. We're sure he's a member of the gang." (a very/very/very much/very many)

§§ 14 a/b/c; 16 a/b/d; 62

6 Translate the following expressions and sentences into English.

1. weitere Auskünfte
2. eine gute Nachricht
3. sehr gute Englischkenntnisse
4. wenige Beweise
5. viel Schaden
6. wenige nützliche Ratschläge
7. Keine Nachrichten sind gute Nachrichten.
8. Diese Hausaufgaben sind viel zu schwierig.
9. Ich bin sicher, daß diese Möbel aus Kunststoff sind.

§§ 14 b/c; 16 a

•7 Put in the right noun, in the plural form if necessary, and choose the correct determiner from the brackets.

conveyor-belt, country, decorator, damage, information, knowledge, luck, news, progress, radio

Dear Mr Werdenberg,

Thank you for your letter of 25th August.

Having heard so (1. many/much/a lot of) bad . . . (2) recently, I am particularly delighted that you have agreed to represent our company in Switzerland and Italy. You not only have (3. an/a lot of/a lot) experience in our field; fortunately, you speak German and English perfectly and have (4. a/some/a lot of) working . . . (5) of both French and Italian. With (6. few/little/a little) . . . (7) I am convinced that we will be able to export (8. a lot/a lot of/much) more of our . . . (9) to (10. this/these) . . . (11) in the next (12. few/a few/little) months.

In answer to your question I am pleased to tell you that the fire at our new factory last month did not do as (13. many/much/a lot of) . . . (14) as we had at first estimated, and the . . . (15) have now started to run normally again. The . . . (16) are at work, too, and they have already made (17. a lot/many/a lot of) . . . (18).

Next week I will be sending you (19. little/a little/a few) . . . (20) about our latest cassette model for small cars, which you should find very interesting.

I am looking forward to meeting you at the conference on 13th October.

Yours faithfully,

J. Hanby

(John J. Hanby)

§§ 14 a/b; 16 a; 62

8 **Pair nouns**

Finish these short dialogues by choosing the right form from the brackets. ("–" means no additional word is needed.)

1. *Mr Lee:* How can I repair the car radio if I can't find my pliers?
   Robert: I think I noticed ... in the hall, Dad. (it/them/one)
2. *Tom:* I like your new jeans, Sue. ... expensive? (Was it/Were they)
   Sue: No. Cheaper than my old ..., in fact. (one/–/ones)
3. *Martin:* Do you happen to know where the big scissors ... ? (is/are)
   Frank: Why? What do you want ... for? (it/them/one)
4. *1st Stewardess:* Have you heard the latest? We're getting a new uniform. Same jacket, but with dark blue trousers.
   2nd Stewardess: The Europair crew wear dark blue ..., too, don't they? (one/ones/some)
   1st Stewardess: I'm not sure. But I know one thing. It isn't a new ... trousers that we need. What they really ought to give us is a longer break between flights. (pair of/–/pair)
5. *Ed:* Have you seen my tennis racket, Al? And have you got any idea where my tennis shorts ... gone? (is/has/have)
   Al: Yes. Mum has just washed ... . (it/them/one)
   Ed: Oh no! What can I wear now? I wish I had two ... . (ones/–/pairs)

§§ 15; 39

The definite article

•9 Put in an abstract noun, made from the verb/adjective in brackets. Add the definite article if necessary.

Example: How will Jeff cope with ...*the disappointment*... (disappoint) if he fails to get that job he's applied for?

1. The new town council is doing a lot to fight ...(pollute), I think.
2. Dr Fields believes that certain illnesses are the result of the way in which ... modern ...(social) has developed.
3. Tom is helped in his new job by ...(know) he gained in Africa.
4. Apartheid is practised in South Africa, but different kinds of ...(discriminate) are practised in other countries, too.
5. "Who gave you ...(permit) to come in here?" Miss Evans asked.
6. Believe me, ...(live) is worth living, even if you've got problems.
7. This early record by the Beatles is ...(proud) of Ed's collection.
8. Yesterday Helga saw an interesting documentary film about the unemployment problems in ... rural ...(Spanish).
9. Will ...(electrical) be cheaper if it comes from nuclear power stations?
10. Can too much money stop you from finding ... real ...(happy)?
11. Our local MP is thinking of retiring from ...(political) soon.
12. Some taxpayers think the government should spend less on ...(defend) and more on ...(modernize) of our factories.

§§ 24 a/b; 25 b

10 Finish the translations by translating the nouns that are underlined and adding the definite article if necessary.

1. Ab morgen wird <u>das Benzin</u> viel billiger.
   From tomorrow ... will be a lot cheaper.
2. Wie heißt der Abgeordnete, der deine Stadt im <u>Parlament</u> vertritt?
   What's the name of the MP who represents your town in ... ?
3. Martina hält nicht viel von <u>den Schulbüchern</u>, die ihre Großeltern benutzen mußten.
   Martina doesn't think much of ... her grandparents had to use.
4. Uta liebt <u>die Natur</u>, ihr Mann geht lieber ins Kino.
   Uta loves ... , her husband prefers going to the cinema.
5. Die Stadtverwaltung tut zu wenig für <u>die Jugend</u>.
   The council doesn't do enough for ... .
6. Stimmt es, daß <u>die amerikanische Gesellschaft</u> wenig auf Formen achtet?
   Is it true that ... pays little attention to form?
7. Herr Richter war mit dem Essen in seinem Hotel in Manchester generell zufrieden, aber er mochte <u>das Brot</u> nicht: Es war ihm zu weich.
   Generally speaking, Mr Richter was satisfied with the food at his hotel in Manchester, but he didn't like ... , he thought it was too soft.
8. Die Schüler sahen einen Film, der einen Tag aus <u>dem Leben</u> einer Krankenschwester darstellte.
   The pupils watched a film about a day in ... of a nurse.
9. Ursula hat <u>dem Großvater</u> gerade erst geschrieben.
   Ursula has only just written to ... .
10. Wir sind Freitag bei <u>Kellers</u> zum Abendessen eingeladen.
    We've been invited to dinner at ... on Friday.
11. Werden <u>die Frauen</u> heute genauso benachteiligt wie früher?
    Are ... discriminated against as much now as they used to be?

§§ 24 a/b/c; 25 a/b

11 Put in the definite article if it is needed.

1. As soon as Paul has packed his satchel he's going to ... school.
2. Janet hopes to go to ... university and study medicine.
3. Liz and Fiona are both nurses. They're on their way to ... hospital now.
4. Mrs Barlow drove very dangerously after leaving the pub – and killed a man on a zebra crossing. Now a judge is sending her to ... prison.
5. Jill's boy-friend is in ... hospital. This afternoon she's going to visit him and take him some flowers.
6. Jeff knows it will be hard to find a job after 9 years in ... prison.
7. Mrs Shaw wants to talk to Alan's headmaster. So she's going to ... school tomorrow afternoon after work.
8. Don is a very religious man. He goes to ... church every Sunday.
9. There was a fire at a church in St. John Street last week. Two fire-engines rushed to ... church within minutes.

§ 27

12 The indefinite article

Put in the indefinite article if it is needed.

1. Is it true that Helga's husband is ... Irishman?
2. Shirley isn't going to vote ... Liberal at the next election.
3. Freddy Baker used to be ... pilot, didn't he?
4. The church Andrew goes to is ... Catholic, I believe.
5. The new director of our company in Hong Kong isn't British, it seems, though she's married to ... European.
6. Justin is training to be ... air traffic controller.
7. Graham belongs to the Labour Party, but he isn't really ... socialist in my opinion.
8. Brigitte studied law for several years and later became ... university professor in Heidelberg.
9. Ben Cohen is a New York taxi driver. He's ... Jew and he sometimes thinks of emigrating to Israel.
10. Lisa has always been interested in electronics. When she leaves school, she'd like to get a job as ... electronics engineer.

§ 32

13 Definite or indefinite article?

Put in the definite or indefinite article – but only where necessary. In some cases you mustn't add anything at all.

When Heidi Frommelt from ... (1) Switzerland visited London last year, she took ... (2) advice of the hotel receptionist and visited one of the city's traditional street markets. And what ... (3) interesting experience it was!

The market was ... (4) such ... (5) colourful sight and full of ... (6) life, with stalls selling everything from ... (7) fresh fruit to a variety of products of ... (8) modern society, such as transistor radios, ... (9) scissors for ... (10) left-handed people, ... (11) latest pop records and rather ... (12) ugly second-hand furniture. Almost all ... (13) clothes that Heidi saw seemed to come from Commonwealth countries, such as India and Hong Kong, and ... (14) most of them struck her as cheap – only about ... (15) half ... (16) price of what she usually bought in Zurich. Some things seemed more expensive, however. For example, she saw some tomatoes selling at 70 p ... (17) pound.

Heidi liked the atmosphere. Although ... (18) most of ... (19) people selling the items shouted loudly at the people walking past, ... (20) most of them did this in ... (21) friendly way. They made ... (22) noise, but they made their customers laugh, too.

After spending about three hours at ... (23) market, ... (24) poor Heidi had ... (25) awful headache – and almost felt as if she should be in ... (26) hospital! However, she had really enjoyed herself and had bought some unusual presents for her friends.

§§ 14 a/b/c; 16 a; 24 a/b/c; 25 b; 26; 27; 29; 30 b; 33; 34 a/b; 35

The adjective and the adverb

Test yourself

A Read the following sentences carefully and make the necessary changes to the words in brackets. In some cases no changes are required.

1. "Have they arrived ...(safe)?" their mother asked ...(anxious).
2. How do you feel today? I hope as ...(good) as you did yesterday.
3. Each word in this dictionary is explained as ...(simple) as ...(possible).
4. Jean was nervous about the interview. But the manager spoke to her ... (friendly).
5. Journalists cannot report ...(free) from all countries in spite of the agreement reached in Helsinki in 1975.
6. When she heard that her husband hadn't been ...(serious) injured, she looked ...(relieved).
7. It may be true, but I find it ...(hard) to believe.
8. What's wrong with you? You look ...(unhappy).
9. Waiter, this fish smells ...(bad).
10. Why don't you tell the truth? It would make things ...(easy).
11. If I were you, I wouldn't take her warning too ...(serious).
12. The thief looked ...(nervous) round the corner.
13. "Sit up ...(straight), John," his mother said ...(impatient).
14. If you want to catch the first train, you'll have to get up ...(early).

B **Anything missing?**

Look carefully at the following sentences and decide if "one", "ones", "man" or some other noun is missing to complete a sentence.

15. Hope for the best and expect the worst.
16. If this exercise is too difficult for you, let's try an easier.
17. Lots of old are lonely and really appreciate a visit from a young.
18. Society should take care of the old and the lonely.
19. Brown bread is better for your health than white.
20. I hope you bought Helen a nice present. After all you're the rich in the family.
21. By the end of the year all the old furniture will have been replaced by new.
22. More than 140 dead or missing have been reported.
23. "But what about him?" asked the detective looking at the dead.
24. Liz has failed her driving-test again. – The poor.
25. Get me my pills. – Which? The yellow?

C Fill in the gaps with English equivalents for the German words given in brackets.

26. ...is that he's always helpful. (Das Nette an Peter)
27. Thank you. I don't need any ... . (weiteren Auskünfte)
28. The quick reaction of a passenger saved ... . (uns das Leben)
29. Elderly people should remain ... as long as possible. (im eigenen Heim)
30. Imagine yourself sitting here ... . (mit einem eigenen kleinen Baby)
31. Jane can jump even ... Bert. (höher als)

32. Have you tasted our new marmalade? - Yes, it tastes .... (sehr gut)
33. Kevin seems to be out of form. Last Sunday he played .... (schlechter als je)
34. What's wrong with Terry? I haven't seen him .... (in der letzten Zeit)
35. Something was wrong in the garden. Jane ... and looked outside. (öffnete langsam die Tür)
36. You never listen to what I tell you. You ... the same mistakes. (machst immer)
37. When she heard that Susan was at the club, ... (ging sie sofort dorthin)
38. ... from Poland sounds alarming. (Die letzten Nachrichten)
39. The ... street is the ... way to the station. (nächste; nächste)
40. Jane has a beautiful voice and she plays .... (sehr gut Gitarre)

D Spot the mistakes.

There is one mistake in each of the following sentences or groups of sentences. Spot the mistakes and write down what you think is the correct version.

41. On November 11th we remember the deads of two world wars.
42. He will sooner or later come.
43. He knows when to keep the mouth shut.
44. I don't need your car. I've got an own car outside.
45. The name at the top is my own one.
46. She could hardly keep the eyes open.
47. My brother can't help you. He's got an own family to worry about.
48. These animals become very wildly in a storm.
49. The boss threatened to sack Diane, and she took his threats quiet seriously although she should have known better.
50. Obviously, Sarah was embarrassed. That's why she behaved so sillily.
51. The wages oilmen receive are good earned.
52. I was stopped for driving too fast, but the policeman only told me to be carefuller in future.
53. I met yesterday Rose. It's hard to believe that she's been away for two years.
54. The drug problem is worser now than it was ten years ago.
55. Our firm is looking for ways to produce goods more economic.

Key

A

1.	... arrived **safely** ... asked **anxiously**.	§ 46
2.	How do you feel ... as **well** as	§ 48 f
3.	... explained as **simply** as **possible**.	§ 48 b
4.	... **in a friendly way**.	§ 48 e
5.	... report **freely**	§ 50
6.	... **seriously** injured, she looked **relieved**.	§§ 46; 51 b
7.	... I find it **hard** to believe.	§ 50
8.	... You look **unhappy**.	§ 51 b
9.	... this fish smells **bad**.	§ 51 a
10.	... It would make things **easier/easy**.	§ 51 a
11.	... take her warning too **seriously**.	§ 46
12.	The thief looked **nervously** round the corner.	§ 51 b
13.	"Sit up **straight**, John", ... **impatiently**.	§§ 49; 46
14.	... get up **early**.	§ 49

B

15.	Hope for **the best** and expect **the worst**.	§ 38
16.	... let's try **an easier one**.	§ 39 a
17.	Lots of **old people** ... a visit from **a young person**.	§ 37 b
18.	... take care of **the old** and **the lonely**.	§ 37 a
19.	Brown bread is better ... than **white**.	§ 39 a
20.	... **the rich one/person** in the family.	§ 37 b
21.	... the old furniture will have been replaced by **new**.	§ 39 a
22.	More than **140 dead or missing** have been reported.	§ 37 a
23.	... **the dead man/boy**.	§ 37 b
24.	... **The poor thing/girl**.	§ 37 b
25.	... my pills." – "**Which (ones)? The yellow ones**?"	§ 39 a

C

26.	**The nice thing about Peter**	§ 38
27.	... **further/more/extra information**.	§ 42 b
28.	The quick reaction ... saved **our lives**.	§ 44 b
29.	Elderly people should remain **in their own homes**	§ 45
30.	... **with a little baby of your own**.	§ 45
31.	Jane can jump even **higher than**	§§ 40 a; 43 a; 50
32.	... it tastes **very good**.	§ 51 a
33.	... he played **worse than ever**.	§ 53
34.	I haven't seen him **recently/lately**.	§§ 55 b; 57 b
35.	... Jane **opened the door slowly**	§§ 56 c; 57 a
36.	... **You always make**	§§ 56 b; 57 c
37.	... **she went there immediately/at once**.	§ 57 f
38.	**The latest news**	§ 42 b
39.	The **next** street is the **nearest** way	§ 42 b
40.	... plays **the guitar very well**.	§ 56 c

D

41.	… we remember **the dead** … .	§ 37 a
42.	**Sooner or later** he will come **(sooner or later)**.	§§ 56 a; 56 c; 57 b
43.	He knows when to keep **his mouth** shut.	§ 44 b
44.	… I've got **my own car/a car of my own** … .	§ 45
45.	The name at the top is **my own**.	§ 45
46.	She could hardly keep **her eyes** open.	§ 44 b
47.	He's got **a family of his own/his own family** … .	§ 45
48.	These animals become very **wild** … .	§ 51
49.	… **quite** seriously … .	§ 55 d
50.	… she behaved **in such a silly way/so stupidly**.	§ 48 e
51.	The wages … are **well** earned.	§ 50
52.	… the policeman told me to be **more careful** … .	§ 40 c
53.	I met Rose **yesterday./Yesterday** I met Rose.	§§ 56 c; 57 b
54.	The drug problem is **worse** now … .	§ 42 a
55.	… ways to produce goods **more economically**.	§§ 48 c; 52

Exercise finder

Test yourself	ENGLISH G Grammatik	Exercises
1, 6, 11	§ 46	•8, 11, 14
2	§ 48 f	9
3	§ 48 b	9, 11
4, 50	§ 48 e	9, 11
5, 7, 31, 51	§ 50	10, 11, 14
6, 8, 9, 10, 12, 32, 48	§ 51 a/b	12
13, 14	§ 49	14
15, 22, 26	§ 38	2, 3
16, 19, 21, 25	§ 39 a	1 :8; 3
17, 18, 20, 22, 23, 24, 41	§ 37 a/b	1, 3, 4
27, 38, 39	§ 42 b	6, 13
28, 43, 46	§ 44 b	7
29, 30, 44, 45, 47	§ 45	7
31, 52	§ 40 a/c	4, 5, 13, 14
33	§ 53	13
34	§§ 55 b; 57 b	15, •16
35	§ 57 a	15, •16
35, 40, 42, 53	§ 56 c	15, •16
36	§§ 56 b; 57 c	15, •16
37	§ 57 f	15, •16
42	§§ 56 a; 56 c; 57 b	15, •16
49	§§ 55 d; 57 d	15, •16
54	§ 42 a	5, 14
55	§§ 48 c; 52	9, 11, 14

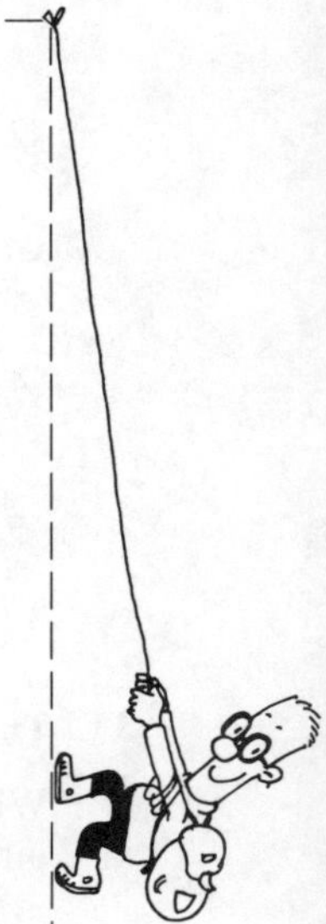

Exercises

Adjectives used as nouns

1 Put in a suitable noun, but only where this is necessary.

1. Is ours a society in which the strong ... look after the weak ... ?
2. What was the name of the boring ... who wanted to tell you his life history at Henry's party?
3. All the young ... at the party wanted to dance with the attractive ... from Duisburg.
4. The new French restaurant in Banbury Road seems to be attracting the rich ... and the famous ... , but I can't afford the prices there.
5. A successful ... left all his money to a home for the old ... .
6. It's often difficult to persuade the racially prejudiced ... to re-examine their views.

§ 37 a/b

2 Finish the translations by putting in "the + adjective" or "the + adjective + thing".

1. Unter diesen Umständen wäre es das Sinnvollste, glaube ich, einen Arzt aufzusuchen.
   In the circumstances, I reckon, ... would be to go and see a doctor.
2. Menschen mit altmodischen Ansichten akzeptieren oft nur widerwillig das Neue.
   People with old-fashioned views are often unwilling to accept ... .
3. Redakteure sollten Wichtiges von Unwichtigem unterscheiden können.
   Editors should be able to tell ... from ... .
4. Das Beste an dieser Stelle ist die Gelegenheit, Menschen in der Dritten Welt zu helfen.
   ... about this job is the opportunity you get to help people in the Third World.
5. Die Politik wurde einmal als die Kunst des Möglichen bezeichnet.
   Politics was once defined as the art of ... .

§ 38

3 **The prop-word "one"**

Where possible, put in "one" or "ones". Otherwise, complete the sentences by putting in a suitable noun. e.g. "thing".

1. Children enjoy various games, of course, but these days they often seem to like the electronic ... most of all.
2. All of the students solved the easy problems, but not many of them managed to solve the difficult ... .
3. "Let's have lunch first," the manager said. "We can discuss the financial ... later."
4. Chris kept the bigger apple for himself and gave Carol the smaller ... .
5. "These modern dances are only for the fit and athletic ... ," Gary said.
6. Clyde asked the tall girl for a dance, while Al asked the dark-haired ... .
7. "The new horror film at the Apollo isn't for the nervous ... ," Carl said.

§§ 37 a/b; 38; 39 a

The comparison of adjectives

4 Put in the comparative form of the adjectives in brackets, remembering to use "more" or "less" in some cases. But put in the nouns given in brackets only if they are necessary here.

Clive Shingler's electronics company has started to produce a series of miniature calculators that are very much ... (1. small) than the well-known ... (2. models) they used to produce. These XZ 89 calculators are ... (3. light) than the old ... (4. series) that they're replacing, weighing less than 25 g. The firm's traditional ... (5. calculators) were a lot ... (6. heavy), weighing over 200 g. At the same time the XZ 89 is ... (7. powerful), since it was developed using only the best ... (8. results) of today's technology; and Mr Shingler's chief designer claims that the XZ 89 is much ... (9. attractive) to look at, too.

The keys on the early ... (10. machines) were quite a bit ... (11. large) than the keys on the XZ 89. So people with big fingers might have found the old-fashioned ... (12. models) a little ... (13. easy) to use. However, as the new ... (14. calculators) are as small as a credit card, they're much ... (15. convenient) to carry around with you. Mr Shingler's new ... (16. machines) can be individually programmed, too, like computers, so scientists or students will find them ... (17. useful). His sales manager expects to sell a lot of them because, surprisingly, they're even ... (18. expensive) than the rather basic, old ... (19. series) and people are always keen to buy the new ... (20. products).

§§ 37 a/b; 40 a/b/c

5 Find "the fourth man". Study the relationship between the expressions given in (a), then put in the missing expression that will form a similar relationship in (b).

Example: (a) punctual/more punctual (b) fast/.faster..

1. (a) satisfactory/more satisfactory (b) convenient/...
2. (a) skilled/more skilled (b) big/...
3. (a) educated/(the) most educated (b) sad/...
4. (a) useful/(the) most useful (b) bad/...
5. (a) effective/more effective (b) far/...
6. (a) confident/more confident (b) fit/...
7. (a) responsible/more responsible (b) filthy/...
8. (a) remarkable/more remarkable (b) good/...
9. (a) smart/(the) smartest (b) intelligent/...
10. (a) quick/(the) quickest (b) nice/...
11. (a) clear/(the) clearest (b) a little/...
12. (a) positive/(the) most positive (b) some/...

§§ 40 a/b/c; 41; 42 a

6 Put in the comparative or superlative form of: far, late, near, old. Use each adjective twice.

1. I've got to ring someone up. Where's the ... phone box?
2. Howard's sister is the ... girl in her class.
3. Do you know what's just happened? Have you heard the ... news?
4. I'd like to know more. Can you give me any ... details?
5. The ... woman in our village has just celebrated her 96th birthday.
6. We'd better stop at the ... filling station we come to and get some petrol.
7. I'd like to stay till the end of the party, too, Jack. But what'll we do if the ... bus leaves before the party is over?
8. Do you realize that in Britain the ... point from the coast is only about 125 kilometres from the sea?

§ 42 b

7 **Possessive adjectives/of my, your, his ... own**

Complete the sentences by translating the words given in brackets.

1. The Robinsons have only got one alarm-clock, and Mr Robinson uses it most of the time. So his daughter, Christine, is thinking of buying an ... . (eigenen Wecker)
2. Andrew's car is being repaired, so he's hired a different one. But he isn't happy with it. He'd rather drive ... . (sein eigenes Auto)
3. Susan has offered to look after her sister's children while she's in hospital. But it won't be easy, because Susan has got ... . (fünf eigene Kinder)
4. Two of the immigrants arrived for the interview in borrowed suits, because they had practically no ... . (eigene Kleider)
5. Diana really likes the little flat she's sharing with two other girls, even though she hasn't got ... . (ein eigenes Schlafzimmer)
6. A helicopter managed to lower a rope to the boy who'd got stuck half-way up the cliff. He realized how silly he'd been and apologized to the members of the helicopter crew for putting ... in danger. (ihr Leben)
7. One of the tourists had to borrow some money, as all ... was stolen from his hotel room while he was having breakfast. (sein eigenes Geld)
8. Mr and Mrs Taylor are staying with friends until the roof of their house has been repaired. It's a pity this is necessary. They'd have preferred to stay ... . (in ihrem eigenen Zuhause)
9. Sarah and her husband are living with her parents at the moment, though they hope to buy ... one day. (ein eigenes Haus)
10. During that terrible winter in Buffalo, N.Y., recently, when it snowed and snowed and snowed, Chester and Susie Wagner were out in their car one night when it suddenly stopped and refused to start again. They'd heard on the radio how other people had met ... by leaving their vehicles and setting off into the snow. So they stayed in their car, put ... in ... and waited for help to arrive. Fortunately, they were soon helped by a passing truck-driver. (den Tod; die Hände; die Tasche)

§§ 44 b; 45

Adverbs

•8 Use the information given in brackets to make a response that includes an adverb ending in "-ly".

Example: What was the test like? – Well, actually, it was surprisingly difficult. (Everybody was surprised to find how difficult it was.)

1. Why did the house have to be pulled down? – Because it … . (Because the damage to it was so serious.)
2. I'm amazed to see a 13-year-old in the school basketball team. – Yes, well, of course, Tommy … . (It's unusual for a 13-year-old to be as tall as Tommy is.)
3. Why did your team lose, do you think? – Well, we attacked okay, but I suppose we … . (Our defence wasn't effective enough.)
4. Didn't the pupils realize they'd get caught? – Well, no, and, you see, they probably wouldn't have been if … . (Nobody had expected the headmaster to come into the room.)
5. Did the Prime Minister's son go to a comprehensive school? – No, he was … . (He had a private education.)
6. How did the customs officer spot that something was wrong? – Simple really. He just … . (He made a careful comparison of all the documents.)
7. Margaret says she'll let you have her car for £600. – Oh? Why is she selling it … ? (The price is so low I can't believe it.)
8. Look at these two pieces of homework. Wouldn't you agree that Gerald and Natalie have been copying from each other? – Hmm. I must admit that … . (It's amazing how similar their answers are.)

§ 46

9 Put in the right verb from the list, in the form of a past participle, and put in an adverb with it, making this from the adjective in brackets.

Example: hurt: Mr Brown had to give up his job as a brewery worker after he was (serious) seriously hurt in an accident.

organize, look after, elect, choose, discuss, marry, make, discover

1. Mrs Brown is the (democratic) … secretary of the local branch of her trade union.
2. Mr and Mrs Brown have been (happy) … for over 30 years.
3. According to their friends, the couple were (simple) … for each other.
4. Every problem they've ever had has always been (full) … in a friendly way.
5. Five years ago they went on a (good) … coach tour of Ireland.
6. That particular holiday was (probable) … because it was so cheap.
7. However, they made a lot of friends, they were (wonderful) … at all the hotels they stayed at, and they've been back every year since then.
8. The funny thing is that, though they've always known that Mrs Brown's great-grandfather was born in Ireland, they've only (recent) … that Mr Brown's great-grandfather was born there, too – and in the next village!

§ 48 a/b/c/d/f

10 Adverbs with two forms

Complete each sentence by choosing a suitable word from the brackets and adding "-ly" if necessary. Write down every answer you think possible, as in some cases there is more than one correct answer.

1. Jill was amazed. She could ... believe what she saw. (hard/close/pretty)
2. None of our players broke the rules. They all played ... well, too. (hard/pretty/fair)
3. The results of the new research corresponded ... to the results of Dr Frost's own experiments. (close/hard/high)
4. Ed has settled into his new job ... quickly. (hard/fair/pretty)
5. Young voters ... support the same political parties their parents vote for. (just/pretty/most)
6. Steve used to go and watch Manchester United regularly, but for some reason or other he hasn't been ... . (hard/near/late)
7. It was an excellent chance to score a goal, but unfortunately Phil kicked the ball too ... . (fair/high/wide)
8. The boy ... admitted that he'd managed to get into the stadium without paying. (free/near/late)
9. The Air Force helicopter didn't fly ... enough above the roofs of the houses and a lot of people complained. (high/hard/close)
10. The police stopped people from coming ..., because they knew the chemicals might explode. (close/near/just)
11. Pamela was ... delighted when she heard the news. (high/hard/pretty)
12. The judge entered the court ... before the bomb was thrown. (just/late/pretty)

§ 50

Adjective or adverb?

11 Read the text and put in the words in brackets, either as adjectives or – after making any necessary changes – as adverbs.

In the early 1980s the Minister for Education asked 15 teachers from ... (1. different) parts of Britain to watch TV ... (2. regular) for a few weeks. He wanted them to comment on the picture of adult life that schoolchildren might get from TV, because some research had shown that young people between five and fourteen spent an average of ... (3. rough) 23 hours a week watching TV – more time than they spent in class.

The 15 teachers watched a variety of programmes ... (4. general) shown after 5.45 pm, when most children are home from school, and before 10.30 pm. Then they discussed these programmes with their own pupils and ... (5. final) they published their report, "Popular TV & Schoolchildren", in 1983.

In particular, the report attacked the aggressive attitude to women and sex shown in American TV series such as "Dallas". It also ... (6. heavy) criticized Kenny Everett's popular comedy series, a programme watched ... (7. enthusiastic) by ... (8. near) one-third of all four to fifteen-years-olds, for linking sex and violence in an ... (9. unacceptable) unpleasant way. According to the report, children were attracted to the show because Everett was ... (10. naughty), behaved ... (11. silly), and said and did ... (12. rude) things.

Not ... (13. surprising), teenagers and adults reacted to the report ... (14. different). For example, 15-year-old Lisa Poole said it wasn't Kenny Everett's taste that worried her. "I ... (15. just) can't stand him," she said, "he's stupid. I don't find him ... (16. funny) at all."

Julie Matthew, aged 14, said she ... (17. real) enjoyed U.S. series such as "Dallas" and "Dynasty" – they were her favourites. But she denied taking them ... (18. serious), as she knew they weren't ... (19. real). And ... (20. similar), Martin Berry, aged 16, admitted enjoying ... (21. violent) police programmes on TV, but he denied that they made him want to go out and hit people.

However, Mrs Joy Valentine, a grandmother with four children and six grandchildren, said some programmes could affect children ... (22. negative) if they watched "the box" on their own. And Mrs Yvonne Fields, who was expecting a baby at the time she was interviewed, said that, although she didn't ... (23. necessary) agree with the teachers' report, she would ... (24. certain) choose the programmes her child saw in later life very ... (25. careful).

§§ 46; 48 a/b/c/e; 50

12 Finish the translations.

1. Vor dem Spiel schienen beide Mannschaften nervös.
   Before the match both teams ... .
2. Deine Aussichten klingen sehr gut.
   Your prospects ... .
3. Hans wird immer wütend, wenn er ein Spiel verliert.
   Hans always ... when he loses a match.
4. Die Suppe schmeckt wirklich fabelhaft.
   The soup ... .
5. Götz kostete den Wein gründlich, bevor er seine Meinung äußerte.
   Götz ... before giving his opinion.
6. Ich bin erkältet. Daher kann ich nicht gut riechen.
   I've got a cold. So I can't ... .
7. Der Mann am Apparat klang sehr aufgeregt.
   The man on the phone ... .
8. Die neue Sekretärin wurde innerhalb kurzer Zeit sehr beliebt.
   Within a short time the new secretary ... .
9. Diese Birnen fühlen sich sehr weich an.
   These pears ... .
10. Der blinde Kunde tastete jede Münze vorsichtig ab, ehe er zahlte.
    The blind customer ... every coin ... , before he paid.
11. Der Tierarzt tastete das Bein des verletzten Hundes sanft ab.
    The vet ... .
12. Der Plan hört sich gut an.
    The plan ... .
13. Vom Hubschrauber aus sah das Meer ruhig aus.
    From the helicopter ... .
14. Paul dachte an Irene und wurde sehr traurig.
    Paul remembered Irene and ... .

§ 51 a/b

13 Find "the fourth man".

Example: (a) punctual/punctually (b) shameful/...shamefully..

1. (a) fatal/fatally (b) historic/...
2. (a) good/well (b) bad/...
3. (a) rare/rarely (b) funny/...
4. (a) glad/most gladly (b) bad/...
5. (a) fluent/more fluently (b) sensible/...
6. (a) hungry/hungrily (b) friendly/...
7. (a) quickly/most quickly (b) fast/...
8. (a) nervously/most nervously (b) a little/...
9. (a) worthwhile/more worthwhile (b) good/...
10. (a) sooner/soon (b) worse/...
11. (a) quick/quickly (b) effective/...
12. (a) equal/equally (b) full/...

§§ 40; 42; 46; 48; 52; 53

14 **The comparison of adjectives and adverbs**

Complete the text by putting in the comparative form of an adjective or an adverb. But be careful, in some cases "less ... " is required.

At the beginning of 1983 two different TV companies in Britain followed the example of the U.S.A. and began broadcasting early morning programmes of up-to-date news and interviews. The programme run by the BBC, called "Breakfast Time", was launched a few weeks ... (1. soon) than the other programme – run by TV-am and called "Good Morning Britain" – and it was also much ... (2. popular) than its rival. However, TV-am, which pays its employees out of the profits it makes from showing commercials between programmes, didn't give up trying to win a ... (3. big) audience. In fact, it tried ... (4. hard) than ever.

Its employees knew that their jobs would be ... (5. secure) and they'd be able to earn ... (6. high) wages if they could succeed in attracting ... (7. many) viewers, because then they'd be able to demand ... (8. fat) fees for showing commercials. So they agreed to work ... (9. long). "Good Morning Britain" started broadcasting at 6.25 am, i.e. five minutes ... (10. early) than "Breakfast Time", and it finished a few minutes ... (11. late), too, at about 9.20 am.

In addition, the programme-makers at TV-am decided to give their viewers ... (12. exact) what they wanted to see at that time of the day. It seems that the majority of viewers prefer jokes and ... (13. serious) interviews early in the morning. So TV-am sacked three of the ... (14. intelligent) members of the team working on the show and introduced a few new faces instead, one or two ... (15. famous) people who were supposed to look ... (16. ordinary) than the stars they replaced and also ask ... (17. difficult) questions when they interviewed their studio guests.

However, some people wondered whether all these changes would really lead to ... (18. high) audience figures or instead, in the long run, to ... (19. expensive) commercials and even ... (20. boring) programmes.

§§ 40; 42 a; 46; 48 a; 49; 50; 52

The word order with adverbs

15 Find the right word order. If you can spot an alternative answer, write it down, too.

1. in – clapped – most of the people – enthusiastically – the crowd – .
2. going – the anti-apartheid demonstration – is – tomorrow – to – who – ?
3. before – come across – have – a case – the police – like this – ?
4. closed – was – unfortunately – that day – the office – .
5. visits – her aunt – usually – Lucy – a month – once – .
6. at the garage – Peter's car – last year – luckily – often – wasn't – .
7. in Hamburg – two years ago – a conference – twice – David – to – went – .
8. thoroughly – her camping holiday – last year – generally speaking – enjoyed – Rosemary – in France – .
9. been – she – already – probably – there – has – .
10. extremely – the violin – well – Vanessa – plays – .

§§ 56; 57

•16 Complete the sentences by putting in the adverbs given in brackets. If you think an adverb can go in two (or more) positions, write down these extra possibilities, too, but in brackets.

Example: Tom spoke Russian. (fluently; ten years ago)
(Ten years ago) Tom spoke Russian fluently
ten years ago.

1. Why does California appear to be a separate country from the rest of the United States? (so often)
2. This is a topic that writers discuss – because many of them choose to live. (there; so; perhaps; a lot)
3. Christopher Isherwood, author of "Goodbye to Berlin", said about California, "This is where the mistakes are made first, which means that we get to the answers." (a few years ago; soonest)
4. An example of this, according to Neal R. Pierce, is the way California's farmers and scientists rush to try new chemical and biological methods of growing things in their fields, only to discover that some of their techniques can cause permanent damage to useful birds, insects and other wildlife. (frequently)
5. But Pierce emphasizes that Californians give up searching for a better way of life. (never)
6. You can't escape the feeling that things are changing, he says, and he points out that one in three moves house. (definitely; each year)
7. California, according to Pierce, is the place from which America gets its signals about what is going to happen to it. (tomorrow)
8. For example, it was in this state that Ronald Reagan entered politics – in the actors' trade union, as Governor of California – before he went. (in 1981; to the White House)
9. What a lot of tourists enjoy about California is the sun and the surf as well as the state's traditional tourist sights – such as the Yosemite National Park or San Francisco's cable-cars, Golden Gate and Chinatown. (particularly)

§§ 56; 57

Quantifiers, the pronoun, question words, word order

Test yourself

A Fill in the gaps with English equivalents for the German words given in brackets.

1. Has … brought their camera? (jemand)
2. It looks like a time bomb that could explode … moment. (jeden)
3. She gave … a drink. (allen)
4. … dictionary is better than … at all. (Jedes; keins)
5. Annie talks …, but most of what she says is rubbish. (viel)
6. … eyes were injured in an explosion. (Ihre beiden)
7. He's lived in London and Birmingham, but he doesn't like … . (keine der beiden Städte)
8. I could come on Tuesday or on Wednesday, … would suit me. (jeder der beiden Tage)
9. … wants to be killed in a war. (Keiner von uns)
10. This is Mrs Schaefer, Inspector Derrick. She's a neighbour … . (von uns)
11. We must try to help the handicapped to learn to help … and … . (sich; einander)
12. She … down and five minutes later she was fast asleep. (legte sich)
13. … when you first … ? (Erinnert ihr euch; euch getroffen habt)
14. When they left, they promised to write … every two months. (sich)
15. The first and the third lines rhyme with … . (sich)
16. What … next? (ereignete sich als)
17. Could you … once more how to do this exercise? (uns erklären)

B Choose the right word from the list on the left to complete the following sentences.

all
all the
any
anybody
anything
anywhere
both
each
either
every
everybody
neither
no
nobody
none
nothing
some

18. There isn't … bread left. Do you want me to get you … ?
19. Won't you have … more tea?
20. Was there … interesting on the 8 o'clock news? – No, … at all.
21. I'm starving. I haven't had … to eat since breakfast.
22. … was cheering and laughing when they heard that they'd won the world championship.
23. … could do that if they tried hard enough.
24. Accidents can happen … – even in hospitals.
25. … men are created equal.
26. … pupils in my class are looking forward to our trip to France.
27. I don't know who to believe. … of them gave me a different version of what happened.
28. The doctor looked very serious. Obviously there was … hope at all.
29. Please take my advice and stay here. – … asked your advice.
30. How much did your moped cost you? – … – it was a birthday present.
31. Many solutions have been offered, but … of them is satisfactory.
32. Jane and Derek had an accident and they … had to be treated in hospital.

33. Have you seen Jane and Susan recently? – No, I haven't seen ... of them.
34. Which of the two umbrellas are you going to buy? ..., I'm afraid. They're too expensive.

C Who/What/Which?

Choose the right question word to complete the questions. Add other words where necessary and use the right form of the verbs in brackets.

35. ... left the lights burning? – Eric, I think.
36. ... look like? – She's tall and black-haired.
37. ... that joke? – It was Peter that told me it.
38. ... of the boys ... ? – I invited them all.
39. ... is the shortest way to the school? – Along the river.
40. ... do you like best? – Love poems.
41. ... (wake) the baby up? – Well, there was a party next door.
42. ... fool (say) that? – John, but I don't think he's a fool.

D Spot the mistakes.

There is one mistake in each of the following sentences or groups of sentences. Spot the mistakes and write down what you think is the correct version.

43. That's child's play. Every schoolboy could tell you that.
44. There are only a little potatoes left.
45. How many orange juice is left in the jug?
46. Nobody of us has seen Jane since she failed the exam.
47. In volley ball there are six players on every side of the net.
48. Derek and Jean are great friends from us.
49. Take your dirty hands off that white dress of me.
50. The door opened itself.
51. There's so much noise I can hardly concentrate myself.
52. Margie and John are attracted to themselves.
53. Who of you hasn't made any mistakes?
54. How much costs this painting? Is $ 200 your last word?
55. Who did light the candle?
56. Did he say her anything?
57. Not only he was impolite but he was stupid as well.
58. Under no circumstances he would ever agree to their suggestion.

Key

A

1. Has **anybody/anyone** brought their camera? .... §§ 59 a; 59 c; 61
2. ... **any** moment. .... § 60 a (3)
3. She gave **everybody/everyone** a drink. .... § 60 a (1)
4. **Any** dictionary ... **none** at all. .... §§ 60 a (3); 63 (5)
5. Annie talks **a lot** ... . § 62
6. **Both her** eyes ... . § 64 a
7. ... he doesn't like **either of the cities**. .... § 64 b
8. ... **either day** would suit me. .... § 64 b
9. **None of us** ... . § 64 c
10. ... a neighbour **of ours**. .... § 67 b
11. ... help **themselves** and **each other/one another**. .... §§ 68 a; 69
12. She **lay** down ... . § 68 b
13. **Do you remember** when you first **met**? .... § 68 b
14. ... write **to each other** ... . § 69
15. ... rhyme with **each other**. .... § 69
16. What **happened** ... ? .... § 77 b
17. ... **explain to us** ... ? .... § 78 c

B

18. There isn't **any** bread ... . Do you want me to get you **some**? .... §§ 59 a (2); 59 b
19. Won't you have **some** more tea? .... § 59 a (3)
20. Was there **anything** interesting ... ? No, **nothing** ... . § 59 c; 63 (4)
21. I haven't had **anything** to eat ... . § 59 c
22. **Everybody** was cheering ... . § 60 a (1)
23. **Anybody** could do that ... . § 60 a (3)
24. Accidents can happen **anywhere** ... . § 60 a (3)
25. **All** men are created ... . § 60 b
26. **All the** pupils in my class ... . § 60 b (1)
27. ... **Each** of them gave ... . § 60 a (2)
28. ... there was **no** hope ... . § 63 (1)
29. ... **Nobody** asked your advice. .... § 63 (4)
30. How much did ... cost you? **Nothing** ... . § 63 (4)
31. Many solutions have been offered, but **none** of them ... . § 63 (5)
32. ... they **both** had to be treated ... . § 64 a
33. ... I haven't seen **either** of them. .... § 64 b
34. Which of the umbrellas ... ? **Neither** ... . § 64 c

C

35. **Who** ... ? .... §§ 72 a; 77 b
36. **What does she** ... ? .... § 72 a (2)
37. **Who told you** ... ? .... §§ 72 a; 77 b
38. **Which** ... **did you invite**? .... § 73
39. **Which** ... ? .... § 73
40. **What poems** ... ? .... § 73
41. **What woke** ... ? .... §§ 72 a; 77 b
42. **What** fool **said** that? .... §§ 73; 77 b

D

43. ... **Any** schoolboy ... . § 60 a (3)
44. ... **a few** potatoes ... . § 62
45. How **much** orange juice ... ? .... § 62
46. **None** of us ... . § 63 (5)
47. ... on **either**/on **each** side ... . §§ 64 b; 60 a (2)
48. ... great friends **of ours**. .... § 67 b
49. ... that white dress of **mine**. .... § 67 b
50. The door **opened**. .... § 68 b
51. ... I can hardly **concentrate**. .... § 68 b
52. Margie and John are attracted to **each other**. .... § 69
53. **Which** of you ... ? .... § 73
54. How much **does** this painting **cost**? .... § 77 a
55. Who **lit/lighted** the candle? .... § 77 b
56. Did he say anything **to her**? .... § 78 c (2)
57. Not only **was he** impolite ... . § 79 a
58. Under no circumstances **would he** ever agree ... . § 79 a

Exercise finder

Test yourself	ENGLISH G Grammatik	Exercises
1, 18, 19	§ 59 a	1, 2
1, 20, 21	§ 59 c	2, 3
2, 3, 4, 22, 23, 24, 25, 26, 27, 43, 47	§ 60 a/b	4
4, 20, 28, 29, 30, 31, 46	§ 63	5, 6
5, 44, 45	§ 62	**1** : 5, •7
6, 7, 8, 9, 32, 33, 34, 47	§ 64 a/b/c	7
10, 48, 49	§ 67 b	8, 9
11, 12, 13, 50, 51	§ 68 a/b	10, •11, 12
11, 14, 15, 52	§ 69	12
16, 35, 37, 41, 42, 54, 55	§ 77 a/b	13
17, 56	§ 78	15
35, 36, 37, 41	§ 72 a	13
38, 39, 40, 42, 53	§ 73	14
57, 58	§ 79 a	16

Exercises

1 **"Some" or "any"?**

Christine: Hallo, Janet. Hallo, James. You both look very brown. How was your holiday?

Janet: What do you think? Two weeks in sunny Spain? It was great!

Charles: Did you go to lots of bull-fights?

James: We didn't go to ...(1) at all, Charles, actually. We spent most of the time on the beach. It was just what we needed.

Janet: Hmm, we made ...(2) nice friends and we had ...(3) really super weather. Really hot.

Christine: You're lucky. We haven't had ...(4) good weather here for ages.

Janet: Why don't you go to Spain then? Like we did? I'm sure you'd enjoy it, both of you. You especially, Christine.

Charles: It's easy for ...(5) people to say that. I suppose you didn't read ...(6) newspapers or watch ...(7) TV programmes while you were away?

Janet: No, we tried to forget about everyday things like that. We just wanted to relax. Why? What's happened?

Charles: Well, the Government has brought in ...(8) new laws. They were worried about the amount of money being taken out of the country, you see, because of the economic situation.

Janet: I don't understand. Do you mean people aren't allowed to take ...(9) money out of the country now?

Christine: Not exactly, though you've got the general idea. You can take ...(10) out with you, but not very much. Not enough for two weeks' holiday in Spain.

James: Never mind, cheer up. We bought ...(11) wine over there. In fact, we bought quite a lot. Why don't you come to dinner tonight and help us to drink ...(12) of it?

§ 59 a/b

"Some", "any" and their compounds

2 Make sensible questions by putting the correct pairs together. For example, if you think sentence 1 can be completed by adding A, write 1/A.

1. I'm going out later. Would you like me to take ...	A. ... anything exciting ever happen to me?
2. What did you say earlier? That you would like me to take ...	B. ... somebody call a doctor, please?
3. You must play better. Can't you try and score ...	C. ... any letters to the post office for you?
4. What was the result? Did our team score ...	D. ... some letters to the post office for you?
5. When the accident happened, why didn't ...	E. ... any good discos around here?
6. I feel ill. Would ...	F. ... some good discos around here?
7. I'm new in town. Are there ...	G. ... any goals?

8. Would you like me to tell you where there are ... H. ... some goals?
9. I'm bored. Why doesn't ... I. ... anybody call a doctor?

§ 59 a/c

3 Finish the sentences by putting in a word from list A together with a word or phrase from list B.

A: somewhere, anywhere, somebody, anybody (2 x), something (2 x), anything
B: from Germany, terrible, to deliver, carrying, near Bordeaux, cold, newer, in Asia

1. Oh dear, ... is going to happen. I can feel it.
2. Will this be your first visit to Japan? – Oh yes. I've never been ... before.
3. You can't wear that old dress tonight! – But, Dad, I haven't got ... .
4. Did you speak to ... at the conference, Dieter?
5. Ed and Liz spent their holidays on a caravan site ... last year.
6. How's the campaign going? – Well, we still need ... leaflets in your neighbourhood.
7. Coffee? – No, thanks. Actually, I'd prefer ... to drink.
8. The customs officers had orders to search ... a red suitcase.

§ 59 c

4 **Every, each, any, all**

Choose the right form from the brackets. If you think both forms are equally suitable, write down both.

... (1. All the/All) computers used to be huge, heavy machines. Whenever you wanted to take one ... (2. everywhere/anywhere), you needed a crane and a lorry. But these days you can carry a powerful computer in a suitcase. You see an advertisement for a new model practically ... (3. every/each) time you open a magazine. And as a result almost ... (4. every/each) teenager in the country, it seems, wants to own a personal home computer.

The cheapest machines for beginners cost under £ 30 each, but this price doesn't include the extra equipment that ... (5. all the/all) typical users soon want, e.g. a special screen, a printer, and a system of tapes or disks for saving programmes. Of course, ... (6. every/each) sales assistant claims that all you really need is a TV set, which can be used as a screen, and ... (7. every/any) ordinary cassette recorder. However, cassette tapes are very slow for some purposes – you really need a disk system – and these are expensive. What is more, ... (8. every/each) computer seems to understand only its own individual version of computer "language" (or code), which makes it difficult for people who own different computers to exchange programmes or use ... (9. every/each) other's machines.

These differences also mean that ... (10. every/each) computer needs its own special series of books about how to use it, which helps to explain why a new computer book seems to get published ... (11. every/each) day. Already roughly 3 % of all the books published in the U.S.A. deal with computers, and it's a growing market. As far as Britain is concerned, it has been estimated that within the next year or two more than 3 million people will ... (12. every/each) have a micro in their home.

§ 60 a/b

No, nobody, etc., none

5 Put in the right word from this list: none, no (2 x), nobody (2 x), nothing (5 x), nowhere (2 x).

The mechanics were checking one of the engines, and ... (1) seemed to know when the plane would take off. It was hot in the airport lounge. Petra wished she'd taken the ferry instead. On days like this, travelling by air was ... (2) quicker, only more expensive, than going by boat and train.

Having ... (3) to read, she studied her fellow passengers. Were the four big, tough-looking men in grey raincoats crooks? Fortunately, Petra knew, ... (4) guns were allowed on the plane! Two attractive young women in low-cut dresses, who looked very smart in spite of their heavy, rather old-fashioned boots, were having an argument. "How could you forget to book a hotel?" one of them said. "Now we've got ... (5) to stay!"

"You can go on board now," an official said. "Everything is okay, there's ... (6) to worry about." ... (7) complained about having been delayed.

Later, when the stewardess offered everyone a drink, ... (8) of the tough-looking men wanted anything except coffee. "... (9) alcoholic for us, thanks," Petra heard one of them say. "How unusual," she said to herself, "though at least there's ... (10) illegal about it."

... (11) else that could be described as unusual happened until they'd landed at Heathrow and were going through customs. At first the four big men had been standing behind Petra in the queue, talking to the two attractive women. Then, suddenly, all six of them were ... (12) to be seen. The next day Petra read in the paper that her four "crooks" had actually been policemen in disguise. It was the two young women who'd been arrested – for smuggling heroin inside their boots.

§ 63

6 Make sensible pairs.

A: nowhere (2 x), nothing (2 x), nobody (2 x).
B: to park, to see, worth watching, to discuss, to put, to meet.

1. All of Jill's friends are busy, so there'll be ... her at the station.
2. Old Mrs Hall has had ... her problems with since her husband died.
3. Did you enjoy your sight-seeing tour, Hilda? – No, it was boring. There was ... really, apart from an old Roman wall.
4. Mr Lee hates taking his car into the city centre, because there's practically ... .
5. There's ... on TV tonight, so Pamela and Cyril are going to the cinema.
6. Professor Goldsmith's shelves are crowded with books already. If he buys any more, he'll have ... them.

§ 63

7 Both, either, neither

Rosemary and Becky are dark-haired twins, but there are some differences between them. Rosemary's favourite colour is brown, for example, and Becky's is green. Rosemary likes classical music and Becky prefers pop. However, Rosemary's hair is short and so is Becky's. They look like each other, wear similar clothes, work as clerks at the same small bank on the outskirts of Lewisham, and even talk like each other. When one of them is on the phone, the person at the other end has no hope of telling which of them is speaking.

Being a twin can be useful. One day a man wearing a mask rushed into their little bank and pointed a gun at Rosemary. Then he looked round and noticed Becky behind the second counter. He was obviously nervous already and this was a surprise he wasn't expecting. He couldn't believe his eyes – and ran out of the bank again at once.

Answer the following questions about the text. Each answer must contain one of these words: both, either, neither, none.

1. Which of the twins has got long, blonde hair? – Actually, ... blonde hair.
2. Is the twins' favourite colour red? – No, ... likes red.
3. Which of the twins is it who likes music? – Well, in fact ... music.
4. If you heard somebody talking about a girl who wasn't interested in music, would this be Rosemary or Becky? – It would be ... .
5. If you saw a girl with long hair, would it be Rosemary or would it be Becky? – It wouldn't ... them.
6. Do they work at difference places? – No, ...
7. Are their voices similar? – Well, ... friends can hear a difference.
8. When one of the twins rings you up, why have you got to ask: "Is that Rosemary or Becky speaking?" – Because it could be ... them.
9. If you found a hanky with the letter 'R' on it, would it belong to Rosemary or to Becky? – Well, it could ... girls.
10. What gave the bank robber a shock? – The clerks behind ... .

§ 64 a/b/c

The possessive pronoun

8 Write the sentences in a different way. Make a noun (from the adjective or verb) and use a possessive pronoun.

Example: (Andy was the one who decided.) The ...decision... was ...his... .

1. (I am responsible.) The ... is ... .
2. (We'll choose, won't we?) The ... will be ..., won't it?
3. (Joe is more able than Anne.) His ... is greater than ... .
4. (Lucy behaves better than Al or Ed.) Her ... is better than ... .
5. (We suggested that, you know.) That ... was ..., you know.
6. (What was it that you were planning?) What was that ... of ... ?

§ 67 a/b

9 Complete the translations.

1. Wir sahen rein zufällig einen alten Klassenkameraden von uns.
   We happened to see an … .
2. Ich lernte neulich einen Verwandten von Ihnen kennen.
   I met a … recently.
3. Er ist ein ehemaliger Schüler von Inge.
   He's a former … .
4. Hast du meine beiden Bücher noch, Peter?
   Have you still got those two …, Peter?
5. Ein Nachbar von Mrs Kirkley hat den Dieb erkannt.
   … recognized the thief.
6. Wo ist Brigitte? Einer ihrer Freunde rief mich gestern an.
   Where's Brigitte? A … rang me up yesterday.
7. Die Journalisten fanden eine Bemerkung des Präsidenten äußerst interessant.
   The journalists found one … extremely interesting.
8. Sie kennen Tom und Helga, nicht wahr? Können Sie sich eine bessere Ehe vorstellen als ihre?
   You know Tom and Helga, don't you? Can you imagine a better … ?

§ 67 a/b

The reflexive pronoun

10 Put the verb in the simple past and – if necessary – add a reflexive pronoun.

Example: You ..enjoyed..yourself.. at the party, didn't you? (enjoy)

1. Sue had an accident when she was working in the garden yesterday. She … very badly. (cut)
2. A surprising thing happened. The door … before Christine had time to ring the bell. (open)
3. When their parents went on holiday for a few days last summer, the children …, you know. (look after)
4. After the race Steve and Sebastian … for a while. (relax)
5. Nobody had expected us to win. In fact, we even … . (surprise)
6. As he lay in bed, George … what it might be like to be the President of the United States of America. (imagine)
7. A reporter interviewed Liz in the street yesterday. Later in the day she … on the radio. It was a strange feeling. (hear)
8. Tom used to look serious all the time. But when he married Helga, he … . He always seems happy now. (change)
9. One after the other the members of the team walked up and … to their new coach. (introduce)
10. As soon as the detective was shown the photo, he … seeing the man outside the bank. (remember)
11. In my opinion the children shouldn't have been playing on the cliffs. I can't say I'm surprised that they … . (hurt)
12. Norman … how to tell the employees the bad news. (wonder)
13. When … Irene … to do this voluntary social work, Mike? (decide)

§ 68 a/b

•11 Translate the infinitives given in brackets, then put them in in the correct form to complete the sentences.

Irene Riley, who together with her husband runs a small restaurant in Mablethorpe, was preparing some vegetables in the restaurant kitchen yesterday when an accident ... (1. sich ereignen).

Some Scottish folk music was on the radio at the time and, almost automatically, Irene ... (2. sich erinnern an) the holiday in Scotland ten years earlier when she and John had first had the idea of running a restaurant. It had been a harder job than they ... (3. sich vorstellen). In fact, if they ... (4. sich klarmachen) just how difficult it was going to be, they might even have stayed in their secure jobs with the local brewery. But, though they ... (5. nicht kaufen) many new clothes or ... (6. sich gönnen/erlauben) a holiday since the restaurant had opened, it had all been worth it.

Irene listened to the music and began ... (7. sich bewegen) in time to the beat, "We'll be able to have a holiday next year," she ... (8. sich sagen), "it would be nice to go to Scotland again." She ... (9. sich fühlen) happier than she had done for days. Unfortunately, she was no longer ... (10. sich konzentrieren) on what she was doing – and she ... (11. sich in die Hand schneiden).

John heard her call out and rushed into the kitchen. "It's okay," Irene said, "I haven't ... (12. sich verletzen) badly. It was just the shock. Don't ... (13. sich sorgen)."

"You should ... (14. auf sich aufpassen) better," her husband said, "we can't afford to pay anybody to take your place if you have to go to hospital!"

Irene smiled. She knew what her husband was really thinking. He hadn't ... (15. sich verändern) a bit since the day they got married.

§ 68 a/b

12 **The reflexive pronoun or "each other"?**

Complete the translations, remembering to put in "each other" or a reflexive pronoun where necessary.

1. Unsere Nachbarn haben sich gerade ein neues Auto gekauft.
   Our neighbours have just ... a new car.
2. Wo sollen wir uns deiner Meinung nach treffen?
   Where do you think we should ... ?
3. Wir haben beschlossen, uns dieses Jahr nichts zu Weihnachten zu schenken.
   We've decided not ... anything for Christmas this year.
4. Die Polizei hat sich überzeugt, daß kein Verbrechen vorlag.
   The police ... that a crime hadn't been committed.
5. Die Kinder freuen sich auf den Film, nicht wahr?
   The children ... to the film, aren't they?
6. Robert und sein neuer Chef können sich leider nicht ausstehen.
   Unfortunately, Robert and his new boss can't ... .
7. Annette und ihre Brieffreundin schreiben sich regelmäßig einmal in der Woche.
   Annette and her pen-friend ... once a week.
8. Wenn man Kinder vor elektrischen Geräten nicht schützt, können sie sich weh tun oder sich sogar tödlich verletzen.
   If children aren't kept away from electrical equipment, they can ... or even ... .

§§ 68 a/b; 69

Question words

13 Translate the questions in brackets. But be careful with the word order and the tenses.

When Gabi Lemmel went to a three-day conference in Coventry recently, she stayed at the home of an old friend of hers, Jean Munroe. While they were having a cup of tea, Jean started to talk about one of her neighbours. "You must remember meeting her last time you were here," Jean said, "because she came to dinner one night." – "... (1. Wen meinst du?)" Gabi asked. – "Angela Pickering," Jean said, "you talked to her about space or astronomy or something." – "Oh, yes, I remember."

"Well, she doesn't live here any more. She's moved to Cornwall." – "Oh, I've been to Cornwall," Gabi said. "... (2. In welcher Stadt wohnt sie?)"

"Padstow. It's a little harbour. Very pretty. I visited her last month."

"... (3. Seit wann wohnt sie da?)" Gabi asked. – "Just over a year." – "... (4. Und was macht sie?)" – "She paints. You know, pictures. A lot of painters live in that part of the world." – "... (5. Was für Bilder malt sie?)" – "The sea, boats, the beach, cliffs, birds. That sort of thing." – "... (6. An wen verkauft sie ihre Bilder?)" – "Tourists mostly," Jean explained, "but her reputation seems to be growing."

"How interesting," Gabi said. "... (7. Was kostet ein Angela Pickering Bild?)" – "About £150. More for a really big picture." – "... (8. Und kann sie genug Bilder verkaufen, um die Miete zu zahlen?)" – "I don't know exactly. I hope so." – "... (9. Wäre es möglich, sie am Samstag zu besuchen?)"

"I'm afraid not. I've arranged for us to go to a party. I forgot to mention that." – "... (10. Wer hat uns eingeladen?)" – "My boss. He's looking forward to meeting you." – "... (11. Worauf freut er sich? Mich kennenzulernen?)" – "Yes, he thinks you might be able to help us with an export problem." – "... (12. Und wer gab ihm den Eindruck, daß ich Euch helfen könnte?)" Gabi wanted to know.

Jean changed the subject. "More tea?" she asked.

§§ 72 a; 77 a/b

14 Put in "what" or "which" – or both, if you think both are possible.

1. ... time does the plane arrive in Montreal? – At about 10.35.
2. ... of the bigger cities in Canada has got the largest number of French-speakers? – Oh, Quebec definitely.
3. ... is the capital of Canada? – Ottawa, of course.
4. ... would you have to pay if you stayed at a top hotel in Montreal, say, the Ritz Carlton? – About £70 a night, I think.
5. ... is the highest mountain in Canada? – Mount Logan, isn't it?
6. ... European tourist would ever visit Toronto without going to see the Niagara Falls? – A good question.
7. If you had to get from Halifax to Vancouver, ... way would you prefer to go – by road, rail or air? – I'd fly.
8. If you left Edmonton and flew north-west, ... super-power's frontier would you reach first? – America's, I guess (Alaska).

§ 73

Word order

15 Finish the translations, paying particular attention to the word order. If you think two possibilities are equally good, write them both down.

1. Peter sagte seiner Frau, er würde seinem Sohn kein neues Fahrrad kaufen.
   Peter ... a new bike.
2. Hast du ihm auch das Schlimmste erzählt? – Ja, das sagte ich ihm zuerst.
   Did you ... the worst part, too? – Yes, I ... first.
3. „Ihren Führerschein, bitte," sagte ihr der Polizist. „Zeigen Sie ihn mir."
   "Your driving licence, please," the policeman ... .
4. Er sah ihn genau an, dann gab er ihn ihr zurück.
   He studied it closely, then ... .
5. Der Präsident stellte den Spielern ihren neuen Trainer vor.
   The president introduced ... .
6. Der Trainer war nicht bereit, ihnen alle seine Pläne zu erklären.
   The coach wasn't willing to explain ... .
7. Du hättest ihm etwas sagen sollen.
   You should have said ... .
8. Beschreiben Sie mir die Maschine. Wie sieht sie aus?
   Describe ... . What does it look like?
9. Frage Lisa, ob sie mir ein paar Briefmarken aus der Stadt mitbringt.
   Ask Lisa whether she'd mind ... .
10. Beim Interview mußte Rita einige merkwürdige Fragen beantworten. Sie fragte später ihren Boß, warum er sie ihr gestellt hätte.
    During the interview Rita had to answer several strange questions. Later, she asked her boss why he'd ... .

§ 78 a/b/c

16 Finish the sentences, using the words in brackets and deciding whether to use inversion. Be careful with the tenses.

Only rarely ... (1. a fashion – last) for more than a year these days. If you think about all the people whose jobs depend on designing, making or selling clothes, you'll spot the reason. Not only ... (2. they – want) to make their customers happy, they also need to keep earning a salary. So under no circumstances ... (3. their customers – must) lose the habit of buying new clothes every year.

In other words, no sooner ... (4. the people in the industry – introduce) a new fashion for 1984 than they start to work on a different style for 1985, a style that's intended to make all the items in 1984's wardrobe look hopelessly old-fashioned. Of course, only once in 20 years ... (5. you – see) an idea that isn't very obviously based on an earlier fashion. But that's not the point.

For example, never in all her life ... (6. my next-door neighbour – wear) boots together with a short skirt until this year. Now, as far as I can see, ... (7. she – wear) boots with everything. Yet next year without a doubt ... (8. the fashion experts – make) her feel that, say, tennis shoes are "in" and boots are "out". What is more, ... (9. she – consider) hardly anything in her wardrobe suitable to wear with tennis shoes. Not till the year after next, if this suits the experts, ... (10. she – discover) that, actually, tennis shoes only look smart when you're playing tennis!

§ 79 a

Modals

Test yourself

A Complete these sentences using the verbs in brackets.

1. The bank is closed this afternoon. – Too bad, I ...(have to + go) tomorrow morning then.
2. There was so much noise that I ...(have to + shout) to make myself heard.
3. Sorry if you ...(have to + wait) for me, but I got held up.
4. If Steve isn't here, he ...(must + wait) at the south entrance. I saw his car near there.
5. Where can my glasses be? Now I remember. I read the paper in the garden so I ...(must + leave) them there.
6. Hurry up. Anne is still waiting for you. – Oh dear, she ...(must + wait) for a long time.
7. At the customs we had to show our passports but we ...(not have to + open) our luggage.
8. You ...(needn't + buy) the book. You could have borrowed it from any library.
9. So far nobody ...(be able to + solve) this problem.
10. She looked at the photo but couldn't recognize the street. She put on her glasses and suddenly she ...(be able to + see) every detail.

B Complete the following sentences, using a suitable modal from the list at the right with the verbs in brackets.

not be to
can't
couldn't
may not/mightn't
won't
wouldn't
shouldn't/oughtn't to
must not
needn't

11. You ...(understand) a film if you arrive in the middle.
12. I ...(get) into the house because I'd forgotten the key.
13. He has no idea what the report is about, so he ...(read) it.
14. You ...(forget) to bring some cake, will you?
15. Mary is in hospital again. – It serves her right. The doctor told her what to do, but she ...(listen) to him.
16. The letter ...(be written) today. It can wait till tomorrow.
17. There's still plenty of beer in the fridge. So I ...(bring) all these heavy bottles home with me.
18. Let's go to the pub and talk to Jim. – Well, I'm not sure; he ...(be) there tonight. He had a cold this morning.
19. The news I'm going to tell you is rather strange. You ...(believe) it, although it's true.
20. Passengers ...(lean) out of the window.
21. You ...(make) such a noise last night. Right in front of your English teacher's house, too.
22. Did Mum leave a message for me? – Yes, you ...(stay) out late.

C Fill in the gaps with English equivalents for the German words given in brackets.

23. Janet's parents ... three times since 1975 and they're afraid ... again next year. (mußten umziehen; sie müssen umziehen)
24. Reading between the lines of your letter I imagine ... a very good time during your holidays. (du kannst nicht gehabt haben)
25. I was so angry that ... . (ich ihn hätte umbringen können)
26. The work ... , but it was at least interesting. (mag schwierig gewesen sein)
27. I'm sorry about my behaviour last night. I drank too much ... . (wie Sie sicher bemerkt haben werden)
28. I don't know how I ... ever get my jeans dry in time. (soll)
29. People who work very hard ... be rewarded for their hard work. (sollten)
30. ... for your final exam now, instead of reading comics? (Solltest du nicht arbeiten)
31. The taxi ... five minutes ago, but it hasn't turned up yet. (hätte kommen sollen)
32. Cars ... in front of the main entrance. (dürfen nicht geparkt werden)
33. ... now. There's plenty of time for that. (Du brauchst es nicht zu tun)
34. I talked to Tom for a long time, and in the end ... to lend me his car. (konnte ich ihn überreden)
35. As the thief confessed, ... give evidence. (brauchten sie nicht)
36. There has been a call from the library. ... return the book you borrowed six weeks ago. (Du sollst)
37. Sarah ... drive her father's car so far. (durfte nicht)
38. ... if you want to get home before it gets dark. (Es wäre besser, wenn du dich beeilen würdest)

D **Spot the mistakes.**

There is one mistake in each of the following sentences or groups of sentences. Spot the mistakes and write down what you think is the correct version.

39. We were late – we missed the bus, so we must walk.
40. Didn't you ask John to help? – No, he wasn't there, and he hadn't carried it anyway because he isn't strong enough.
41. I had done the same thing if I had been in that situation.
42. I rang you up yesterday. A girl answered the phone, but I didn't recognize her voice. – Oh, it had to be my sister.
43. Betty has taken a job, though she mustn't have. Her husband earns a very good salary.
44. There was a funny noise in the TV set during the news. Since then we can only get black and white.
45. The ring cost too much. He wouldn't have had to give her such an expensive one.
46. The boss says you shall leave at seven, not earlier.
47. I shall return this book to the library today, but I haven't really got time. Could you take it back for me?
48. It's raining. You would better bring in the washing.

Key

A

1. ... **I'll have to go** tomorrow morning ... . §§ 83 b; 97 b
2. ... I **had to shout** ... . §§ 83 b; 97 b
3. ... you've **had to wait/you had to wait** ... . §§ 83 b; 97 b
4. ... he **must be waiting** ... . §§ 93 b; [189 b]
5. ... I **must have left** them ... . §§ 93 b; [189 b]
6. ... she **must have been waiting** for a long time. ...... §§ 93 b; [189 b]
7. ... we **didn't have to open** our luggage. .... § 97 b
8. You **needn't have bought** the book ... . §§ 97 b; [189 b]
9. So far nobody **has been able to solve** this problem. .. §§ 96 a; 96 b
10. ... suddenly she **was able to see** every detail. .... §§ 96 a; 96 b

B

11. You **can't understand** a film ... . § 85 a
12. I **couldn't get** into the house ... . §§ 86 a; 96 b
13. ... he **can't have read** it. .... §§ 85 c; [189 b]
14. You **won't forget** ... , will you? .... § 89 a (2)
15. ... she **wouldn't listen** to him. .... § 90 c
16. The letter **needn't be written** today. .... §§ 95; 97 b; [189 b]
17. ... **I needn't have brought** ... . §§ 97 b; [189 b]
18. ... he **may not/mightn't be** there tonight. .... §§ 87 a; 88; 105
19. ... You **may not/mightn't believe it** ... . §§ 87 a; 88; 105
20. Passengers **must not/mustn't** lean out of the window. § 94
21. You **shouldn't have/oughtn't to have made** such a noise ... . §§ 98 (2) [189 b]
22. ... you **aren't to stay** out late. .... §§ 98 (4 b); 100 (2)

C

23. ... **have had to move** ... since 1975 ... **they'll have to move** again ... . §§ 83 b; 97 b
24. ... **you can't have had** a very good time ... . §§ 85 c; [189 b]
25. ... **I could have killed him.** .... §§ 86 c; [189 b]
26. The work **may have been difficult** ... . §§ 87 a; [189 b]
27. ... as **you will have noticed.** .... §§ 89 b; [189 b]
28. ... how I **shall** ever get my jeans dry ... . § 91 (3)
29. People ... **should be/ought to** be rewarded ... . § 92 a (3)
30. **Shouldn't you be/Oughtn't you to be working** ... now ... ? .... §§ 92 a (4); [189 b]
31. The taxi **should have/ought to have arrived/come** five minutes ago ... . § 92 a (5)
32. Cars **mustn't be parked** ... . §§ 94; 100 (2)
33. **You needn't do it** now. .... §§ 95; 97 b
34. ... in the end **I managed to/I was able to persuade him** ... . § 96 b (2)
35. ... **they didn't have to** give evidence. .... § 97 b (1 b)
36. ... **You are to** return the book ... . § 98 (4 b)
37. Sarah **hasn't been allowed to** drive ... . § 100 (1 b 7)
38. **You had better hurry up** ... . § 104 b (4)

D

39. ... we **had to** walk. .... § 83 b
40. ... he **couldn't have carried** it anyway ... . § 86 c (3); [189 b]
41. **I would have done** ... . §§ 90 b; 106 b (3)
42. ... it **must have been** my sister. .... § 93 b; [189 b]
43. ... she **needn't have**. .... § 97 b
44. ... Since then we'**ve** only **been able to** get black and white. .... §§ 96 b; [189 b]
45. He **needn't have given** her such an expensive one. ... § 97 b; [189 b]
46. The boss says you **are to** leave at seven ... . § 98 (4 b)
47. **I'm supposed to** return this book ... . § 98 (1 b 3)
48. ... You **had better** bring in the washing. .... § 104 b (4)

Exercise finder

Test yourself	ENGLISH G Grammatik	Exercises
1, 2, 3, 7, 8, 16, 17, 23, 33, 35, 39, 43, 45	§ 97 b	1
4, 5, 6, 42	§ 93 b	1
9, 10	§ 96 a	2
9, 10, 12, 34, 44	§ 96 b	2
11	§ 85 a	2
12	§ 86 a	2
13, 24	§ 85 c	2
16, 33	§ 95	1
18, 19, 26	§ 87 a	5
18, 19	§§ 88; 105	5
20, 32	§ 94	1
21, 22, 36, 46, 47	§ 98	3
22, 32, 37	§ 100	2, 3
25, 40	§ 86 c	2
27	§ 89 b	4
28	§ 91	3
29, 30, 31	§ 92 a	3
4, 5, 6, 8, 13, 16, 17, 21, 24, 25, 26, 27, 30, 40, 42, 44, 45	§ 189 b	**8** 1, •2, •10; 6, 7

Exercises 8–•15 contain a mixture of modals (§§ 83–106)

Exercises

1 Must, mustn't and needn't

At the Bolts' house early one morning, Tom and Pam are getting ready to go to work. Fill in the gaps in their conversation, using "must", "mustn't" or "needn't."

Tom: Oh by the way, could you take my grey trousers to the cleaner's on your way to work? I ... (1) have got some oil on them, I think.

Pam: Oh, Tom, your best trousers! You ... (2) have been wearing them for cleaning the car again. I've asked you so often to wear old clothes for dirty jobs. You simply ... (3) be more careful – we can't afford the cleaner's bills.

Tom: All right, I'll try, but you ... (4) be so upset, because I hate to see you unhappy. And now I'll go and make the tea for you – the water ... (5) be boiling by now.

Pam: You ... (6) have bothered to put water on for tea. I've no time now if I'm to go to the cleaner's. I ... (7) be late for work.

Tom: Oh, I've just remembered. You ... (8) go to the cleaner's after all. I'll be passing near there myself today.

Pam: Well, let me see your trousers anyway. – Oh, you ... (9) take those to be cleaned – I can do it. That spot isn't oil, I'm sure, but all the same you ... (10) wear your best clothes to work on the car in future!

§§ 93 a/b/c; 94; 95; 97 b; 100; 103 b

2 Can/could and related verbs

Complete the following text, using "can/could (not)" or, where that is not possible, "manage to" or "(not) be able to."

Last Monday Martin Pitt woke up with a sore throat. He ... (1) get out of bed, but his legs were so weak that he ... (2) hardly stand. When his mother saw him, she said, "You ... (3) go to school – you've got a temperature." "But Mr Carter has been trying to arrange a visit to a TV studio for weeks, and at last he ... (4) fix it for Thursday," Martin protested, "and we're going to prepare for it today and tomorrow. If I don't go to school today, I ... (5) visit the TV studio with the others."

Mrs Pitt ... (6) see how disappointed Martin was at the thought of not ... (7) go, so she said, "Well, you ... (8) ring up George now and ask him to make notes for you and bring them round. And if you stay in bed for a couple of days, perhaps you ... (9) go back on Thursday." "Oh, I do hope so, but the last time I had flu I ... (10) go back to school for a fortnight. Let's ask the doctor for something to help me to get well quicker," Martin suggested. "There are pills you ... (11) take to bring down a high temperature," Mrs Pitt agreed, "but Dr Watts doesn't like using them if it ... (12) be avoided."

On the telephone Dr Watts said, "Of course it ... (13) be measles, but it's probably just a cold." Fortunately it was, and Martin ... (14) go to the TV studio with the others.

§§ 85; 86; 96; 99; 100

3 English equivalents for "sollen"

Use a modal verb from the following list to fill in the gaps: be to, be supposed to, ought to, shall, should. Sometimes more than one answer is possible.

1. I'm worried. Don ... be home by four, and it's six already. Do you think I ... phone the police?
2. ... I put the basket on the kitchen table or do you want it in the living-room?
3. You ... have bought the big size – it's cheaper.
4. A new car park ... be built here. The town council decided this yesterday.
5. I don't think we ... put our bikes against the wall. We ... not ... leave them here at all – only in the bike-shed behind the school.
6. The teacher wants Jane to collect the exercise-books, and Tony ... put the maps in the cupboard.
7. I don't know the restaurants here very well, but the Chinese one ... be very good.
8. Hey, you ... be working instead of sitting there in the sun! The boss says you ... finish this job as quickly as possible.

§§ 91; 92; 98; 100; S. 147

4 Will/won't to express probability

Complete the following conversation, using "will ('ll)/won't" and the verbs given in brackets in the simple or progressive form.

Jim: That's Bill's car outside the newsagent's, isn't it? I wonder what he's doing there at this time?

Example: He ..'ll be buying.......... (buy) some cigarettes, I expect.

Tim: He ... (1. buy) a newspaper, more likely. He ... (2. want) to know whether his team won yesterday.

Ann: I think you're both wrong. He ... (3. fetch) his girl-friend. She lives above the newsagent's, you know.

Jim: Oh well, that ... (4. be) why his car is there – he ... (5. give) her a lift to work today, I suppose.

Tim: Yes, I expect so. His car is still there, because she ... (6. keep) him waiting. Girls are always late.

Jim: Be fair. Her mother is ill just now, you know, so she ... (7. do) the housework before she leaves.

Ann: In that case Bill ... (8. help) her, I expect. He's very good at housework, I know.

Tim: Well, he ... (9. not get) to work in time if he doesn't hurry. And his boss ... (10. make) a fuss, because he's so often late.

§§ 89 b; 106 b

5 May/might

John hasn't arrived at work yet. What possible explanations can you think of? Re-write the possibilities suggested below, using "may/might."

Example: Perhaps he missed the bus.
He may have missed the bus/
He might have missed the bus.

1. Perhaps he's ill.
2. Perhaps he had to go to the doctor's first.
3. Perhaps he decided to drive to work when he missed the bus.
4. Perhaps he's had a breakdown.
5. Perhaps he hasn't been able to get a taxi.
6. Perhaps he's had an accident.
7. Perhaps he didn't hear the alarm clock.
8. Perhaps he isn't coming to work at all today.
9. Perhaps he was told to see the boss first.
10. Perhaps he's looking for a new job!

§§ 87 a; 88; 105 b

Modals with infinitives

6 Choose the right infinitive form (present or perfect) for the verbs given in brackets.

Example: There is no chocolate left. Clare must ...have taken...(take) the last piece.

1. John's car is still outside the front door, so he can't ...(go) to London yesterday after all.
2. I'm dead tired this morning. I shouldn't ...(stay up) so late last night.
3. I don't think you should ...(ask) Mrs Blair now. She won't ...(have) lunch yet, and she'll ...(be) very tired and hungry because she'll ...(have to) work all morning without even a break for a cup of tea.
4. I'm afraid I don't know where Miss Bates is. She may ...(go out) to do something for Mr Morton.
5. Of course I could ...(ask) someone to help me to repair the car, but I decided to try and do it myself, and I actually managed!
6. "Good heavens, someone must ...(break in)," I thought when I saw the open window, but of course Mr Jones may ...(climb in) himself because he had forgotten his key.
7. He gave the job to Jane, but I think he should ...(give) it to Rose.
8. Dad can't ...(leave), because his car is still in the garage, and he can't ...(be) in the house, because I've looked everywhere, so he must ... (go) into the garden.
9. Is this all the paint you bought this morning? You really should ...(buy) more than this. It wouldn't even ...(do) for a doll's house.
10. Ask Katy for some eggs. She might ...(remember) to get some really fresh ones when she was at the market this morning. Take this bowl – it'll ...(hold) all the eggs you need.

§ 189 b

7 Choose the right infinitive form (present simple or progressive) for the verb given in brackets.

Example: That's the school band playing, isn't it? They must .be practising. (practise) for the school concert.

1. Ask Greg. He might ...(know) them.
2. I've forgotten to post your letter. Never mind, I'll ...(post) it on my way to the pub.
3. I can hear someone in the house - Mike must ...(be) at home, and what's more he must ...(work) on his radio.
4. I can ...(read) French not too badly, but I can't ...(speak) it well, so my teacher thinks I should ...(go) to France in the summer holidays.
5. I simply must ...(go) now. Alan will ...(wait) for me at the gate.
6. I'm not sure where he is, but he can't ...(work) in the garden, because his boots are still here. Perhaps he's gone into town.
7. Why don't you go and ask him now? He won't ...(do) anything important at the moment, and anyway he won't ... (bite) your head off!
8. There's a terrible noise coming from next door. They must ...(have) a party.
9. *Liz:* Isn't it wonderful - Rod has passed his exam!
   Ben: Great! We must ...(have) a party to celebrate.
10. *Stella:* Mary was going to play golf today, wasn't she?
    Joe: Yes, but surely she won't ...(play) in this rain? She would be wet through by now.

§ 189 b

Mixed modals

8 Fill in the gaps with a modal verb from the following list: can, can't, couldn't, may/might, must, mustn't, needn't, shall, should/ought to, will ('ll), would.

1. Roger has broken his leg. That means he ... play football this afternoon.
2. If you want my advice, I think you ... buy a new car.
3. I ... see a light in the living-room, so Frank ... be at home after all.
4. I've got some important news for Dick. Do you think he ... be at home this afternoon?
5. I'm not sure where your exercise-book is, but I ... have put it in the cupboard.
6. Sue is very good at languages - she ... speak three!
7. No, you ... stay up a minute longer - I've already let you stay up an extra hour.
8. I've already found three people to help me, so you ... come if you're busy.
9. I looked everywhere, but I ... find it.
10. ... I get you some cigarettes when I'm out shopping?
11. ... you like another piece of chocolate cake?
12. I ... stay any longer, I'm afraid. It's Mum's birthday, so I ... be late home today.

§§ 83–106

9 Complete the translations, using a modal or related verb.

1. Du brauchst nicht auf mich zu warten. Tom nimmt mich mit.
   You ... for me. Tom is going to give me a lift.
2. Sie müssen zu Hause gewesen sein. Ich habe ihre Stimmen gehört.
   They ... at home. I heard their voices.
3. So was darfst du nicht sagen.
   You ... things like that.
4. Vielleicht war er im Kino gestern abend.
   He ... at the cinema last night.
5. Er wird den Artikel inzwischen gelesen haben.
   He ... the article by now.
6. Glücklicherweise konnte ich ihn schließlich überzeugen.
   Fortunately I ... him in the end.
7. Man hat ihm gesagt, daß er um zwei Uhr hier sein soll.
   He's been told that he ... here at two o'clock.
8. Er kann nicht gekommen sein – der Brief, den ich ihm hinterlassen habe, ist noch da.
   He ... – the letter that I left for him is still here.
9. Ich finde, er sollte vorsichtiger sein.
   I think he ... more careful.
10. Er sollte gestern kommen, aber statt dessen mußte er nach London fliegen.
    He ... yesterday, but he ... to London instead.
11. Leider konnte ich nicht länger warten.
    I'm afraid I ... any longer.
12. Mach dir keine Sorgen – sie rufen sicher bald an.
    Don't worry – I'm sure they ... soon.

§§ 83–106

10 Complete the translations, using a modal or related verb.

1. Was tut Tim hier? Er müßte eigentlich an seinen Hausaufgaben arbeiten (do).
   What is Tim doing here? He ... his homework.
2. Meine Eltern werden am Bahnhof auf uns warten, wenn wir ankommen.
   My parents ... for us at the station when we arrive.
3. Ich muß jeden Tag um sieben Uhr zur Arbeit gehen.
   I ... to work at seven o'clock every day.
4. Ich weiß nicht, was er will. Vielleicht sucht er jemanden.
   I don't know what he wants. He ... for somebody.
5. Du mußt nicht einkaufen gehen – ich habe alles mitgebracht.
   You ... shopping – I've brought everything with me.
6. Ich konnte seinen Brief nicht verstehen.
   I ... his letter.
7. Tim wird jetzt wissen, ob er die Prüfung bestanden hat.
   Tim ... now whether he's passed the exam.
8. Soll ich morgen ein bißchen früher kommen?
   ... I ... a little earlier tomorrow?
9. Es ist niemand da. Ich höre überhaupt nichts.
   There's nobody here. I ... anything at all.
10. Es wird ihm bestimmt nicht gefallen.
    I'm sure he ... it.

§§ 83–106

11 Choose the right verb form.

Example: The Martins have packed four suitcases into their car. They
a) must go
b) have to go } on holiday.
c) must be going

They must be going on holiday.

1. If your book isn't here, you
a) must leave
b) had to leave } it at school.
c) must have left

2. There was nobody at home, so I
a) had to put
b) must have put } the parcel on the window-sill.
c) had to be putting

3. There's a parcel on the window-sill. It
a) has to be
b) must have been } lying there all morning.
c) must be

4. If my umbrella isn't here, I
a) had to leave
b) must have left } it on the bus.
c) 've had to leave

5. We
a) wouldn't have to
b) don't have to } forget to take Tom the video cassette.
c) mustn't

6. That was Linda on the phone – they're not coming this afternoon after all, so I
a) needn't have made
b) didn't have to make } all this cake.
c) needn't make

7. I missed the last bus, so I
a) must have taken
b) had to take } a taxi.
c) have to take

8. Oh, Jane, I've got a message for you. You
a) 're to phone
b) should phone } the boss right away.
c) should be phoning

9. My American cousins
a) can be coming
b) could have come } for Christmas this year. We do hope they will.
c) might be coming

10. Let me do it. It
a) mustn't
b) isn't to } be too difficult.
c) shouldn't

11. I think you
a) are to take
b) should take } the green one. It's nicer than the red one.
c) should be taking

§§ 83–106

12 Pair each of the numbered sentences with a), b) or c) in the same group.

Example: 1. You mustn't tell Philip.
2. You needn't tell Philip.
a) It's a secret.
b) Mary has already said she'll tell him.
1 + a) You mustn't tell Philip. It's a secret.
2 + b) You needn't tell Philip. Mary has already said she'll tell him.

1. 1. We managed to open a tin of fruit
   2. We could open a tin of fruit
   a) even though we had lost the tin-opener.
   b) if anyone is still hungry.
2. 1. You needn't go out today.
   2. You mustn't go out today.
   a) Your cold will only get worse if you do.
   b) I can bring home anything you want from town.
3. 1. He should leave after lunch
   2. He was to leave after lunch,
   a) but he had to work late.
   b) if he wants to arrive before it gets dark.
4. 1. We could walk all the way
   2. We were able to walk all the way,
   a) when we were young.
   b) and I'm glad we didn't have to take the bus.
5. 1. I needn't have bought any food,
   2. I didn't have to buy any food,
   a) because I noticed that the fridge was already full.
   b) but how was I to know that you were going to do the shopping?
6. 1. She was supposed to be at Tony's by seven,
   2. She should have been at Tony's by seven,
   a) she promised to be on time, after all.
   b) but she missed the bus and arrived late.
7. 1. Grandad will be having a little sleep now.
   2. Grandad would be having a little sleep now.
   a) Don't wake him up.
   b) It's too bad you woke him.
8. 1. Shall I get you the Telegraph?
   2. Should I get the Telegraph or the Times?
   3. Am I to get the Telegraph or the Times?
   a) Or do you want me to get you the Daily Mail?
   b) Which did John say he wanted?
   c) Which do you think is better?
9. 1. They were allowed to go swimming
   2. They may have gone swimming
   3. They might go swimming
   a) later this afternoon.
   b) even though they knew the river is polluted.
   c) whenever they liked.

§§ 83–106

13 Mary, Diana and Sally have just left school and taken a flat together, but they are finding that leaving home is not so easy, as the following conversation shows. Translate the underlined parts into English.

Mary: Was (1) wollen wir heute abend machen – an unserem ersten Samstag in der neuen Wohnung? Vielleicht eine Party geben?

Sally: Aber (2) müßten wir nicht vorher die Küche fertig streichen? Mit einem solchen Durcheinander da drin (3) können wir sowieso nichts für eine Party kochen.

Diana: (4) Wir brauchen überhaupt nicht zu kochen. (5) Es muß hier irgendwo ein Geschäft geben, wo (6) man Pizzas kaufen kann, oder?

Mary: Na ja, es gibt ein kleines Geschäft um die Ecke, das Tiefgefrorenes verkauft – also (7) müßten wir wenigstens Tiefkühl-Pizzas bekommen können. Aber (8) wir hätten früher an eine Party denken sollen, dann (9) hätte ich gestern auf dem Heimweg in die Lebensmittelabteilung von Marks & Spencer gehen können.

Sally: (10) Wir können uns eine Party überhaupt nicht leisten, nicht einmal wenn wir bei Marks & Spencer einkaufen. Vergeßt nicht, (11) wir müssen für die Küche mehr Farbe kaufen.

Diana: Sei kein solcher Spielverderber!

Mary: He, ihr zwei! (12) Wir dürfen nicht anfangen, einander anzuschreien. Laßt mich einen Vorschlag machen. (13) Könnten wir nicht einfach ein paar Sandwiches machen? (14) Das dürfte nicht zu teuer sein, und morgen (15) können wir früh aufstehen und den ganzen Tag anstreichen.

Diana: Was! Bei meinen Eltern (16) durfte ich Sonntag morgens nicht im Bett bleiben, und jetzt (17) willst du mich auch nicht schlafen lassen! Aber (18) ich muß zugeben, daß der Vorschlag fair ist. – Ach du liebe Zeit! Es ist schon zehn. (19) Peter wird an der Bushaltestelle auf mich warten. (20) Wir sollen Tim um viertel nach in der High Street treffen. (21) Macht ihr zwei den Abwasch? Seid mir nicht böse. (22) Ich bringe Farbe eimerweise aus der Stadt mit – ich versprech's!

§§ 83–106

•14 Fill in the gaps with a modal verb. The underlined words before the numbered gaps will help you to choose the right modal from the following list: can, could, may/might, should/ought to, needn't, will ('ll), would ('d).

Example: Mary advised Tom not to stay out in the snow. "I think you .should. come in or you'll catch cold," she said.

Mrs Pratt was expecting a neighbour, so when the doorbell rang, she thought it was probably her visitor and said to her daughter, "That ... (1) be Mrs Jay." But Sara was not so sure. "It ... (2) be Betty. She promised she ... (3) come this afternoon." Betty's parents were to be out till late, so Sara hoped her mother would allow Betty to stay to supper. " ... (4) Betty have supper with us this evening?" she asked. "Of course, she ... (5)," her mother replied. It was Betty at the door, and the girls enjoyed their afternoon and evening together.

Sara's father did not consider it advisable for Betty to be out in the streets alone at night, so he offered to drive her home. "I don't think you (6) ... walk home so late. ... (7) you like me to take you in the car?" As Betty thought it likely that her parents had returned by now, she politely asked to be allowed to phone them. "My parents ... (8) be back now," she said. "... (9) I phone them, please?" Betty's father answered the phone and she asked him to fetch her so that it would not be necessary for Mr Pratt to drive her home.

"... (10) you pick me up here?" she asked. "Then Mr Pratt ... (11) bother to get out his car."

§§ 83–106

•15 Complete the following text, using modal or related verbs from the following list: be able to, be said to, can (cannot), have to, may/might (not), must (not), need not, should (not)/ought (not) to, will (not), would. Be careful: in 6, 9, 15, 16 and 18 more than one answer is possible.

Nothing new under the sun – not even pollution.

In Britain the Government has accepted a recommendation that all petrol ... (1) be free of lead within the next ten years. This is the first big success of the Green movement in Britain, and they hope it ... (2) lead to a completely lead-free Europe. This is not, however, Britain's first environmental success. For example, like many Londoners, I ... (3) remember only too well the smog of a generation ago and am grateful for the fact that today only smokeless fuel is burned in homes and factories. London's Thames water is now also much cleaner, and fish ... (4) already be seen in it again for the first time in this century, and there are even those who firmly believe that we ... (5) catch fish from Westminster Bridge in a few years! These examples prove that we ... (6) give up hope; progress ... (7) be made by any country that is seriously convinced that it simply ... (8) be made, whatever the pessimists say. However, we ... (9) be too pleased with ourselves either, for even though lead ... (10) possibly no longer pollute the air quite soon, it still pollutes the drinking water in many parts of Britain, like Glasgow, where the water in some areas still runs through lead pipes. What is more, farmers' fertilizers are raising the level of certain chemicals in our drinking water so much that many people think that there ... (11) be a tax on fertilizers so that farmers ... (12) use less.

And it is not only our drinking water that is in danger: Shakespeare's "silver sea" ... (13) long remain as Shakespeare knew it if we are not careful; we ... (14) continue to pollute the sea without the risk of spoiling our beaches and making it dangerous to eat the fish from our coasts, and so our politicians ... (15) act soon to reduce the amount of domestic and industrial waste pumped into the sea.

Pollution, by the way, is a very old problem. It ... (16) have been an indirect cause of the fall of the Roman Empire, for some people believe that the Romans ... (17) almost certainly have been slowly poisoned by their lead water pipes. The future ... (18) be so black for us, it is true, but we ... (19) pay constant attention to possible sources of danger. If we do not, the price that we ... (20) pay ... (21) certainly be very high indeed.

§§ 83–106

The main verb: forms and tenses

Test yourself

A Mind your spelling.

Write the simple past tense of the following verbs.

1. prefer, develop, occur, play, die, offer, admit, enjoy, enter
2. hear, make, choose, feel, fall, hold, go, leave, grow, teach, broadcast, pay, beat, quit, lay, mean, lead

Write the past participle of the following verbs.

3. travel, destroy, rely, justify, expel, cry, drop, discover, delay, visit
4. fly, cut, lose, be, rise, forget, hide, know, leave, see, sew, fight, dream, go

B German "Präsens"

Translate the words underlined in the following sentences into English. Remember that German "Präsens" cannot always be translated by simple present or present progressive.

5. Das ganze Haus riecht wieder nach Zigarettenrauch.
6. Hör auf! Ich habe jetzt genug von deinem Blödsinn.
7. Derek spricht Englisch mit einem starken Akzent. Wo kommt er denn her?
8. Unterhaltung ist wichtig für Menschen, die eine langweilige Arbeit haben.
9. Peters Schwester, die in England lebt, hält sich für drei Monate in Bremen auf.
10. Diese Szene des Stücks zeigt, daß Biff seine Einstellung geändert hat.
11. Ich bedaure, Ihnen mitteilen zu müssen, daß Sie nächsten Monat entlassen werden.
12. Wenn du diese Frage richtig beantwortest, freut sich dein Lehrer.
13. Guten Tag. Ich hoffe, ich störe Sie nicht.
14. Frau Miller ist im Krankenhaus. Aber eine Freundin von ihr schaut nach dem Baby, solange sie dort ist.
15. Susan hat heute Geburtstag und wir feiern heute abend (have a party).
16. Jane läßt immer die Türen offen, weil der kleine Tom die Klinke noch nicht erreichen kann.
17. Wie lange weißt du schon, daß Kathy vor sechs Wochen einen Unfall hatte?
18. Eine Freundin von mir geht schon seit Jahren in die Sauna. Sie sagt, es täte ihr wirklich gut.
19. Es ist nett, dich in Heidelberg zu sehen. Wie lange bleibst du noch?
20. Wer macht den nächsten Satz?
21. Mach sofort die Tür auf, oder es gibt Ärger.
22. Mein Messer ist runtergefallen. – Sarah holt dir ein anderes.
23. Wenn ich heimkomme, sitzen die andern vorm Fernseher – du wirst schon sehen.
24. Wir lassen Sie am Bahnhof abholen. Ein Firmenwagen wartet auf Sie am Südeingang, wenn Sie ankommen.
25. Sobald Terry zurückkommt, sag' ich ihm, er soll sofort anrufen.

C German "seit" – English "since" or "for"

Find the ten phrases that can only be used with "for".

26. ... 1982, ... six months, ... last night, ... a long time, ... this morning, ... twenty minutes, ... three days, ... the last week, ... last week, ... their mother's death, ... she died, ... the break, ... they've had a new car, ... thousands of years, ... ages, ... half an hour, ... two weeks, ... the last few days

D Present perfect or simple past?

Put the verbs in brackets into the present perfect or the simple past. Be careful with the word order in questions.

27. Oh bother! Someone ... (borrow) my bike! I'll just have to walk.
28. You ever ... (be) here before? – Yes, I ... (be) here several times. In fact it's the fifth time I ... (be) here.
29. This is the best news I ... (hear) in months.
30. Jane ... (have) a red Mini as long as I ... (know) her.
31. I ... (not see) Derek since he ... (be) out of work. I wish I could do something for him.
32. Some young people who ... (begin) using drugs two years ago are no longer alive.
33. I ... (see) that film before, but I can't remember when I ... (see) it. Anyway it ... (be) more than a year ago.
34. I ... (not see) Paul this morning and it's nearly lunch time. I ... (be) late for work this morning and Paul ... (not be) in his office when I ... (get) here.
35. Mary ... (work) at the local hospital for five years after leaving school. But when she ... (get married) her husband ... (want) her to leave.
36. Christine ... (not write) to her boy-friend since she ... (meet) Tony.

E Translate the following sentences into German.

37. Derek has been in Munich for two weeks.
38. Helen has been to Scotland three times, but I've never been there.
39. Gerald is going to work for two years in the London branch of his firm.
40. Kevin played for the local team for two years.
41. Grace has been visiting the old lady for a year now and has never regretted it for a single minute.
42. Tim has been out of work since his firm had to close down.
43. Since Bill has been driving that fast car, he's had two accidents.
44. Since you're going to watch that game, I'll watch it, too.

F Spot the mistakes.

There is one mistake in each of the following sentences or groups of sentences. Spot the mistakes and write down what you think is the correct version.

45. Have you looked at the time-table? – Yes, our train is going to arrive at Heidelberg at 2.16.
46. Tom can't come to your party. He plays in a football match on Saturday afternoon.
47. I just have a good idea. Are you doing anything tonight?
48. This shop is getting on my nerves. I have enough of you and your TV set. I just want my money back.
49. Since we're using this new machine, the working conditions have improved.
50. I've dropped a coin inside the piano. – How have you managed that?
51. The new assistant is working in this department since this morning.
52. ☐ I'm afraid I can't go dancing tonight. I've worked in the garden and my back is aching terribly.
53. I was reading at midnight. Suddenly the door has opened. There stood Peter.
54. Dave has been in hospital since last week. – Oh, I haven't known about that.
55. I've just been doing the washing up when you rang up.
56. What on earth were you doing last night? Why weren't you coming to the disco?
57. Wait and see. When he's seventy he's still running around.

There are two mistakes in each of the following sentences or groups of sentences. Find them and write down what you think is correct.

58. Her new job is much better payed and she's soon able to afford a new car.
59. When she came in, I sat in front of the TV set - something I'm not doing often.
60. Havn't you seen Jane since she's back from Canada?
61. I've worked for BAB so I know quite well what this place is like. But that has been five years before. How time flies.
62. I remember that you always have been the black sheep when you were a child.
63. At two o'clock in the morning we've been talking still.
64. I'm looking forward to watching the Olympic Games since weeks.

"We're going to look like damn fools if this is just a shower."

Key

A

1. **preferred, developed, occurred, played, died, offered, admitted, enjoyed, entered** .... §§ 114; 115
2. **heard, made, chose, felt, fell, held, went, left, grew, taught, broadcast, paid, beat, quit, laid, meant, led** .... § 115; S. 152–153
3. **travelled, destroyed, relied, justified, expelled, cried, dropped, discovered, delayed, visited** .... §§ 114; 115
4. **flown, cut, lost, been, risen, forgotten, hidden, known, left, seen, sewn, fought, dreamt, gone** .... § 115; S. 152–153

B

5. The whole house **smells** of cigarette smoke again. .. § 119
6. Stop it, **I've had enough** of your nonsense. .... § 138
7. Derek **speaks** English with a broad accent. **Where does he come from**? .... §§ 123; 124
8. Entertainment is important for people who **have** boring jobs. .... § 124
9. Peter's sister, who **lives** in England, **is staying** in Bremen **for three months**. .... §§ 124; 134
10. **This scene** of the play **shows** that Biff has changed his attitude. .... § 125
11. **I regret** to inform you that you are to be dismissed next month. .... § 126
12. If **you answer** this question correctly, your teacher will be pleased. .... § 129
13. Good afternoon. **I hope I'm not disturbing you**. ...... §§ 118 c; 132
14. Mrs Miller is in hospital. But **a friend of hers is looking after the baby as long as she's there**. .... §§ 134; 129
15. It's Susan's birthday today and **we're having a party tonight**. .... § 135
16. Jane always **leaves** the doors **open** because little Tom can't reach the handle yet. .... § 122
17. **How long have you known** that Kathy had an accident six weeks ago**?** .... § 140
18. **A friend of mine has been going** to the sauna **for years. She says** it really does her good. .... §§ 143; 126
19. Nice to see you in Heidelberg. **How long are you staying/ going to stay**? .... §§ 134; 162
20. **Who is doing/going to do the next sentence**? .... §§ 135; 162
21. Open the door this minute or **there'll be trouble**. .... § 166
22. I've dropped my knife. – Sarah **will get you another one**. .... § 167
23. When I get home, **the others will be sitting in front of the TV** – you'll see. .... § 171 (1)
24. We'll have you met at the station. A company car **will be waiting for you** at the south entrance **when you arrive**. §§ 171; 129
25. **As soon as Terry comes back, I'll tell him** to ring you up immediately. .... §§ 129; 171 (1)

C

26. **for six months, for a long time, for twenty minutes, for three days, for the last week, for thousands of years, for ages, for half an hour, for two weeks, for the last few days** § 159

D

27. ...**has borrowed**... ! .... §§ 157 (1); 138
28. **Have** you ever **been**...**I've been**...**I've been**... . .... §§ 157 (2); 139
29. ...**I've heard**... . ... §§ 157 (3); 139
30. ...**has had**...**I've known** her. .... §§ 157 (4); 140
31. I **haven't seen**...he's **been**... . ... §§ 157 (5); 159 (2)
32. ...**began**... . ... §§ 157 (6); 146
33. **I've seen**...**I saw**...it **was**... . ... §§ 157 (1); 146
34. I **haven't seen**...I **was**...Paul **wasn't**...I **got**... . .... §§ 139; 157 (8)
35. Mary **worked**...she **got married**...her husband **wanted**... . ... §§ 157 (9); 157 (6)
36. Christine **hasn't written**...she **met**... . ... §§ 159 (2); 157 (10)

E

37. **Derek ist seit zwei Wochen in München.** .... § 159 (3)
38. **Helen war schon/ist schon dreimal in Schottland gewesen, aber ich war noch nie dort/bin noch nie dort gewesen.** .... § 139
39. **Gerald wird zwei Jahre in der Londoner Filiale seiner Firma arbeiten.** .... § 162
40. **Kevin spielte zwei Jahre/hat zwei Jahre für den hiesigen Verein gespielt.** .... § 159 (3)
41. **Grace besucht nun schon ein Jahr/hat nun schon ein Jahr die alte Dame besucht und hat es noch keinen Augenblick bereut.** .... § 143 (2)
42. **Tim ist arbeitslos, seit seine Firma schließen mußte/hat schließen müssen.** .... § 159 (2)
43. **Seit Bill den schnellen Wagen fährt, hatte er/hat er zwei Unfälle gehabt.** .... § 159 (2)
44. **Da du das Spiel anschauen willst, werde ich es auch anschauen.** .... §§ 162; [245]

F

45. ...our train **arrives**... . ... § 128
46. ...He'**s playing/going to play**... . ... §§ 135; 162
47. **I've** just **had**... . ... § 138
48. **I've had** enough... . ... § 138
49. ...we'**ve been using**... . ... § 143
50. ...**did** you **manage**... ? .... § 141
51. ...**has been working**... . ... § 143
☐ 52. ...**I've been working**... . ... § 144
53. ...the door **opened**... . ... § 146
54. ...I **didn't know**... . ... § 146
55. I **was** just **doing**... . ... § 149
56. ...**didn't** you **come**? .... § 146
57. ...he'**ll** still **be running**... . ... § 171
58. ...**paid**...she'**ll** soon **be able**... . ... § 166; S. 153
59. ...I **was sitting**...I **don't often do**. .... §§ 149; 122; 176 b; [57 c (1)]

60. **Haven't**... she's **been** back... . ... §§ [81 c]; 140
61. ... **was** ... **ago**... . ... § 146
62. ... **were always**... . ... §§ 146; [56 b]
63. ... **were still talking**. .... §§ 149; [56 b]
64. **I've been** looking forward ... **for** weeks... . ... §§ 143; 159 (3)

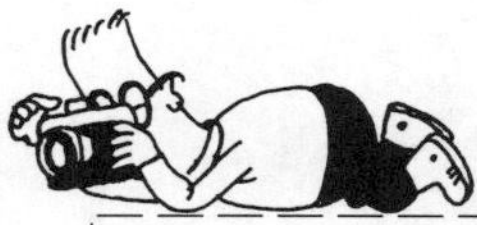

Exercise finder

Test yourself	ENGLISH G Grammatik	Exercises
5	§ 119	**6** : 3, 12, •19
6, 27, 47, 48	§ 138	**6** : 6, 8, 12, 13, •14, •19; 4, 6, •14
7	§ 123	**6** : 4; 1
7, 8, 9	§ 124	**6** : 3, 4; 1
9, 14, 19	§ 134	**6** : 3, •19
10	§ 125	**6** : 2, 3
11, 18	§ 126	**6** : 3, 4
12, 14, 24, 25	§ 129	**6** : 3, 4, •17, 18, •19; •14
13	§ 118 c	**6** : 3, 4
13	§ 132	**6** : 1, 2, 3, 4, •19
15, 20, 46	§ 135	**6** : 1, 2, 3, 4, •17, 18; •14
16	§ 122	**6** : 1, 2, 3, 4; 1
17, 30, 60	§ 140	**6** : 5, 6, 7, 8, 12, 13, •19; 2
18, 41, 49, 51, 64	§ 143	**6** : 5, 6, 7, 8, 11, 12, 13, •14, •19; 5
19, 20, 39, 44, 46	§ 162	**6** : •17, 18; 11, 13, •14
21, 58	§ 166	**6** : 15, •17, 18, •19; 11, 12, •14
22	§ 167	**6** : 18, •19; 11, 13, •14
23, 24, 25, 57	§ 171	**6** : 15, •17, 18, •19
26, 31, 36, 37, 40, 42, 43, 64	§ 159	**6** : 5, 7, 8, 12, 13, •14, •19; 2, 7
27, 28, 29, 30, 31, 32, 33, 34, 35, 36	§ 157	**6** : •14; 5, 10
28, 29, 34, 38	§ 139	**6** : 5, 6, 7, 8, 11, 12, 13, •14, •19; 2, 4, 5, 7, 10, •14
32, 33, 53, 54, 56, 61, 62	§ 146	**6** : 9, 10, 11, 12, 13, •14, •19; 3, 4, 5, 6, 7, 8, •9, 10, •14
45	§ 128	**6** : 2, 4, •17, 18, •19
50	§ 141	**6** : 11, 12, 13; 6
52	§ 144	**6** : 11
55, 59, 63	§ 149	**6** : 9, 10, 11, 12, 13, •14, •19; 3
44	§ 245	**12** : 14
59	§ 57 c	**2** : 15, •16
62, 63	§ 56 b	**6** : 15, •16

Exercises

1 Simple present

Tom and Sue are teenagers. Their grandmothers are talking about them. Fill in the gaps in their conversation.

Example: Sue gets up at six on weekdays.
– Really? Tom never ...gets up... before eight.

1. Sue always washes up the breakfast dishes.
   – Not Tom! He never ... up at all.
2. Does Tom tidy his room before breakfast every day like Sue?
   – Oh no, he only ... it when he can't find anything any more.
3. Sue walks to school.
   – Not Tom. He ... n't ... anywhere if he can help it.
4. Sue takes the dog out for a walk every evening.
   – Tom never ... the dog out. I've just told you that he never ... anywhere.
5. Sue does her homework straight after school. And Tom?
   – Oh, he ... his homework at once, too; he wants to play football as soon as possible.
6. Sue never eats hamburgers, she eats a lot of fruit and vegetables.
   – Not Tom! He ... n't ... much fruit, but he ... hamburgers whenever he can.
7. Sue is always polite and doesn't interrupt her parents.
   – Tom is polite too, but he often gets excited and then he ... everybody.
8. Sue plays the piano very well and practises every day.
   – Tom ... n't ... any instrument well, because he never ... .
9. Sue never goes to horror films and doesn't watch TV very often, because it's too violent.
   – Tom loves horror films and often ... TV, especially the late-night films.
10. The trouble is the other children don't like Sue very much.
    – No wonder! She sounds awful. But everybody ... Tom!

§§ 122; 123; 124

2 Present perfect with "since" and "for"

Fill in the gaps in the dialogues with verbs in the simple form of the present perfect and "since" or "for".

1. *Bob:* You said Sandra had the flu, didn't you?
   Ann: Yes. She ... it ... ten days now, and she's still very ill.
2. *Mum:* You can stop writing now. Tea's ready.
   Kate: Oh, good. I ... six thank-you letters ... two o'clock, and I'm fed up.
3. *Mrs Grey:* I expect your daughter helps with the cooking.
   Mrs Benn: Oh, yes. She ... often ... our lunch ... I had the accident.
4. *Mary:* The Martins live near you, don't they? Do you know them well?
   Ruth: Of course I do. They ... next door ... twenty years.
5. *Simon:* The exhibition is very interesting, but what a lot of people are here to see it today!
   Paul: Yes. I wonder how many people ... it ... the opening day.

6. *Mark:* I'm looking forward to playing football again on Sunday.
Melanie: Well of course you are. You ... n't ... months.
7. *John:* Have there been many applications for the job?
Jeff: Oh, yes. Three hundred people ... for it ... last week.
8. *Rachel:* Is Matthew still working for ITC?
Deborah: Goodness, no! He ... for two other firms ... he left there.
9. *David:* Isabel was at the Stardust Disco last Saturday, wasn't she?
Paula: Oh, yes. She ... there every Saturday ... it opened.
10. *Kathy:* Don phones me every second night.
Delia: That's nothing. Jerry ... me twice every night ... the last month!
11. *James:* Did you hear our song on Harry's Hit Parade last night?
Katie: Yes, it was a lovely surprise! I ... n't ... it ... ages.
12. *Ben:* Will you make a trifle for pudding on Sunday, Mum?
Mum: Good idea. I don't think I ... one ... Christmas, have I?
13. *Muriel:* You're always losing things, aren't you?
Pamela: I know. I ... two pairs of gloves ... the winter started.
14. *Janet:* Has Susan had her computer long?
Carol: No, she ... only ... it ... a few weeks.
15. *Harry:* Do they go skiing a lot?
Bobby: They ... skiing in Scotland every winter ... the last ten years.
16. *Ken:* The rain has left pools of water on the tennis court.
Joe: But it ... n't ... last night, so perhaps the court will be dry by this afternoon.
17. *Eileen:* The car looks awful. Don't you ever wash it?
Martin: Well, I ... n't ... it ... quite a while. It's not worth it in this weather.
18. *Daisy:* I like that scarf Betty knitted for Jill's birthday.
Peggy: She ... two more ... then. They make nice presents, don't they?
19. *Dick:* Are you allowed to keep animals in these flats?
Tony: Oh, yes. We ... a dog ... years.

§§ 139; 140; 159

3 Simple past and past progressive

Last Wednesday Tony rang up Pam, but only spoke to her sister Helen.

Tony: Can I speak to Pam?
Helen: Well, I'm afraid she's busy. She's washing her hair. And she has an awful lot of homework to do later. She plans to finish her history essay, too. Peter is playing his guitar and making a terrible noise, so she doesn't know how she's supposed to manage. She can't even hear herself think! She doesn't expect to be able to finish until very late, so she can't go out with anyone tonight. She thinks she's getting a headache, too, with all the noise, so she wants to go to bed early if she can finish her essay before supper.
Tony: OK, OK. I'm not stupid!

Now describe the situation last Wednesday afternoon, when Helen spoke to Tony. Begin like this:
Last Wednesday afternoon Pam was busy. She ... .

§§ 145; 146; 148; 149

Simple past or present perfect?

4 Fill in the gaps in the following text, using the verbs given in brackets.

Tom ... (1. write) to Joe last week, but he ... (2. not receive) an answer yet. In the letter he ... (3. ask) Joe whether he could stay with him when he is in London next week for an interview with the British Papermaking Company. Poor Tom ... (4. not be able to) find a job since leaving university last June. He ... (5. apply) for nearly thirty jobs meanwhile, but he ... (6. have) no luck so far. In October he even ... (7. answer) an advertisement for a typing job, but without success – they ... (8. tell) him he had too many qualifications! However, Tom ... (9. not give up) hope, and so he ... (10. borrow) several books about papermaking from the public library to read before next week's interview.

If he doesn't get the job, he ... (11. make up your mind) to look abroad. His cousin Oliver ... (12. emigrate) to Australia when he ... (13. leave) school, and is doing so well there that last year he ... (14. be able to) invite Tom over to spend his Christmas holidays with him. As a Christmas present, Oliver ... (15. offer) him a job. But Tom ... (16. refuse), and although Oliver ... (17. offer) him the job again several times since, he ... (18. not accept) – not yet, anyway. Of course, he ... (19. enjoy) the sunshine, the sailing and the surfing in Australia, but he doesn't really want to go so far away. His girl-friend, who ... (20. leave) university at the same time as Tom, ... (21. find) work with the EEC in Brussels and is going there next month. Tom ... (22. suggest) her keeping her eyes open for work for him when she gets there. So who knows what will happen in the end?

§§ 138; 139; 146

5 Sally Trent has applied for a job in a travel agency. She has to answer the following questions on the application form. Write the answers, using the words in brackets and a verb in either the simple past or simple present perfect.

1. Have you had any previous experience of office work? (so far – two office jobs in the school holidays)
2. Have you ever used a computer? (at school – not – since)
3. Have you ever been to a French-speaking or German-speaking country? If so, for how long? (France for six weeks on an exchange visit last summer – never – to a German-speaking country)
4. Have you learned any other languages? At school? Abroad? (some Arabic when my father worked in Cairo)
5. Have you ever used the above language(s) professionally? (once or twice to interpret for Arab visitors to the town)
6. Have you ever studied any subject/learned any skill out of school, e.g. at evening classes? (typing and shorthand at evening classes last winter)
7. Have you ever done voluntary work, e.g. with children or old people? (at our local children's home every week since last Christmas)
8. Organizing ability: have you ever organized any activity, at school for example? (concert given by our school choir this spring)

§§ 139; 143; 146; 157

6 Complete the following translations, using the simple past or simple present perfect.

1. Er ist nicht hier. Er ist ins Kino gegangen.
   He's not here. He ... to the cinema.
2. Wann ist sie einkaufen gegangen?
   When ... she ... shopping?
3. Wir können das Fenster wieder öffnen. Len hat es endlich repariert.
   We can open the window again. Len ... it at last.
4. Ich habe einen tollen Witz gehört. – Los, erzähl mal!
   I ... a great joke. Come on, tell me it!
5. Wir haben vorgestern ein Diktat geschrieben, aber unser Lehrer hat es noch nicht korrigiert.
   We ... a dictation the day before yesterday, but our teacher ... it yet.
6. Sieh' mal. Ich habe dir einen neuen Schal mitgebracht. Ich habe ihn bei Dickinson gekauft.
   Look. I ... you a new scarf. I ... it at Dickinson's.
7. In welchem Jahr ist Shakespeare gestorben?
   In what year ... Shakespeare ... ?
8. *Pat:* Jemand hat mein Portemonnaie gestohlen!
   Ben: Wann hast du es bemerkt?
   Pat: Somebody ... my purse!
   Ben: When ... you ... it?

§§ 138; 141; 146

7 Complete the following translations, using the simple past or simple present perfect.

1. Ich habe ihn seit Ostern nicht mehr gesehen.
   I ... him since Easter.
2. Im August sind wir drei Wochen an der See gewesen.
   We ... at the seaside for three weeks in August.
3. Er ist pensioniert. Aber er hat zwanzig Jahre hier gearbeitet.
   He's retired. But he ... here for twenty years.
4. Hast du Don heute morgen gesehen, als du in der Bank warst?
   ... Don when you were in the bank this morning?
5. Ich weiss von ihrem Plan, seit ich am Dienstag einen Brief von Peter bekommen habe.
   I ... about their plan since I ... a letter from Peter on Tuesday.
6. Seit er diesen Hund hat, ist er nicht einmal mit mir ausgegangen!
   Since he ... that dog, he ... with me even once!
7. *Fred:* Wie lange kennt ihr euch schon?
   Harry: Wir sind Freunde, seit wir zusammen zur Schule gegangen sind.
   Fred: How long ... each other?
   Harry: We ... friends since we ... to school together.
8. Maggie ist verrückt nach Paul McCartney seitdem sie ihn 1964 in einem Konzert gesehen hat.
   Maggie ... crazy about Paul McCartney since she ... him in a concert in 1964.

§§ 139; 146; 159

Simple past or past perfect?

8 Fill in the gaps, using a simple form of the verbs given in brackets.

1. When I ... (arrive) home last night, my wife was out, but she ... (leave) a meal for me in the oven.
2. Last month I ... (go) to Bilston to look after my father for a few days. He ... (not have) a good meal since my mother ... (go) to hospital.
3. The Watsons ... (not live) here very long when Mrs Watson ... (become) ill.
4. The house was no longer there. It ... (burn) down two years before.
5. I went out to get my bike from the shed, but I ... (have) to go back again, because I ... (forget) the key.
6. We had supper early. We ... (be) very hungry, because we ... (have) nothing to eat since breakfast.
7. The police came into the pub and ... (arrest) the man. He ... (break) a shop window nearby.
8. He ... (work) for the firm for only two years when he ... (become) manager.
9. Andrew ... (introduce) me to his wife, not realizing that we ... (meet) at the last office party.

§§ 146; 153

•9 Fill in the gaps in the following text, using a simple past or simple past perfect form of the verbs given in brackets.

The Death of Admiral Nelson

It was on October 20th, 1805 that the French admiral, Villeneuve, and his fleet at last ... (1. leave) Cadiz, where they ... (2. be) at anchor since the summer, because now Napoleon ... (3. order) him to return to the Mediterranean. The next morning he ... (4. see) Nelson's ships waiting for him. On board the 'Victory' Nelson ... (5. feel) certain that the day of the decisive battle against the enemy fleet ... (6. arrive). After he ... (7. put) his private papers in order, he ... (8. go) up on deck again, and soon the signal flags ... (9. appear) with Nelson's famous message to his ships before the Battle of Trafalgar: "England expects that every man will do his duty". By midday the British fleet ... (10. come) close enough for the French to open fire. One of the first shots ... (11. kill) Nelson's secretary, who ... (12. join) him on deck.

Earlier Nelson ... (13. tell) Hardy, who ... (14. be) captain of the 'Victory', to steer anywhere through the French line. By chance he sailed between the flagship and the 'Redoutable', in those days the best fighting ship the French ... (15. have – ever). Then the 'Victory' ... (16. hit; passive) by heavy gun-fire and thrown against the 'Redoutable'. Nelson and Hardy ... (17. walk) up and down the deck, hidden from the French only by gunsmoke. They ... (18. walk) up and down for half an hour, when, at their usual turning point, Hardy ... (19. notice) that Nelson ... (20. be) no longer beside him. Turning round, he ... (21. find) that Nelson ... (22. fall), hit by gunfire from the 'Redoutable'.

Sailors ... (23. carry) him below deck, where someone ... (24. ask) him why he ... (25. cover) his face with his handkerchief. He ... (26. do) so, so that no-one would see that the French ... (27. wound) him was the answer. Nothing ... (28. can) save Nelson's life now, but before he ... (29. die) at half past four on October 21st, 1805, he ... (30. learn) that his ships ... (31. beat) the combined French and Spanish fleets, which ... (32. mean) that 'Britannia ruled the waves' for more than a hundred years.

§§ 146; 153

10 Mixed past tenses

Pair each of the numbered sentences with a), b) or c) in the same group, using each only once.

1. 1. Have you seen Mr Williams this morning?
   2. Did you see Mr Williams this morning?
   a) No, he wasn't on the bus.
   b) No, I can't imagine where he is.
2. 1. Tess wore this dress
   2. Tess has worn this dress
   3. Tess had worn this dress
   a) only once when someone spilled tea on it.
   b) at Jenny's seventeenth birthday party.
   c) lots of times.
3. 1. Jerry hadn't finished his work
   2. Jerry hasn't finished his work
   3. Jerry didn't finish his work
   a) yet.
   b) last night.
   c) so I waited for him.
4. 1. Carla has lived here
   2. Carla lived here
   3. Carla had lived here
   a) since last year.
   b) for two years when she moved to Ohio with her family.
   c) for two years.

§§ 139; 146; 153; 157

Will-future or going-to future?

11 Fill in the gaps in the following sentences.

1. *Jeff:* Mary told me about their plans last night. They ... paint the kitchen on Saturday.
   Jack: Oh, I like painting – I ... help them!
2. I expect you ... be able to buy a picture postcard at the chemist's.
3. *Jill:* Oh dear, there's no tea left.
   Anne: Never mind. I ... make you some more.
4. I could borrow my parents' car tonight. They've got tickets for the theatre, but they ... take the bus, because it's so difficult to find somewhere to park.
5. Go and ask George. He ... know where Queen Street is – he was born here after all.
6. We've booked a holiday house on the Costa Brava for next June. We ... find out if there are any evening classes in Spanish this winter.
7. My husband usually gets home at five-thirty, so ring up again about six, and I'm sure he ... be here then.
8. You ... find the documents you need in the second drawer from the top.
9. Sooner or later he ... realize his mistake.

§§ 162; 165; 166; 167

12 Complete the following translations, using "will ('ll)" or "going to".

1. Warum ziehen sie nach Pittsburgh? Meiner Meinung nach wird es ihnen dort nicht gefallen.
   Why are they moving to Pittsburgh? I don't think they ... like it there.
2. Alle sehen glücklich aus. Ich freue mich, daß der Abend offensichtlich ein Erfolg werden wird.
   They all look happy. I'm glad the evening ... obviously ... be a success.
3. Ich schwitze jetzt schon. Es wird heute sehr heiß werden, fürchte ich.
   I'm sweating already. It ... be very hot today, I'm afraid.
4. Wenn Frank nach Amerika geht, wird er seine Schulfreunde bestimmt vermissen.
   When Frank goes to America, I'm sure he ... miss his school-friends.
5. Ich habe ihm einen Brief auf dem Tisch hinterlassen. Glaubst du, daß er ihn sehen wird?
   I've left a letter for him on the table. Do you think he ... see it?
6. Ich habe beschlossen, diesen Pullover nochmal anzufangen, weil er zu groß wird.
   I've decided to start this pullover again, because it ... be too big.
7. Sieh dir die Wolken an! Es wird gleich regnen und ich habe keinen Mantel dabei.
   Look at the clouds! It ... rain any minute, and I haven't got a coat with me.
8. Meine Frau wird voraussichtlich ungefähr um elf Uhr zu Hause sein.
   My wife ... be home at about eleven o'clock, I expect.

§§ 163; 166

13 Complete the following translations, using "will ('ll)" or "going to".

1. Warte mal. Du hast ja keine Tasche für die Einkäufe. Ich geb' dir eine.
   Wait a moment. I see you haven't got a bag for the shopping. I ... give you one.
2. Hast du's schon gehört? Peter geht von der Schule weg, um in einer Bank zu arbeiten.
   Have you heard? Peter ... leave school to work in a bank.
3. Ich habe mein Auto verkauft. Statt dessen kaufe ich mir ein Fahrrad.
   I've sold my car. I ... buy a bike instead.
4. *Ann:* Darf Nicole am Samstagnachmittag zum Spielen kommen?
   Mum: Sicher. Und ich backe euch einen Kuchen!
   Ann: Can Nicole come to play on Saturday afternoon?
   Mum: Of course. And I ... bake you a cake!
5. Meine Eltern müssen für ein Jahr nach Amerika und sie nehmen mich mit!
   My parents have got to go to America for a year, and they ... take me with them!
6. Ach, wie dumm von mir! Die Tasse ist leider kaputt. Ich besorge dir natürlich eine neue.
   How stupid of me! The cup is broken, I'm afraid. I ... get you a new one, of course.
7. *Dave:* Wie soll ich bloß rechtzeitig hinkommen?
   Jack: Ganz einfach. Ich leih' dir mein Fahrrad!
   Dave: How on earth am I to get there in time?
   Jack: That's easy. I ... lend you my bike!

§§ 162; 167

Mixed tenses

•14 Fill in the gaps in the text, using the verbs in brackets either in a simple tense form or with "will ('ll)" or "going to". Be careful with the word order.

Murder at the Duck Club

November Joe was a trapper who lived near a lake north of the St. Lawrence River in Canada. One autumn evening Eileen East, who ... (1. know) him since childhood, ... (2. knock) at the door of his hut, calling his name. "November Joe, something terrible ... (3. happen). My uncle ... (4. shoot; passive)! Everyone thinks Ted Galt ... (5. shoot) him". – "Impossible. Ted would never shoot anyone, and certainly not a fine man like Judge Harvey."

"Please come with me, Joe," said Eileen. "Mr Hart – he's a new member of the Duck Club who ... (6. drive up) from Quebec with his wife only this morning – well, he ... (7. set off) to call the police, but it's a long way to the nearest telephone. Then he ... (8. wait) where the track meets the main road to show them the way here. But I'm sure you ... (9. find out) what really happened before anyone from the police ... (10. get) here."

"Well, I ... (11. do) my best. But why everyone ... (12. think) Ted killed your uncle?" – "Two hours ago my uncle, Ted, Mr Hart and Mr Carter, the only other man at the club, ... (13. go out) to shoot some ducks. Ted hid in the bushes furthest from the clubhouse, Uncle was quite close to him, and the others were near the house. These two ... (14. hear) Ted and Uncle arguing in loud voices. You see, Ted ... (15. ask) me to be his wife, and we ... (16. get married) as soon as possible. And – well, Uncle ... (17. not be) too happy about it. Another thing against Ted is that his footsteps are the only ones to be seen in the mud near where Uncle was hiding and where his body ... (18. find; passive)."

After Joe ... (19. examine) all the guns and ... (20. speak) to Ted, Mr Carter, Mrs Hart and Sally Mackenzie, the woman who ... (21. look after) the clubhouse, her face ugly from a bad cut on her lip, he and Eileen ... (22. walk) up the track to the lake, following the footsteps the men ... (23. make) earlier that evening. "Nobody else ... (24. walk) this way since it ... (25. rain) this morning," said Joe. "Look, Ted ... (26. walk) back by the side of the lake, stopping here nearly opposite the scene of the tragedy. Why don't you sit on that log, and I ... (27. see) what I can find out." Eileen watched Joe study the ground. Suddenly picking up something close to her foot, he said, "Look what I ... (28. find) – a cartridge that is not from Judge Harvey's gun and not from Ted's either. I expect this ... (29. need; passive) in evidence, so we must mark the place where I ... (30. find) it. But how it ... (31. get) here?"

Joe and Eileen walked on along the edge of the lake till they came to the boathouse where the canoes were kept. "When ... (32. be) anyone last out in a canoe?" he asked, looking down at a spot of fresh blood in one of them. – "None of us ... (33. take) a boat out at all this weekend," was the answer. – "Well," said Joe, "I suppose you ... (34. guess) who ... (35. kill) your uncle – it's so obvious." Eileen looked at him in surprise. "Sally Mackenzie of course. From the canoe she jumped onto that log where that cartridge was found, walked along it in mocassins so that she left no marks on the log and no footsteps in the mud and then she shot him. Her lip was cut by the kick of the gun. The only thing that is not clear is why, but I suppose the police ... (36. discover) that."

§§ 118 a/b; 129; 135; 138; 139; 146; 153; 162; 166; 167; 181

The main verb: the simple form and the progressive form in different tenses

Test yourself

A State verb or activity verb?

Verbs which cannot normally be used in the progressive forms are state verbs. Verbs which can be used in the simple and progressive forms are activity verbs. In each of the following four groups of state verbs there are three verbs which can be used as activity verbs as well. Try to spot them.

1. contain, consist, hold, exist, have got, belong, own, possess, include, weigh, have
2. agree, believe, think, see, know, doubt, disagree, understand, realize, suppose, imagine, remember, expect, recognize, mean
3. matter, depend, fit, suit, look, cost, stink, smell, seem, measure, hear
4. like, love, feel, want, be tired, be rich, be silly, hate, dislike, need, taste, wish

B Simple present or present progressive?

Complete the sentences with the simple present or present progressive of the verbs in brackets. Be careful with the word order in questions.

5. I ...(hold) something in my hand that ...(feel) like a coin. Guess what it is.
6. We ...(think) of moving to Spain. What you ...(think) of it?
7. You ...(realize) that you ...(stand) on my foot?
8. You ...(hear) that noise? It ...(come) from upstairs.
9. So you ...(come) from Barcelona? I didn't know you were Spanish.
10. Something ...(seem) to be wrong with this soup. It ...(taste) of soap.
11. Most people ...(drive) too fast. They shouldn't be allowed to do more than 50 mph anywhere. – You ...(be) a bit hard on drivers with fast cars.
12. She ...(have) a beautiful voice, but it is well known that she ...(not sing) with much expression.
13. This brochure ...(contain) all the information you ...(need).
14. Bill ...(write) in his letter that he ...(come) tomorrow.
15. What ...(happen) in the film 'A Man's Man'? – Well, a father ...(try) to make his son like him, but ...(discover) that there are many ways to prove one's manhood.
16. I ...(realize) I should have been more careful. I ...(apologize) and ...(promise) to be more careful next time.
17. I can't leave yet. I ...(expect) an important telephone call any minute.
18. The police ...(look) for the escaped prisoner who is supposed to ...(hide) in a forest near here.
19. Look, the lights in Pete's office still ...(burn), so he must ...(work).

C Simple and progressive forms in context

Put the verbs in brackets into the correct form. Be careful with the word order in questions.

20. Why you ...(smell; present) the fish? It ...(not smell) bad, does it?
21. What you ...(use; present) this thing for? It looks dangerous.
22. In our city park ...(stand; present) a statue of an old man holding a boy by the hand.
23. In this book the author ...(provide; present) a clear introduction to the nature of language.
24. The story is about a housewife who ...(become; present) the millionth customer of a supermarket and the ridiculous prize she ...(win; present).
25. The doctor can't see you yet. He ...(see; present) someone else at the moment.
26. Yes, you're right. Mary ...(live; present) here, but she ...(stay; present) with friends in the country at the moment.
27. The East School football team just ...(lose; present perfect) an important match. Their coach ...(have; present) an argument with the players.
28. She ...(be; present perfect) in the shop for an hour and she still ...(not find; present perfect) a suitable present.
29. Jim ...(look; present perfect) for that letter since his girl-friend ...(leave; past) him.
30. ☐ What you ...(do; present perfect) all afternoon? You look exhausted.
31. ☐ What ...(go on; present perfect) here? The place is in a terrible mess.
32. The child ...(look; past) half frozen; she ...(need; past) a hot drink.
33. After what ...(happen: past) last night, Joan ...(feel; present) that Terry ...(not love; present) her any longer.
34. Poor Mary ...(fail; present perfect) her driving test. But I ...(expect; present) she ...(pass; future) it the next time.
35. Tomorrow's wind generators ...(look; future) quite different from the windmills we ...(know; present perfect) for nearly 2000 years.
36. When Tom ...(become; past) ill last year, his mother ...(fear; past) the worst.
37. The murderer ...(think; past) what to do next when the police ...(arrive; past).
38. When I ...(enter; past) the room, the boy ...(lie; past) on the floor.
39. Mrs Ferber ...(wait; past) for us when we ...(return; past).
40. This time next week I ...(have; future) my first judo lesson.

D Spot the mistakes.

Of the following sentences or groups of sentences 7 are wrong, 3 are entirely correct. Spot the mistakes and write down what you think is the correct version.

41. Are you having any advice for me?
42. I can't make up my mind before I'm knowing the facts.
43. Gerald and Harry know each other for a long time.
44. Tom's father is seriously ill, his doctor is fearing the worst.
45. Sarah is going to the seaside twice a year, in the spring and in the summer.
46. Can I help you? – No, thank you. I just look.
47. I seem to be losing my voice so I won't be able to speak any louder.
48. The water boils. Shall I make some coffee?
49. We're having our club meeting next Saturday.
50. He's had three accidents since he got his driving licence.

Key

A

1. **hold, weigh, have** .... §§ 117 b; 118 a
2. **think, see, expect** .... §§ 118 b; 117 b
3. **look, smell, measure** .... §§ 117 b; 119
4. **feel, be silly, taste** .... §§ 119; 118 a; 119

B

5. **I'm holding** ... that **feels** .... §§ 117 b; 119
6. We're **thinking** ... What **do** you **think** of it? .... § 118 b
7. **Do** you **realize** ... you're **standing** ... ? .... §§ 118 b; 132
8. **Do/Can** you **hear** ... ? **It's coming** .... §§ 119; 132
9. ... you **come** ... ? .... § 124
10. ... **seems** ... **tastes** .... §§ 118 a; 119
11. ... **drive** ... You're **being** .... §§ 122; 118 a (1)
12. ... **has (got)** ... **doesn't sing** .... §§ 118 a; 123
13. ... **contains** ... **need**. .... §§ 124; 118 c
14. ... **writes** ... he's **coming** .... §§ 125; 135
15. What **happens** ... **tries** ... **discovers** .... § 125
16. ... **realize** ... **apologize** ... **promise** .... § 126
17. **I'm expecting** .... § 132
18. The police **are looking** ... supposed to **be hiding** .... §§ 132; [189 b]
19. ... **are** still **burning** ... must **be working**. .... §§ 132; [189 b]

C

20. Why **are** you **smelling** .... It **doesn't smell** ... ? .... § 119
21. What **do** you **use** ... ? .... § 122
22. ... **stands** .... § 124
23. ... **provides** .... § 125
24. ... **becomes** ... **wins**. .... § 125
25. ... He's **seeing** .... §§ 117 b; 132
26. ... **lives** ... she's **staying** .... §§ 124; 134
27. ... **has** just **lost** ... **is having** an argument .... §§ 139; 132; 118 a (2)
28. She's **been** in the shop ... she still **hasn't found** .... §§ 140; 139
29. ... **has been looking** ... **left** .... §§ 143; 159 (2)
30. ☐ What **have** you **been doing** ... ? .... § 144
31. ☐ What **has been going on** ... ? .... § 144
32. ... **looked** ... **needed** .... §§ 146; 118 a; 118 c
33. ... **happened** ... **feels** ... **doesn't love** .... §§ 146; 118 b; 118 c
34. ... **has failed** ... **expect** ... she'**ll pass** .... §§ 138; 118 b; 166
35. ... **will look** ... we've **known** .... §§ 166; 140
36. ... **became** ... **feared** .... §§ 147; 118 c
37. ... **was thinking** ... **arrived**. .... §§ 149; 118 b
38. ... **entered** ... **was lying** .... § 149
39. ... **was waiting** ... **returned**. .... § 149
40. ... **I'll be having** my first judo lesson. .... §§ 171; 118 a (2)

D

41. **Have you got/Do you have** ... ? .... § 118 a
42. ... **I know** .... § 118 b
43. ... **have known** each other ... . § 140
44. ... **fears** .... § 118 c
45. ... **goes** .... § 122
46. ... **I'm** just **looking**. .... § 132
47. **Correct sentence** .... §§ 132; [189 b]
48. ... **is boiling** .... § 132
49. **Correct sentence** .... § 135
50. **Correct sentence** .... §§ 139; 159 (2)

Exercise finder

Test yourself	ENGLISH G Grammatik	Exercises
1, 4, 10, 11, 12, 27, 32, 40, 41	§ 118 a	5 : •14; 2, 3, 4, 9, 12, 13, •14, •19
2, 6, 7, 33, 34, 37, 42	§ 118 b	5 : •14; 2, 3, 4, 9, 12, •19
3, 4, 5, 10, 20	§ 119	3, 12, •19
7, 8, 17, 18, 19, 25, 27, 46, 47, 48	§ 132	1, 2, 3, 4, •19
9, 13, 22, 26	§ 124	5 : 1; 3, 4
11, 21, 45	§ 122	5 : 1;1, 2, 3, 4
12	§ 123	5 : 1; 4
13, 32, 33, 36, 44	§ 118 c	3, 4,
14, 15, 23, 24	§ 125	2, 3
14, 49	§ 135	5 : •14; 1, 2, 3, 4, •17, 18
16	§ 126	3, 4
26	§ 134	3, •19
27, 28, 50	§ 139	5 : 2, 4, 5, 7, 10, •14; 5, 6, 7, 8, 11, 12, 13, •14, •19
28, 35, 43	§ 140	5 : 2; 5, 6, 7, 8, 12, 13, •19
29	§ 143	5 : 5; 5, 6, 7, 8, 11, 12, 13, •14, •19
29, 50	§ 159	5 : 2, 7; 5, 7, 8, 12, 13, •14, •19
30, 31	§ 144	11
32, 33	§ 146	5 : 3, 4, 5, 6, 7, 8, •9, 10, •14; 9, 10, 11, 12, 13, •14, •19
34	§ 138	5 : 4, 6, •14; 6, 8, 12, 13, •14, •19
34, 35	§ 166	5 : 11, 12, •14; 15, •17, 18, •19
36	§ 147	9, 12, 13
37, 38, 39	§ 149	5 : 3; 9, 10, 11, 12, 13, •14, •19
40	§ 171	15, •17, 18, •19
18, 19, 47	§ 189 b	8 : •2, •10; 15

Exercises

Simple present or present progressive?

1 Fill in the gaps with a present simple or progressive form, using the verbs given in brackets. Be careful with the word order in questions.

1. We usually ...(go) to the seaside in August, but this year we ...(spend) our holidays in Bavaria.
2. What you ...(read)? Oh, a western. I never ...(read) westerns.
3. Tim ...(go) to school? Or isn't he old enough yet?
4. Mary can't help you just now. She ...(type) an important letter.
5. We ...(buy) all our fruit and vegetables at the market, because they are fresher there.
6. My parents ...(come) on Friday for the weekend. They always ...(come) at Easter.
7. Whenever Joe ...(visit) his grandmother, he ...(take) her some flowers.
8. Tell Billy I want him. He ...(play) in the garden.

§§ 122; 132; 135

2 Pair each of the numbered sentences with a) or b) in the same group.

1. 1. He has a party for all his friends
   2. He's having a party for all his friends
   a) on Saturday.
   b) on his birthday every year.
2. 1. He's going to see his grandmother
   2. He goes to see his grandmother
   a) this afternoon.
   b) on Wednesdays.
3. 1. Do you think
   2. Are you thinking
   a) that it's a good idea to go to Scotland this winter?
   b) of going to Scotland this winter?
4. 1. The book
   2. Professor Pringle
   a) is examining the problems of ethnic minorities in Birmingham.
   b) examines the problems of ethnic minorities in Birmingham.
5. 1. Hurry up, the film is beginning
   2. Hurry up, the film begins
   a) so there's no time to wash up.
   b) at seven-thirty and not eight.
6. 1. The Prime Minister
   2. The documentary
   a) deals with conditions in the steel industry.
   b) is dealing with conditions in the steel industry.
7. 1. Most of our electronic equipment
   2. A new piece of electronic equipment
   a) is being made for us in England.
   b) is made for us in England.

§§ 118 a/b; 122; 125; 128; 132; 135

3 Fill in the gaps with a present simple or progressive form, using the verbs given in brackets. Be careful with the word order in questions.

1. Pam ... (walk) to work this week, though she usually ... (go) by bus.
2. I ... (cook) my father's meals until my mother ... (come) home from hospital.
3. I ... (be) busy. I ... (clean up) my room, because my cousin ... (come) at the weekend.
4. *Jane:* Hallo, Jill. Where you ... (run) off to in such a hurry?
   Jill: I ... (go) to Brown's Bookshop to buy a good dictionary. You see, we ... (read) "Faust" at school.
5. *Peggy:* Oh, good! A letter from Bill.
   Clare: What he ... (say)?
6. Clare is a country girl. She ... (live) in Cornwall, but this summer she ... (stay) with her aunt in London.
7. I never ... (go) to the cinema, but I often ... (watch) films on TV and sometimes someone ... (give) me a ticket for the theatre.
8. Bobby ... (want) to be an astronaut when he ... (grow up), but I ... (expect) he'll change his mind.
9. *Liza:* The jam ... (taste) super. Can I help to put it in the jars?
   Mum: Just a minute, Bobby ... (taste) it first to see if it's sweet enough for him, too.
10. We ... (have) a party in the garden next Saturday if the weather ... (stay) fine.
11. *Patsy:* Oh, hallo. You ... (do) the weekend shopping, too?
    Sally: Yes. I usually ... (try) to do it on Fridays, because I ... (hate) the crowds on Saturdays.
12. I've heard from Alec at last. He ... (say) he ... (look forward) to seeing us all on Sunday.
13. Ted and I ... (help) Diana to decorate her room this week. She ... (think) we can finish it by Monday.
14. *Bobby:* What is that song the band ... (play) just now?
    Fiona: Well, it ... (sound) like "Blue Grass".
15. To get to the Houses of Parliament you ... (take) any bus going west along the Strand and then you ... (change) buses at Trafalgar Square.
16. I've got tickets for a concert tonight. I ... (hope) you ... (like) Bach.
17. *Diana:* I ... (not know) what to wear. You ... (take) a coat?
    Jenny: Well, a coat would be too warm in this weather, but it ... (look) like rain, so I ... (take) my umbrella.
18. *Molly:* What a nice dog!
    Carole: Yes, he ... (belong) to my sister. I ... (look) after him while she ... (be) on holiday.
19. *Peter:* Will you help me hang this picture, Dad?
    Dad: Well, I must go to the post-office before it ... (shut), but I ... (promise) I'll help you when I ... (get) back.
20. That was Joan on the phone. She ... (come) back tomorrow, and she ... (want) us to meet her at the station. Her train ... (arrive) at five-thirty.

§§ 118 a/b/c; 119; 122; 124; 125; 126; 127; 129; 132; 133; 134; 135

4 Fill in the gaps in this letter with a present simple or progressive form, using the verbs given in brackets.

Seaview Hotel
Lynton, Devon
22nd July

Dear Fiona,

Thank you for your letter from New York. How lucky you are to have relatives in America! My sister Mandy is in the States at the moment, too. She . . . (1. stay) with her pen-friend in Boston, and she . . . (2. enjoy) herself very much. This is her second visit, and she . . . (3. like) Boston so much that she . . . (4. think) of trying to get a job there for a year when she . . . (5. leave) school and before she . . . (6. go) to university. I . . . (7. feel) quite envious whenever I . . . (8. think) of all the exciting things you and Mandy . . . (9. do) this summer, and all the interesting people you . . . (10. meet). However, Mandy . . . (11. say) my turn will come. Anyway, when you . . . (12. arrive) back from New York, you must ring me up at once. I . . . (13. look forward) very much to hearing all the details of your holiday.
I . . . (14. spend) a fortnight by the sea with my parents. We . . . (15. have) our bikes with us, and sometimes Dad and I . . . (16. go) for quite long tours of the country round Lynton. Churchyards . . . (17. interest) Dad in particular. You . . . (18. see) very funny things on some of the stones. I . . . (19. take) photos of the gravestones for him. At first I was rather bored, but now I . . . (20. get) quite interested in churchyards myself. And some of my photos . . . (21. look) really super. Dad . . . (22. think) he can use them for an article he . . . (23. write) for 'History Today'. It certainly will be exciting if they actually . . . (24. publish) my pictures! Mum . . . (25. suggest) I should try and find out if there are any evening classes in photography when we . . . (26. get) home to Swindon.
We . . . (27. leave) here on Friday, but we . . . (28. not drive) straight home. My brother – the one who . . . (29. live) in Bristol – . . . (30. get married) on Saturday. Fortunately, I . . . (31. like) the girl he . . . (32. marry) very much. She always . . . (33. treat) me as if I was a friend of her own age. We . . . (34. stay) in Bristol only till Sunday, because Dad . . . (35. have) to go back to work on Monday.
That's all for now, Fiona. Mum . . . (36. call) me to go for a swim with her.

Love, *Alison*

§§ 118 a/b/c; 122; 123; 124; 126; 128; 129; 132; 133; 135

Present perfect or present perfect progressive?

5 Fill in the gaps, using a suitable verb and "since" or "for".

1. *Andy:* It's nearly midnight, and John is still working.
   Bill: Do you mean he ... this morning without stopping?
2. *Paul:* Does Diana still go to the youth club? Do you ever see her there?
   Dave: I ... n't ... her at all ... weeks.
3. *Jane:* If you're looking for Lucy, she's out on the tennis court.
   Jeff: Still? That means she ... tennis ... three whole hours.
4. *Mum:* Has Mike done his homework?
   Sue: He can't have. He ... TV ... tea-time.
5. *Clare:* I expect you have a lot of visitors.
   Sally: Yes, I ... nineteen different visitors ... I came into hospital.
6. *Don:* Do you hear from Joe sometimes?
   Tom: I ... n't ... from him ... years.
7. *Mum:* Can't you find your penknife?
   Joe: No, I ... for it ... the last half hour, but it's nowhere to be seen.
8. *Policeman:* Have you seen anyone go into the house?
   Old man: No-one ... through that door ... three o'clock.

§§ 139; 140; 143; 159

6 Fill in the gaps, using the verbs given in brackets. Be careful with the word order.

Anke always ... (1. want) to visit Edinburgh, so she ... (2. save) her pocket-money for three years now, and on each of her last three birthdays she ... (3. put) her money presents into her savings account, too. What's more, for the last few weeks she ... (4. make) some summer dresses which her aunt is going to sell in her shop in Aachen. At last she ... (5. save) almost enough. Just a few more more months now!

She already ... (6. prepare) everything she thinks she'll need for the trip; for example, she ... (7. buy) a history of the city and a street-map too. She is still worried about her English, however. Although she ... (8. learn) English at school for six years now, she feels she is not fluent enough yet, so for the last few weeks she ... (9. practise) her spoken English by going out with an English au pair girl who is living next door just now. Anke ... (10. improve) a lot already. Her uncle has a powerful radio, and she ... (11. listen) to the BBC World Service in the late evenings. She can understand it quite well now.

For weeks she ... (12. get) more and more excited as the summer and her trip to Edinburgh come closer. Tomorrow she is going to book a place on the night ferry to Hull for July 1st, though she says she ... (13. look forward) to the trip for so long now that she can hardly believe that the time ... (14. come) at last to take such a definite step.

§§ 138; 139; 140; 143

7 Complete the following translations, using the present perfect or present perfect progressive. Be careful with "schon" as there is not always an equivalent word in English.

1. Wir warten seit Anfang der Woche auf die Maler.
   We ... for the painters ... the beginning of the week.
2. Ich weiß seit Monaten, daß seine Arbeit ihm nicht gefällt.
   I ... months that he doesn't like his work.
3. Die Männer arbeiten schon seit drei Stunden und haben jetzt Hunger.
   The men ... three hours, and they're hungry now.
4. Seit dem Brand in der Fabrik ist Raymond arbeitslos.
   Raymond ... unemployed ... the fire at the factory.
5. Anna sucht dein Buch schon seit dem Mittagessen.
   Anna ... for your book ... lunch.
6. Andrew reinigt sein Moped schon seit zwei Stunden. Es kann nicht mehr lange dauern.
   Andrew ... his moped ... two hours. It can't take much longer.
7. Ich bin seit Wochen nicht mehr im Kino gewesen.
   I ... to the cinema ... weeks.
8. Seit den Weihnachtsferien hat er nur einmal geschrieben.
   He ... only once ... the Christmas holidays.
9. Seit wir den neuen Computer haben, habe ich samstags nicht mehr arbeiten müssen.
   ... we ... the new computer, I ... to work on Saturdays.
10. Jane hat schon dreimal angerufen, seit sie von deiner Krankheit gehört hat.
    Jane ... three times ... she ... about your illness.

§§ 139; 140; 143; 159

8 Complete the following translations. Be careful with "schon" as there is not always an equivalent word in English.

1. Hast du schon mal englisches Bier getrunken?
   ... English beer?
2. Es ist sehr spät. Wie lange arbeitest du schon?
   It's very late. ... ?
3. Ich habe einen Kuchen gemacht. Möchtest du ein Stück?
   I ... a cake. Would you like a piece?
4. Thomas hat schon immer einen Sportwagen gewollt.
   Thomas ... a sports car.
5. Ich füttere ihre Katzen schon seit drei Monaten.
   I ... their cats ... three months ... .
6. Wir diskutieren das Problem seit dem Mittagessen, aber bis jetzt haben wir noch keine Lösung gefunden.
   We ... the problem ... lunch, but we ... a solution ... .
7. Ich habe euch einen Kaffee gemacht. Ihr tapeziert mein Zimmer schon den ganzen Nachmittag – ihr habt bestimmt Durst.
   I ... you some coffee. You ... my room ... – you must be thirsty.
8. Karen sucht ihren Hund schon stundenlang. Sie hat ihn gerade gefunden – unter ihrem Bett.
   Karen ... for her dog ... . She ... him – under her bed.

§§ 138; 139; 140; 143; 159

Simple past or past progressive?

9 Fill in the gaps in the text, using the verbs given in brackets.

Early on December 5th, 1872, which ... (1. be) a fine, cold, clear day, a British sailing-ship ... (2. cross) the Atlantic. On board, a sailor who ... (3. clean) the deck suddenly ... (4. notice) something far away on the water. He ... (5. suppose) it was another ship. A little later, while he ... (6. wash) the last bit of the deck, he ... (7. look) up again. It was a ship, but there was something unusual about her: no-one ... (8. steer) her, he was sure, so he ... (9. put away) his bucket and ... (10. call) the captain, who ... (11. sleep) in his cabin.

When the captain ... (12. come) on deck, most of the sailors ... (13. watch) the strange ship to which they ... (14. get) quite close now, close enough for them to see that she was an American ship called the 'Mary Celeste'. The captain ... (15. shout) her name, but no-one ... (16. reply).

Then the captain ... (17. send) some of his sailors on board the 'Mary Celeste', but there was no sign of her crew: no-one ... (18. read) the map on the table in the captain's cabin, no-one ... (19. cook) a meal below deck, no-one ... (20. repair) ropes and sails. There was no sign of any damage from bad weather, however, and no sign of a fight either. It ... (21. look) as if the sailors had just left the ship and ... (22. spend) the day on land – but this was far out in the Atlantic.

What ... (23. happen) to those on board the 'Mary Celeste'? The mystery has never been solved.

§§ 118 a/b; 146; 147; 149

10 Pair each of the numbered sentences with a) or b) in the same group.

1. 1. Sue made me some tea
   2. Sue was making me some tea
   a) when I asked her to.
   b) when I got home.
2. 1. I was working very hard yesterday,
   2. I worked very hard yesterday,
   a) so I couldn't go swimming with the others.
   b) so I think I deserve a holiday today.
3. 1. Were you driving
   2. Did you drive
   a) all the way to Exeter?
   b) when the sheep ran across the road?
4. 1. I was phoning Jane between 8 and 8.30,
   2. I phoned Jane between 8 and 8.30,
   a) but she wasn't in.
   b) so I couldn't watch the Monty Python show on TV.
5. 1. When Mary came I was reading your letter,
   2. When Mary came I read your letter,
   a) so I asked her to wait till I had finished.
   b) which she had brought with her.
6. 1. Derek repaired his motor-bike this morning,
   2. Derek was repairing his motor-bike this morning,
   a) so he had no time to do his homework.
   b) so he's going to take his girl-friend out this evening.

§§ 146; 149; 151; 153 b

Simple past, past progressive, present perfect or present perfect progressive?

11 Make sensible responses to the following remarks, using the words in brackets where given.

1. I'm going to do the washing now.
   – That's not necessary. Dorothy … . (already)
2. Jerry has bought a super new camera.
   – Where … ?
3. I'm sorry about the mess in my room, Mum.
   – What on earth … ?
4. Are you going to see Grandma this afternoon?
   – No, I … . (yesterday)
5. Was George working when you got there?
   – No, he … . (in a chair in the garden)
6. Why wasn't he working?
   – Well, he … . (ill recently)
7. Harry is tired of hanging pictures.
   – I'm not surprised. He … . (all day)
8. Did Bobby finish that letter last night?
   – No, and what is more, he … ! (not yet)
9. Pauline has applied for a job at Marley's.
   – When … ?

§§ 139; 141; 143; 144; 146; 149

12 Fill in the gaps, using the verbs given in brackets. Be careful with the word order.

1. *Linda:* I'm looking for John. You ... (see) him anywhere?
   Len: Yes. But when I ... (see) him, he ... (leave) the office.
2. *Tim:* You live in Hull, don't you?
   Alan: Not now. We ... (move) to Kent in 1975.
3. *Steven:* You ... (see) what that man ... (do) a moment ago?
   Valerie: No. I ... (look) at these records.
   Steven: He ... (put) a cassette in his pocket while the assistant ... (serve) that lady who just ... (go) out.
4. *Jane:* When I ... (leave) home to catch the bus this morning, it ... (rain) heavily, so of course I ... (take) my umbrella with me, and now I can't find it.
   Lucy: You ... (leave) it on the bus perhaps? Or you ... (be) out again since you ... (get) to the office?
5. *Mary:* You work at the biscuit factory, don't you? I'm sure I ... (notice) you there.
   David: Not now. I ... (work) there for twenty years, but I ... (take) a job at the new electronics factory when it ... (open) a few months ago.
6. *Mary:* Are you married?
   David: Not any more. I ... (get) a divorce a couple of years ago. But I ... (go out) with a very nice girl from the office lately, so you never know ... .
7. *Jake:* Look – I ... (buy) new tyres for my moped. I ... (get) them at that shop in Forth Street that just ... (open). They ... (not cost) very much, so why don't you get some too if they ... (not sell) them all yet?
   Bill: I already ... (buy) some!
8. *Tony:* Where's James? When I last ... (see) him he ... (fish) near those rocks over there, but now he completely ... (disappear).
   Andy: I don't know. I ... (help) Larry to paint his boat all morning, so I ... (not see) James at all yet.
9. *Chris:* There was a fire at our school last week. We ... (have) a history lesson about the Great Fire of London when it ... (start)!
   Alex: The school ... (burn) down?
   Chris: No – only the school kitchen. So Mum ... (give) me sandwiches to take for lunch – something different every day so far!
10. *Anne:* I ... (learn) German for five years now, but I ... (not understand) those people on the boat at all.
    Mona: But they ... (be) Swiss. Germans often don't understand the Swiss either.
11. *Phil:* Christine and I just ... (see) a ghost!
    Mark: What it ... (say)?
12. *Rod:* How long you ... (stay) with the Parkers?
    Chantal: Since August. I ... (see) their advertisement for an au pair girl one day while I ... (wait) for an interview for another job. I ... (read) a newspaper because I had to wait so long.
13. *Andrew:* That ... (be) a terrible storm last night, ... (not be) it?
    Terry: Oh? I ... (not hear) anything. But we ... (watch) TV all evening and we ... (have) it on very loud, because my mother ... (become) rather deaf since she ... (work) at the Magic Machine factory.

§§ 118 a/b; 119; 138; 139; 140; 141; 143; 146; 147; 149; 151; 159

13 Complete the following translations, using a suitable past or perfect tense.

1. Ich habe dir einen Kuchen mitgebracht. Ich habe ihn selbst gemacht.
   I ... you a cake. I ... it myself.
2. Die Kartoffeln kochen schon seit zwanzig Minuten. Ob sie wohl fertig sind?
   The potatoes ... for twenty minutes. Do you think they're ready?
3. Als ich anrief, packten sie schon ihre Koffer.
   When I ... , they ... their suitcases.
4. Charles arbeitet schon den ganzen Morgen. Zuerst hat er Blumen gepflanzt, dann hat er den Rasen geschnitten, und seitdem streicht er die Gartenstühle an.
   Charles ... all morning. First he ... some flowers, then he ... the lawn, and since then he ... the garden chairs.
5. Colin ist um acht nach Hause gekommen. Seine Eltern unterhielten sich gerade im Wohnzimmer.
   Colin ... home at eight. His parents ... in the living-room.
6. Richard hat das Haus um eins verlassen. Seine Familie war beim Mittagessen. Seither hat ihn niemand mehr gesehen.
   Richard ... the house at one o'clock. His family ... lunch. No-one ... him again since.
7. Ich war schon mal in Blackpool. Es hat mir nicht gefallen.
   I ... to Blackpool. I ... it.
8. Ein Schiff mit 600 Passagieren ist vor der französischen Küste gesunken. Das Radio berichtet über das Unglück seit dem frühen Morgen.
   A ship with 600 passengers ... off the French coast. The radio ... on the disaster since the early morning.

§§ 118 a; 138; 139; 140; 141; 143; 146; 147; 149; 159

•14 **Mixed past and perfect tenses**

Fill in the gaps in the following text, using a past or perfect tense of the verbs in brackets. Be careful with the word order.

Every cloud has a silver lining

One morning last week the door bell ... (1. ring) while Mrs Barton ... (2. make) breakfast for her husband, Henry, who ... (3. clear) the snow from the front path. But why he ... (4. ring) the bell, why he ... (5. not come) in, she wondered. Shaking her head, she ... (6. go) to the door after she carefully ... (7. turn off) the gas. When she ... (8. see) her husband, she ... (9. call out) in surprise because he ... (10. sit) on the door-step in the snow. "I ... (11. hurt) my leg," he said, "I suppose I ... (12. slip) on some ice under the snow." – "Oh, dear. I ... (13. be) afraid of something like this for a long time – we're getting too old for this kind of work," his wife replied. However, having helped Henry into the living-room, pulled off his boots, and looked at his foot, Mrs Barton ... (14. realize) that he only ... (15. sprain) it. Just then she ... (16. notice) something else. "Oh, Henry, look – your watch isn't on your wrist. What you ... (17. do) with it?" – "Perhaps it ... (18. drop) off my wrist while I ... (19. work) in the snow," he ... (20. suggest). "But you mustn't go and look for it. It's so cold and you ... (21. cough) such a lot during the last few days. I ... (22. get) quite worried about it."

Out in the kitchen again to finish making the breakfast, Mrs Barton felt rather sad at the loss of the watch, because their grandson Richard ... (23. give) it to his grandfather for his birthday, paying for it out of his very first salary, and so she ... (24. decide) to look for it after all, while she ... (25. wait) for the eggs to boil. "Richard is coming this afternoon, and Henry will hate having to tell him that the watch ... (26. lose; passive). It is only a week since Richard ... (27. give) it to him, too," she thought. And she went out into the snow without even stopping to put on proper boots. She ... (28. search) the snow at the side of the path when she ... (29. find) that she ... (30. have) a hole in her pocket and that her key ... (31. disappear). She hoped she ... (32. leave) the back door open so that she could get back inside without ringing the front door bell for Henry. She ... (33. turn) round quickly – too quickly – and fell. Pulling herself painfully to her feet, she had to ring the bell after all. When a surprised Henry ... (34. open) the door, she ... (35. sit) on the step just where he ... (36. be) a quarter of an hour before!

"How long you ... (37. sit) there?" Henry asked in amazement. "And what on earth are you doing out here?" – "I ... (38. try) to find your watch and all I ... (39. manage) to do is hurt my ankle, too," his wife replied. But she was wrong: she ... (40. find) the watch after all, for after Henry ... (41. help) her to get up, he ... (42. spot) it in the snow just where she ... (43. fall).

§§ 118 a; 138; 139; 143; 146; 149; 153; 157; 159

15 Simple or progressive infinitive?

Tina and Alan Dixon are flying home after spending a year in Africa. Fill in the simple or progressive infinitive of the verbs given in brackets.

Tina: I'm looking forward to seeing the family again of course, but in some ways it'll ... (1. seem) strange to be back in England, won't it? I'm sure I'll ... (2. miss) Africa a lot, especially the evenings there when it's cooler. In about an hour from now the others will ... (3. watch) the sun go down over the river. And only yesterday we were with them.

Alan: Cheer up! We'll ... (4. go) back again in two years, I promise you. And now let's think of England and the family. Guess what I missed most in Africa – English rain! I hope it'll ... (5. pour) with rain by the time we get to London, though by this time next week I expect I'll ... (6. wonder) if it'll ever ... (7. stop)!

Tina: Well, look out of the window – there are dark clouds over the Channel, so it probably will ... (8. rain) in England. I wonder what the family are doing. Of course Father and Rex will ... (9. wait) at the airport when we land. I wonder if Rex will ... (10. recognize) us after such a long time?

Alan: Your mother won't be at the airport, of course – she'll ... (11. make) lunch for us all, and your grandmother will ... (12. help) her. But when they hear the car horn, they'll ... (13. rush) to the door, and they'll ... (14. stand) on the front step when we come up the garden path. And the minute she sees us, your mother will ... (15. say), "Well, my dears, there's no place like home," just the way she always does. And then I'll ... (16. feel) that we are really home at last!

§§ 166; 171; 189 b

16 Future perfect

Complete the following dialogues.

1. Has George mended the iron for me yet?
   – No, but he ... it by the time you need it.
2. Can you tell me when Peter's train arrives?
   – Well, I'm expecting a letter from him. I'll ring you back at twelve – the postman ... here by then.
3. Shall I tell Terry about the meeting when I see him tonight?
   – You needn't bother. Mr Roscoe ... him before then.
4. I've invited the Carrs for the weekend. But they can't come if you haven't finished papering the living-room.
   – Don't worry. I ... it long before they come.
5. Could you read this report soon? I'd like to discuss it with you.
   – Let's meet on Friday. I ... it by then.
6. I've ordered the paint for the boat.
   – Fine. When the season starts, the 'Seagull' ... (passive) shining white with her name in gold!
7. Oh dear. There is still so much to get ready for the party.
   – The twins are very efficient. I'm sure they ... everything ready in plenty of time.
8. I think John should buy some new tyres before he takes the car on holiday.
   – His wife hopes he ... a whole new car by then!
9. The bus is late. When does the film start?
   – At eight, so I'm afraid it ... before we get there.
10. I hear they are going to begin building a school at the end of your road soon.
    – Yes, we're very pleased. It means the school ... (passive) by the time Philip starts school.

§ 174

Simple present, present progressive, will-future, going-to future or future progressive?

•17 Emma and Jeremy both work for an oil firm. Emma is telling her friend Rose about the plans she and Jeremy have made for their future. Fill in the gaps in the conversation, using the verbs given in brackets to express future time. Be careful with the word order.

Emma: I've got some news for you. Jeremy and I have fixed the date of our wedding. We ... (1. get married) on June 25th.

Rose: Why this sudden rush?

Emma: Well, in August the firm ... (2. send) Jeremy to Saudi Arabia for a year and they ... (3. not allow) me to go with him if we ... (4. not get married), you know. According to the instructions Jeremy has been given, we ... (5. fly) to Riyadh on August 8th, so there's not much time left for everything that has to be done. And I expect we ... (6. discover) all kinds of problems that we haven't even thought of yet.

Rose: And what about your job?

Emma: Well, in Saudi Arabia it's impossible for women to do business, so I haven't any choice: I just ... (7. have) to give up my job for a year. But I have already thought about that, and I ... (8. make) good use of the time. I ...

(9. learn) to cook and sew, for example. You ... (10. not know) me when we ... (11. get) back to England!

Rose: But surely you ... (12. hate) having nothing but housework to do. You ... (13. do) anything outside your home? It ... (14. be) difficult, of course. In Saudi Arabia women are not even allowed to drive a car, you know.

Emma: Oh yes. I've begun to learn Arabic, and Jenny Holmes has given me the names of one or two Arab women she managed to get to know in Riyadh, and I hope to visit them. I hope I ... (15. be able) to speak quite well by the time we ... (16. leave) Riyadh again. My old job ... (17. wait) for me then, the firm has promised me that, and I expect my knowledge of Arabic ... (18. improve) my chances of promotion, too. I'm still ambitious, you know. I ... (19. not be) just a housewife for the rest of my life – I've made up my mind about that. In fact – just between ourselves – I ... (20. become) managing director of the firm one day. I'm quite determined. Jeremy says he ... (21. not mind) having me as his boss at work as well as at home! Well, I must go now. I ... (22. meet) Jeremy at five o'clock to do some shopping. There is so much to do and so much to buy that obviously we ... (23. find) it difficult to have everything ready in time.

Rose: Well, if there ... (24. be) anything I can do, just ring me up and I ... (25. come).

Emma: Oh, Rose, sometimes I feel quite nervous. I ... (26. manage) to cope with everything in Riyadh, do you think?

Rose: That's no way for a future managing director to speak, so cheer up. And if I ... (27. get) you an Arabic dictionary as a wedding present, perhaps that ... (28. help)!

§§ 128; 129; 135; 162; 163; 165; 166; 171

18 Pair each of the numbered sentences with a) or b) in the same group.

1. 1. I'm going to complain to the manager about the broken switch,
   2. I'll complain to the manager about the broken switch,
   a) so I've brought the radio with me.
   b) if they don't take the radio back.
2. 1. The play starts
   2. The play is going to start
   a) at seven-thirty.
   b) any minute now – the lights have been turned off already.
3. 1. Think of me when you are celebrating –
   2. The man says the plane to Paris is full, but never mind –
   a) I'll cross the Channel on the ferry.
   b) I'll be crossing the Channel on the ferry.
4. 1. I'm sorry to hear the accident was so serious –
   2. No, I'm afraid we can't go to the match with you –
   a) we're going to see John in hospital on Saturday.
   b) we'll go and see John in hospital on Saturday.
5. 1. I'm afraid we can't accept any invitations for the weekend –
   2. We're sorry to hear you're all ill. But don't worry –
   a) Mary is coming to stay from Friday to Sunday.
   b) Mary will come to stay from Friday to Sunday.

§§ 128; 129; 135; 162; 163; 166; 167; 171

•19 Mixed Tenses

Fill in the gaps in the story, using the verbs given in brackets in a simple or progressive form. Be careful with the word order.

On a Greek Island

In the early evening we decided to take a walk down to the harbour to watch the island ferry come in. It was still fine and sunny, but by now a cool wind ... (1. blow) in from the sea, making the temperature very pleasant. We ... (2. walk) past the little café where we ... (3. have) lunch a few hours before, when I ... (4. realize) that I ... (5. forget) to bring my camera.

"Oh Andrew, I ... (6. leave) my camera at the hotel!" I exclaimed. – "Never mind, I ... (7. go) back for it," Andrew said. "Where I ... (8. find) it exactly?" – "I expect I ... (9. put) it on the table when we ... (10. get) back from the beach this afternoon," I replied. – "Are you sure, Margaret?" Andrew asked. "I ... (11. not remember) seeing it there. In fact, I ... (12. not see) it at all since you ... (13. take) some pictures of the little boy with the two dogs on the beach. You remember – there were two men there, too. They ... (14. stand) at the edge of the water, and they ... (15. chase) the child with the dogs away. When they ... (16. notice) us, they ... (17. turn) their backs."

The lively little scene came back to my mind, and I remembered putting the camera in my beach bag. No doubt, it still ... (18. lie) at the bottom of the bag under my swimming things. "Let's not bother about it," I said. "The ferry ... (19. come) in at six every evening, and we ... (20. miss) it if we ... (21. not hurry). We ... (22. stand) here talking too long already. I know you ... (23. look forward) to a cool drink at one of those little tables on the pier and to watching the excitement when the ferry ... (24. arrive). So let's go on. I ... (25. take) pictures of it another time."

At that moment we ... (26. hear) the sound of a horn coming from the harbour as a warning to the little boats there: the ferry ... (27. come) through the harbour entrance. We were just in time to see everything. The ferry boat still ... (28. glide) along quite fast. "It ... (29. hit) the pier!" I exclaimed. But no, it stopped at the exact spot where two men ... (30. wait) on the pier with the gangway.

In spite of the crowds we found a table outside the café and sat down. Andrew picked up the wine list. "Let me see. Yes – I ... (31. try) some of that Greek wine I ... (32. hear) so much about – retsina," Andrew said. "You ... (33. decide) what you would like yet?" – "Oh, I think I ... (34. wait) and try some of your retsina when the waiter ... (35. bring) it, so just order me a lemonade to start with," I replied, looking round at the busy scene on the pier. Suddenly I noticed someone. "Andrew, you ... (36. see) that man over there in the green shirt, the one who ... (37. sit) at the table by the door to the café? He ... (38. look) familiar somehow. Where I ... (39. see) him before, I wonder?" Andrew looked round: "I think perhaps he ... (40. stay) at our hotel. He ... (41. wander) up the hill when I stopped to look back at the view while we ... (42. climb) back up to the hotel from the beach this afternoon. Ah, here comes the waiter with your lemonade and my retsina!" He drank a little. – "What it ... (43. taste) like?" I asked. – "I can't describe it. It ... (44. not taste) like anything I ever ... (45. drink) before. Here – try it yourself," he said, offering me his glass. As I took it, I saw the man in the green shirt looking at me, and some drops of retsina fell on my blouse. "Be careful, you ... (46. spill) retsina on your blouse," Andrew warned me. – "It ... (47. not matter). I ... (48. wash) a few things tonight anyway, so I ... (49. wash) this blouse with them," I answered. "But that man ... (50. look) at us. In fact, I think he ... (51. watch) us ever since we ... (52. sit down) here. I wonder why. Oh look – he ... (53. get up)! I'm sure he ... (54. come over) and speak to us."

Before the man could reach our table, Andrew signalled to the waiter for the bill and stood up. Quickly drinking the rest of my lemonade, I followed him. "Why you ... (55. do) that?" I asked in surprise. – "Well, for weeks I ... (56. count) the days till the beginning of our holiday, our first holiday together. I don't want a stranger to spoil our very first evening here. Anyway, I ... (57. order) dinner at the hotel for seven-thirty. They ... (58. serve) it to us outside in a quiet corner of the terrace. Just imagine, in an hour or two you ... (59. sit) out there with a glass of wine in your hand, watching the moon rise over the sea. So promise you ... (60. put on) your prettiest dress!"

But when we ... (61. get) to our room, I ... (62. make) a very strange discovery. My camera was indeed at the bottom of my beach bag, but it was empty: the film ... (63. disappear)! "No," I decided, "I ... (64. not tell) Andrew, so that I ... (65. not spoil) the evening he ... (66. plan) so carefully."

But who could have taken the film and why?

118 a/b; 119; 128; 129; 132; 134; 138; 139; 140; 143; 146; 149; 150; 151; 153; 159; 162; 163; 165; 166; 167; 171

The passive

Test yourself

A **Active or passive?**

Complete the following sentences, using the active or passive form of the verb in brackets. Be careful with the tenses.

1. It's a great advantage for English-speaking people that English ...(speak) all over the world.
2. When Latif came to Britain, he ...(speak) English with a strong accent.
3. Ladies and gentlemen, after the film tea ...(serve) in the garden.
4. The French language programme ...(repeat) at the moment.
5. Do you know which firm ...(make) more cars last year – ABV or MRX?
6. □ After the death of his wife George ...(take care of) by his nephew.
7. I'd like this film ...(develop) by Saturday.
8. The employees are not going on strike, because they ...(promise) higher wages at last.
9. Applications by telephone will not be considered. A company application form must ...(fill in) by all applicants for the job.
10. Sometimes foreigners ...(talk to) as if they are stupid.
11. The criminals' passports ought ...(check) much earlier than they were.
12. When the immigrant got to the terminal building, the other members of his family ... already ...(question) by an immigration officer.
13. □ The student teacher told her pupils to return to their desks, but she ...(not take notice of).
14. Yes, Anne's orange hair is certainly different. I think she just wants ...(notice) by everybody.

B Find suitable English equivalents for the German words and sentences given in brackets. Use the passive.

15. Lots of beaches in Cornwall ... when the tanker Torrey Canyon broke in half. (wurden vom Öl verunreinigt)
16. After the match ... for their efforts. (dankte man der Mannschaft)
17. The drinks ... . (sind schon bezahlt worden)
18. We've got to hurry. Dinner ... . (wird schon serviert)
19. Mr Dawson wanted ... by Friday. (seinen Anzug reinigen lassen)
20. Don't worry – Joanne ... in a few minutes. (wird ins Krankenhaus gebracht)
21. A lot of people ... every day. (werden ins Mayflower-Krankenhaus gebracht)
22. ... . (Man glaubt, daß der Gefangene entflohen ist)
23. After the boy had returned from abroad, ... (wurde ihm von fast allen Lehrern geholfen)
24. □ Our house is not finished yet. In fact, a lot of work ... . (bleibt noch zu tun)
25. After the accident ... everywhere. (sprach man von den Kulakowskis)
26. Yes, I know ... to say I wasn't in the office if anyone phoned. But you should have known that my wife wouldn't believe you. (man bat Sie)
27. ... . (Man erwartet von Krankenwagenfahrern, daß sie äußerst vorsichtig fahren)
28. ... . (Dem Wagen des Präsidenten folgten Polizisten auf Motorrädern)

C Spot the mistakes.

There is one mistake in each of the following sentences. Spot the mistakes and write down what you think is the correct version. Be careful: three are not passive mistakes.

29. The building is finished by next spring.
* 30. The police was called immediately after the accident.
31. Sally wanted her fridge to be repairing by Saturday.
32. The children have already be given lots of nice presents.
33. The rooms have already been paid.
34. "At the moment a very important question is discussed", the secretary said.
35. The story sounded strangely because it was told from a different point of view.
36. After the disaster the inspectors discovered that the plane was not been checked thoroughly before the flight.
37. The dead woman's husband ought have been questioned much earlier.
38. Measles should have been unknown among the Indians before the white settlers came.
☐ 39. Foreign children are often made fun by their classmates.
40. Thousands of houses were destroyed through a terrible earthquake in Italy.

"Then again, gentlemen, we're in complete agreement in the sense that nobody knows the answer to any of the questions that have been raised."

Key

A

1. ... English **is spoken** all over the world. .... § 181 a
2. ... he **spoke** English with a strong accent. .... § 179
3. ... **will be served** in the garden. .... § 181 a
4. ... programme **is being repeated** at the moment. .... §§ 182; 181 a
5. ... which firm **made** more cars ... ? .... § 179
6. □ ... George **was taken care of** by his nephew. .... § 184 d
7. I'd like this film **(to be) developed** ... . § 187 b
8. ... they **have been promised** ... . § 184 b
9. ... application form **must be filled in** ... . §§ 181 a; 187 a
10. Sometimes foreigners **are talked to** ... . § 184 c
11. ... passports ought **to have been checked** much earlier ... . § 187 a
12. ... members of his family **were** already **being/had** already **been questioned** ... . §§ 182; 181 a
13. ... she **wasn't taken notice of**. .... § 184 d
14. ... she just wants **to be noticed** ... . § 187 a

B

15. Lots of beaches ... **were polluted by oil** ... . §§ 181 a; 183
16. After the match **the team was thanked/all the members of the team were thanked** ... . § 184 a
17. The drinks **have already been paid for**. .... § 184 c
18. Dinner **is already being served**. .... §§ 182; 181 a
19. Mr Dawson wanted **his suit (to be) cleaned** ... . § 187 b
20. ... Joanne **will be taken to hospital** in a few minutes. § 181 a
21. A lot of people **are taken to Mayflower Hospital** every day. .... § 181 a
22. **The prisoner is believed/is thought to have escaped**. .. § 185
23. ... **he was helped by almost all the teachers**. .... §§ 184 a; 183
24. □ ... a lot of work **still has to be done/is still to be done/ remains to be done**. .... §§ 187 a; 189 c
25. ... **the Kulakowskis were talked about** everywhere. ... § 184 c
26. ... **you were asked** to say ... . § 184 b
27. **Ambulance drivers are expected to drive extremely carefully**. .... § 185
28. **The President's car was followed by policemen on motor-bikes**. .... § 184 a

C

29. The building **will be finished** by next spring. .... §§ 181 a; [165]
30. * The police **were called** ... . § [16 d]
31. ... wanted her fridge (to be) **repaired** ... . § 187 b
32. The children have already **been** given ... . §§ 181 a; 184 b
33. ... have already been paid **for**. .... § 184 c
34. ... question is **being** discussed ... . §§ 182; 181 a
35. The story sounded **strange** ... . § [51 a]
36. ... the plane **had not been checked** ... . §§ 181 a; [153 a]

37. ... ought **to** have been questioned ... . § [92]
38. Measles **is said/supposed to have been** unknown ... . § 185
☐ 39. ... are often made fun **of** ... . § 184 d
40. ... houses were destroyed **by** ... . § 183

Exercise finder

Test yourself	ENGLISH G Grammatik	Exercises
1, 3, 4, 9, 12, 15, 18, 20, 21, 29, 32, 34, 36	§ 181	1, 2, 10
2, 5	§ 179	1
4, 12, 18, 34	§ 182	2, 3, 10
6, 8, 13, 26, 32, 39	§ 184 b/d	5, •6
7, 19, 31	§ 187 b	9, 10
9, 11, 14, 24	§ 187 a	8, 10
10, 17, 25, 33	§ 184 c	5, •6, 10
15, 23, 40	§ 183	4, 10
16, 23, 28	§ 184 a	3, 5, •6
22, 27, 38	§ 185	•7, 10
24	§ 189 c	**8** : 1
29	§ 165	**5** : 11
30	§ 16 d	**1** : 4, 5
34	§ 51 a	**2** : 12
36	§ 153 a	**5** : 8, •9, 10, •14
37	§ 92	**4** : 3

Exercises

1 Active or passive?

Decide whether to put in the verbs in the passive or not, and be careful with the tenses. Can you name the man whose life is referred to here?

Although this man's name ... (1. know) throughout the world today, nobody ... (2. predict) such fame for him when he was young, even though his father and grandfather had been important government ministers.

He ... (3. be born) in 1869 in a part of the British Empire where several forms of discrimination ... (4. practise). At the age of twelve, according to his autobiography, he ... (5. steal) some money in order to buy cigarettes. At the age of thirteen he ... (6. follow) the traditions of his family and ... (7. get married). He ... (8. send) to England at the age of eighteen to become a lawyer. When he visited Paris in 1890, just after the Eiffel Tower ... (9. build), he ... (10. impress) with the size and character of the big churches there, especially Notre Dame. After passing his examinations, he ... (11. return) home in 1891 and studied law in his own country – though he sometimes went to sleep in court!

His life up to then had not changed history. Then, in 1893, he ... (12. invite) to go to South Africa to give legal advice in a commercial case.

A few days after arriving at the port of Durban, he bought a first-class ticket for the train to Pretoria, but he ... (13. throw) off the train at Maritzburg, because the law there ... (14. give) only whites the right to sit in first-class carriages. He complained about discrimination – against himself and against others – and later he ... (15. arrest) several times and had to spend a long time in prison. However, he reached Pretoria in the end and the court case ... (16. solve) with his help.

When his talent and dedication became known, he ... (17. encourage) to stay in South Africa longer to organize a non-violent campaign for the rights of immigrant workers from Asia. And, in fact, it was more than twenty years before he ... (18. leave) South Africa to become a key figure in the independence movement that ... (19. grow) in his native land.

The campaigns of the American civil rights leader, Dr Martin Luther King, who ... (20. shoot) dead in Memphis in 1968, ... (21. base) on this man's ideas and example. And a film about his life, which ... (22. make) by Sir Richard Attenborough, ... (23. win) eight Hollywood "Oscars" in 1983 for being the best film of the year. Who was this man of peace who ... (24. die) in 1948?

§§ 179; 181

2 Put the verbs into the passive. Be careful with the tenses.

Julian: That was a pleasant meal, Herbert, thanks. I ... (1. not feed) like that since Emily died.
Herbert: Oh, you're welcome, Uncle Julian. But would you excuse me for a moment while I make sure that all the windows ... (2. close)?
Julian: Why? Is crime getting worse in this area, too?
Herbert: I'm afraid so. I read an article about it that ... (3. publish) only last week. It seems that seven homes ... (4. break into) every day around here.
Julian: I suppose most of the crimes ... (5. commit) by unemployed teenagers?

Herbert: It's hard to say. In 80 % of the cases, you see, nobody is caught.
Julian: That's bad. Are the police around here on strike or what?
Herbert: It isn't their fault. In nearly all the cases last month, for example, no force ... (6. have to use), because a window ... (7. leave open). In fact, most homes ... (8. enter) via open windows these days, it seems.
Julian: But can't anything ... (9. do)? Can't the police give advice at least?
Herbert: Oh, they keep advising people to get windows that ... (10. can lock). It stressed that in the article. And a special exhibition ... (11. hold) in the town hall next week.
Julian: Exhibition? What sort of exhibition?
Herbert: You know, equipment that ... (12. can fix) in people's homes to make them safer.
Julian: Listen. What's that noise? It sounds as if my car engine ... (13. start)!
Herbert: It could be my next-door neighbour. She drives the same sort of car as you. But we'd better have a look. Quick!

§§ 181; 182

3 What might you say in the following situations? Put the verbs in the passive and finish the sentences.

Example: You're with a friend on the beach when you feel someone's eyes on you.
"You know, I think ...we're being watched..., Peter." (watch)

1. You've got a temporary job as a secretary. After typing some letters, you have to ask another secretary where to find some envelopes.
   "Can you tell me where ... , Janet?" (keep)
2. As you were leaving the cinema last week, you saw something terrible happening. Later you had to tell a court about it.
   "As I came out, I noticed that an old lady ... by two men." (beat up)
3. You lost your camera last week. A policeman has just called at your hotel – with the camera.
   "Oh, that's great! Where ... ?" (find)
4. You think Kate Bradley is the only good candidate in the by-election.
   "If the voters are sensible, ..." (elect)
5. Martin didn't manage to win the tennis championship yesterday.
   "What a shame you ... , Martin. Better luck next time." (beat)
6. You're walking along the street with a friend. Somebody is walking behind you – a detective, perhaps, or a pickpocket?
   "Don't turn round now, Sue, but I'm sure ... ." (follow)
7. You've applied for a job as a junior bank clerk. The bank might accept you. Your name is on the list. You want to impress your pen-friend.
   "I ... for a position in the world of banking." (consider)
8. The new hospital wasn't quite finished when you left Pudley.
   "Is it finished now? It ... still ... last time I was there." (build)

§§ 182; 184 a

4 Passive sentences with "by"

Put in the right verb in the passive form. Be careful with the tenses. Add the phrase in brackets only where it is necessary.

blow off, borrow, deliver, dislike, drive, force, score, steal, take, win

1. Everyone in the football stadium cheered when the winning goal ... . (by a footballer).
2. My motor-bike has gone! Oh no! It must ... while we were sitting in the café! (by a thief)
3. Who won the contest? – Oh, it ... from California. (by a contestant)
4. Is it true that Mr Allen started his new company with some money that ... from the bank? (by Mr Allen)
5. A red sports car overtook us so quickly that we thought it must ... . (by a Grand Prix racing driver)
6. Fortunately, an ambulance arrived quickly and the injured girl ... to hospital at once. (by the ambulance men)
7. The new headmaster is popular with the boys, but he ..., I'm afraid. (by some of the girls)
8. That storm was terrible last week, wasn't it? – Yes, the roof of my garden shed ... . (by the wind)
9. The postman never gets to Martina's house before 9.30. She'd be happier if her letters ... before breakfast. (by a postman)
10. Is it true that the pupils ... to learn a ridiculously huge amount of new French vocabulary last week? (by their French teacher)

§ 183

The passive with different kinds of verbs

5 Margaret Appleton, a candidate in the by-election in Pudley, has worked out ten reasons why people should vote for her. But she doesn't want to express herself in the same words all the time. So she's worked out an alternative to each of these sentences. Can you do the same, using the verb in brackets in the passive form in each new sentence?

Example: If you elect me, I'll save our old town hall. (not knock down)
If you elect me, ...*our old town hall won't be knocked down.*...

1. I won't say that your problems are ridiculous. (not laugh at)
2. I'll help our retired people. (take care of)
3. I'll be interested to hear your views. (take notice of)
4. I'll study the problems of the homeless. (deal with)
5. I'll examine the situation of our ethnic minorities. (not discriminate against)
6. I'll assist people to find jobs. (help)
7. I won't forget the problems of the unemployed. (listen to)
8. I'll mention Pudley wherever I go. (talk about)
9. I'll always give you the facts. (tell)
10. I'll stop people from thinking that Pudley is a funny sort of place in future. (not make fun of)

§ 184 a/b/c/d

•6 Translate these sentences into English, using the verbs in brackets in the passive form.

1. Wann wurde dir diese Nachricht übermittelt? (give)
2. Dem Bürgermeister wurde für seine Unterstützung gedankt. (thank)
3. Man stellte ihr ein paar schwierige Fragen. (ask)
4. Das Essen wird wahrscheinlich von der Firma bezahlt. (pay for)
5. Das wird später erledigt. (take care of)
6. Man hat ihn dreimal um Rat gebeten, aber er hatte nie Zeit. (ask for)
7. Dem Film wird eine kurze Diskussion folgen. (follow)
8. Das ist den Arbeitern vor einem Jahr schon zugesagt worden. (promise)
9. Wenn du vor 100 Jahren vorausgesagt hättest, daß der Mensch eines Tages würde fliegen können, hätte man dich ausgelacht. (laugh at)
10. Man hat dem Manager viel Geld angeboten, aber er wollte nicht nach London umziehen. (offer)

§ 184 a/b/c/d

•7 **The passive with the verbs "say", "think", "believe", etc.**

Finish the sentences by putting in each pair of verbs. Put the first into the passive, then add the second in an infinitive form.

Examples: This horse holds the record, so it ...'s expected to win... the race tomorrow. (expect + win)
The girl ...is said to have been walking... home when the gang attacked her. (say + walk)

Irish police searching for the missing horse, Sherthang, that was stolen from its stable just before the big race yesterday, have now described the three men they want to question. Their information ... (1. believe + come) from the girl who had just fed the horse when the crime took place.

One man was described as "a jockey type". He ... (2. think + work) at the stable at some time in the past, in order to gain the "inside knowledge" that helped the gang to plan their work. A second man ... (3. say + wear) a uniform when the gang attacked, possibly a policeman's uniform. The third man, described as tall and heavy, ... (4. understand + have) an unusually long nose. He ... (5. know + carry) a gun.

The gang ... (6. believe + hide) the horse somewhere in Ireland at the moment, but they ... (7. expect + try) and get it out of the country before the weekend. It seems that a two-way radio conversation, in which code words were used, was picked up by an amateur radio enthusiast late last night. The thirty-minute conversation ... (8. understand + refer to) plans to move an animal. The speakers ... (9. believe + speak) with Irish accents.

Sherthang's owner ... (10. say + have) millions of pounds. However, after taking advice from the police, he ... (11. think + reject) the idea of trying to buy the horse back from the thieves. So far he ... (12. not believe + have) any contact with the gang at all.

§ 185

The passive infinitive

8 Put in one of the following: should, can't, can't have, must have. Then add the correct form of the passive infinitive.

Example: Ed was late again. – Maybe, but I don't think he ...should be sacked... (sack)

1. Will the meeting take place? – Of course. It ... now. (cancel)
2. I feel ill. – I do, too. I reckon we ... something to eat in that café that hadn't been cooked properly. (give)
3. You need a new TV, sir, I'm afraid. – Do you mean this one ... ? (repair)
4. That meal was exceptional. We must come here again. – Mmm. The cook ... his skill and imagination. (compliment on)
5. Has the flight from Berlin arrived yet? – No. It ... because of the weather. (delay)
6. Good heavens, the wallpaper is coming off the wall already! – It ... by a very good decorator. Who did it for you? (put on)
7. Bad news, sir. The bomb might explode at any moment. – In that case the whole area ... at once, Major. (evacuate)
8. I didn't see Cecil at the party. – No, he ... . (invite)
9. Diana looks ill. – Well, she ... to the doctor's at once. (take)
10. Frank's new computer game is super. – Yes, it ... by a real expert. (design)

§ 187 a

9 A group of senior pupils are discussing some complaints with their headmistress. Can you finish their sentences for them? First, choose the right direct object (from the first list). Then add the correct verb from the second list, putting it in in the form of a passive infinitive or just as a past participle.

Example: We'd like more ...money (to be) spent... on the school library. (money – spend)

A: attention, integration, pupils, tax expert, time, timetable, troublemaker
B: change, encourage, expel, give, invite, keep out, pay

1. We find it difficult to concentrate on subjects like maths and physics in the last lesson of the day. We'd like the ... if possible.
2. We're fed up with vandalism. We want every ... from the school in future.
3. We feel pretty ignorant as far as financial affairs are concerned. We'd like a ... to the school to give us a series of talks.
4. Some teachers spend too much time criticizing the clothes we wear. We want less ... to what we put on and more to what we think.
5. We're not in favour of separate classes for the foreign pupils at the school. We'd like ... more actively at the school.
6. We want more ... to careers guidance.
7. Could we have a room where just sixth formers could sit and chat? Obviously, we'd like other ... of it.

§ 187 b

10 Mixed passive sentences

Read the text. Then answer the questions, using a form of the passive.

Mr Andrews is complaining to a member of the town council.

"It's about that nice little park we used to have in Stanley Street."

"Oh yes?"

"First you took the children's slides and swings down."

"Yes, well -."

"Then a team of council workers cut all those beautiful old trees down."

"I know, but -."

"And now you've built an expensive car park on the site - and stopped us from parking in the street by putting up signs saying NO PARKING."

"Look, Mr Andrews, we spent a lot of money on that car park. We must encourage people to use it."

"They say you're doing something similar in Goose Street."

"Well, not exactly -."

"You're knocking down a 17th century pub to make room for another car park. Do you know what I think? You're spoiling this part of town completely! The least you could do is change these latest plans before it's too late!"

1. What happened to the park first? - The children's … .
2. What happened next? - All the beautiful … .
3. And what's happened to the site since then? - An … .
4. Why can't cars be parked in Stanley Street now? - Because signs … .
5. What is the council's attitude towards the car park? - A lot … , so … .
6. What do we know about Goose Street? - The council … similar there.
7. How does Mr Andrews feel about all this? - He thinks this part … .
8. What about the future? - Mr Andrews wants these … .

§§ 181; 182; 183; 184 c; 185; 187 a/b

The infinitive

Test yourself

A **Active or passive infinitive?**

Complete the following sentences, using either an active or a passive infinitive (with or without "to") of the verbs in brackets.

1. This bill ought ... (pay) by tomorrow.
2. Tony is always the last boy ... (understand) a maths problem.
3. Why doesn't Jill let her brother ... (ride) on her bike?
4. Mrs Hancock certainly knows ... (where; find) cheap things.
5. You'd better ... (read) that text again.
6. Mr Shaw would like ... (his son; take) a typing course.
7. The questions ... (ask) by the host of the show were written on a small sheet of paper.
8. Mrs Cable made her daughter ... (take) piano lessons though she didn't want to.
9. Weren't those souvenirs too expensive ... (for Charlie; buy)?
10. ☐ A lot of hard work still remains ... (do).
11. Every morning Grandma Clark was the first ... (see) on the beach.
12. Why not ... (watch) TV tonight?
13. It was a bit difficult ... (for the mayor; smile) for the cameras, as his new shoes were killing him.

B Find suitable English equivalents for the German words or clauses given in brackets, using infinitives wherever possible.

14. Bob and Martin were the only pupils ... when their class went on a trip to France. (die zu Hause blieben)
15. Mrs Dalloway didn't want ... . (daß ihr Mann sonntags das Auto wäscht)
16. Joan told her brother ... . (wo er das Geschenk für ihre Eltern kaufen solle)
17. ☐ John ... . (war nirgends zu sehen)
18. Here's a football magazine ... . (die David beim Arzt lesen kann)
19. When the teacher saw Jill's homework, ... (ließ er sie sie nochmals machen)
20. If you want advice on any problem, ... is Mrs Keene. (die Frau, die man fragen sollte)
21. Before the trip to the Holbein exhibition, ... about the painter in the library. (erwartete der Lehrer von seinen Schülern, daß sie sich informierten)
22. Though he hated racing ... . (ließ er es zu, daß sein Sohn Rennfahrer wurde)
23. Where's Andy? ... . (Um diese Zeit kann er doch nicht mehr beim Tennisspielen sein!)
24. After the strike, Mrs Shields ... . (war die erste, die von der Geschäftsleitung entlassen wurde)
25. He has given us a valuable picture ... for the Red Cross. (das verkauft werden soll)
26. When I arrived, the man who was to unload the lorry ... . (wartete auf jemanden, der helfen könnte)
27. ... . She'll invite herself if we don't. (Wir sollten Lulu lieber zu der Party einladen)

C Spot the mistakes.

There is one mistake in each of the following sentences or groups of sentences. Spot the mistakes and write down what you think is the correct version. Be careful: two are not infinitive mistakes.

28. Here are some magazines to look at for Harry on his trip.
29. The government didn't make the immigrants to leave the country.
30. What a noise! They must have a party next door.
31. Mr Gimson didn't want that his son left school.
32. ☐ Maps of the Underground are to find at all the stations in London.
33. Why doesn't the teacher let the pupils to go home earlier?
34. The policeman said him to drive away immediately.
35. I'm sure the children would rather to spend their holidays on their own than with us.
36. The people which we met at the station will be travelling through Italy now.
37. Mr Black preferred that his wife didn't do the cooking alone.
38. Jack ought be having dinner now.
39. Marcia kept wondering whether go to the pictures or watch TV.

"The Athenians are here, Sire, with an offer to back us with ships, money, arms, and men—and, of course, their usual lectures about democracy."

Key

A

1. ... ought **to be paid** ... . § 189 b
2. ... is always the last boy **to understand** ... . § 192
3. ... let her brother **ride** ... . § 200
4. ... knows **where to find** ... . § 193
5. You'd better **read** ... . § 198
6. ... would like **his son to take** ... . § 196 a
7. The questions **to be asked** ... . § 194
8. ... made her daughter **take** ... . § 199
9. ... too expensive **for Charlie to buy**? .... § 195 a
10. □ ... remains **to be done**. .... § 189 c
11. ... was the first **to be seen** ... . § 192
12. Why not **watch** ... ? .... § 198
13. ... difficult **for the mayor to smile** ... . § 195 a

B

14. ... were the only pupils **to stay at home** ... . § 192
15. ... didn't want **her husband to wash the car on Sundays.** § 196 a
16. ... **where to buy the present for their parents.** .... § 193
17. □ ... **was nowhere to be seen.** .... § 189 c
18. ... **for David to read at the doctor's.** .... § 195 a
19. ... **he made her do it again.** .... § 199
20. ... **the woman to ask** is Mrs Keene. .... § 194
21. ... the teacher **expected his pupils to find out/get information** ... . § 196 b
22. ... **he let his son become/he allowed his son to become a racing driver.** .... §§ 200; 196 b
23. ... **He can't (still) be playing tennis at this time (of the day).** .... § 189 b
24. ... **was the first to be sacked by the management.** .... § 192
25. ... **to be sold** for the Red Cross. .... § 194
26. ... **was waiting for someone to help.** .... § 195 b
27. **We'd better invite Lulu to the party.** .... § 198

C

28. ... magazines **for Harry to look at** ... . § 195 a
29. ... make the immigrants **leave** ... . § 199
30. ... They must **be having** ... . § 189 b
31. ... didn't want **his son to leave** ... . § 196 a
32. □ Maps ... are **to be found** ... . § 189 c
33. Why doesn't the teacher let the pupils **go** ... ? ...... § 200
34. The policeman **told** him to drive away ... . §§ 196 b; [78 c]
35. ... would rather **spend** their holidays ... . § 198
36. The people **we met/who(m)/that** we met ... . § [238 c]
37. ... preferred **his wife not to** do ... . § 196 a
38. Jack ought **to** be having ... . § 189 b
39. ... wondering whether **to** go to the pictures or **(to)** watch TV. .... § 193

Exercise finder

Test yourself	ENGLISH G Grammatik	Exercises
1, 23, 30, 38	§ 189 b	**4** : 6, 7; 1, •2, •10
2, 11, 14, 24	§ 192	3, •10
3, 22, 33	§ 200	**9** : 5; 8, 9, •10
4, 16, 39	§ 193	5, •10
5, 12, 27, 35	§ 198	**9** : 5, 8; 1, •2, •10
6, 15, 31, 37	§ 196 a	**9** : 8; 7, 8, 9, •10
7, 20, 25	§ 194	•2, 4, •10
8, 19, 29	§ 199	8, 9, •10
9, 13, 18, 28	§ 195 a	6
10, 17, 32	§ 189 c	1
21, 22, 34	§ 196 b	**9** : 8, •9; 1, 7, 8, 9, •10
26	§ 195 b	4, 6
34	§ 78	**3** : 15
36	§ 238 c	**12** : 10, 11, 12

Exercises

Different forms of the infinitive

1 Choose the correct form of the infinitive.

1. Why are you reading the magazine, Miss Jones? Shouldn't you ... those letters? (type/to type/be typing)
2. The oldest part of this factory is said ... in the 17th century. (to have built/to be built/ to have been built)
3. According to the contract, these goods must ... by the end of the month. (deliver/to deliver/be delivered)
4. Where are those leaflets about the exhibition? – I think the director might ... them with him. (be taking/have taken/to be taken)
5. Don't type the documents individually, Miss Hall. Use the photocopying machine – unless you intend ... copies at midnight. (to be making/to make/have made)
6. We've decorated the living-room and the dining-room, but a lot of work still remains ... on the house. (to do/to be doing/to be done)
7. I've got to do some shopping, so I hope the boss will let me ... at 4.30. (to leave/leave/be leaving)
8. If we get two new electronic typewriters for the office, will our typists find it difficult ... them? (use/to use/to have used)
9. Where's Dennis? It's late. He can't ... in the office at this time of the evening, can he? (work/to work/be working)
10. No, that isn't true, madam. You must ..., I'm afraid. (mislead/be misleading/have been misled)
11. It was lovely walking through the woods in the snow. There wasn't a sound ... anywhere. (to have been heard/to hear/to be heard)

§§ 185; 189 a/b/c; 191; 196 b; 198

•2 Put in the correct form of the infinitive, adding "to" where necessary.

Since 1973, when suddenly a much higher price had ... (1. pay) for oil, scientists all around the world have been trying ... (2. develop) cheap alternative sources of energy. Some critics say they should ... (3. work) on this problem years ago. Then they might ... (4. complete) the necessary research before the oil crisis hit us. However, already the scientists can ... (5. point to) a lot of progress in this area.

One of the many promising ideas they are known ... (6. study) at the moment is a modern version of the traditional windmill. Windmills are particularly common in the Netherlands, of course, where they are believed ... (7. use) since the tenth century or earlier. But the machines that will ... (8. build) in coming centuries are likely to be much larger – a prototype in Clayton, New Mexico, is over 37 metres high, for example – as well as more powerful. According to recent forecasts, nearly 10 % of the electricity used in the Federal Republic of Germany is expected ... (9. provide) by windmills in the future. And the final figure could even ... (10. be) a lot higher.

§§ 189 b; 194; 198

3 The infinitive after superlatives, ordinal numbers or "the only"

Imagine you're on a package tour to Australia. What questions might you ask in the following situations? Put in "only" or an ordinal number or an adjective in the superlative form, then add a noun + infinitive with "to".

Example: You'd like some advice about the Australian press, because you want to follow political events in Europe.
"Which is the ..best newspaper to read.. if you want news about European affairs?"

1. On visiting Sydney, you enjoy going surfing at Bondi beach. You wonder if there is anywhere else in the country that's as good for this.
"Is Bondi beach the ... in Australia?"
2. Jenny, your guide on the coach, never seems to tell you anything until after she's told everybody else. You wonder why.
"Jenny, why am I always the ... anything?"
3. You discover that a solar power station is being built near Perth.
"Will this be the ... in Australia? Or are there some others already?"
4. Your coach stops at Coolgardie. You've been told there's an interesting museum there, but you've got to find it before the coach leaves again.
"Jenny, can you tell me the ... to the museum?"
5. At a car factory somebody points out that the 1980 World Champion motor racing driver, Alan Jones, was an Australian.
"Alan Jones is the ... this title, though, isn't he?"
6. You want to visit a relative in a town your coach won't go to. But you want to re-join the coach two days later.
"How can I do it, Jenny? Is flying the ... there and back in two days?

§ 192

4 The infinitive after nouns, pronouns, somebody/something, etc.

If you don't know the English for a particular noun, you can sometimes use another noun (or a pronoun) plus an infinitive. Try this technique here, using as few extra words as you can.

Examples: This is an interesting ..thing to talk about.. . (Diskussionsgegenstand)
I'm looking for ..somebody to play tennis with.. . (einen Tennispartner)

1. I think I'm going to need .... (einen Rechtsberater)
2. Your photos would be better if you bought .... (ein Stativ)
3. Can you help me? I need .... (einen Gepäckträger)
4. The storm has damaged the roof. You'd better phone for .... (einen Dachdecker)
5. The doctors say there are no drugs on the market yet that can help our son. We've just got to hope for .... (eine künftige Entdeckung)
6. Can you help me to find ... ? (eine Übernachtungsmöglichkeit)
7. Why don't you have a house specially built for you? – Me? I couldn't afford it. I'd only be able to pay for .... (einen Architekten)
8. We need Peter's help. Let's wait for .... (seine Rückkehr)

§§ 194; 195 b

5 The infinitive after question words or "whether"

Complete the translations. In each case put in a question word, e.g. "how", followed by "to" and an infinitive from the list below.

Example: Können Sie mir bitte sagen, wie ich zum Rathaus komme?
Can you ..tell me how to get to the town hall.., please?

accept (an offer), cash (a cheque), park (a car), accept (an invitation), invite (s.b. to a celebration), get rid of (s.th.), leave out (details), pay attention to (s.b.), wait for (s.b.), start (a conversation)

1. Alfred hat gerade einen Scheck erhalten. Da er aber über kein Bankkonto verfügt, weiß er nicht, wie er ihn einlösen kann.
   Alfred has just received a cheque. But as he hasn't got a bank account, he … .
2. Alle Parkplätze sind besetzt. Ilse ist sich nicht sicher, wo sie ihr Auto abstellen soll.
   All the car parks are full. Ilse … .
3. Der neue Abgeordnete hört sich selber gerne reden. Er scheint nicht zu begreifen, wann er anderen seine Aufmerksamkeit widmen sollte.
   The new MP likes to hear himself talk. He … .
4. Es war die Chefin selbst, die mir sagte, wen ich zur Feier übermorgen einzuladen hätte.
   It was the boss herself … .
5. Andrew möchte gern die neue Sekretärin in der Personalabteilung kennenlernen. Da er jedoch schüchtern ist, hat er keine Ahnung, wie er mit ihr ins Gespräch kommen könnte.
   Andrew would like to get to know the new secretary in the personnel department. However, as he's shy, … .
6. Barbara hat zwei verschiedene Einladungen für morgen abend bekommen. Nun muß sie entscheiden, welche sie annehmen will.
   Barbara has been given two different invitations for tomorrow evening. Now … .
7. Dolmetscher müssen rasch erkennen, ob sie Details unübersetzt lassen dürfen.
   Interpreters … .
8. Pamela ist sich nicht sicher, wie lange sie auf ihren neuen Freund warten soll. Er hat die Verabredung möglicherweise vergessen.
   Pamela … . He might have forgotten about their date.
9. Nach dem Tode ihres Mannes fragte sich Mrs Bull, wie sie sein altes Motorrad loswerden sollte.
   After the death of her husband, Mrs Bull … .
10. Elizabeth hatte wenig Zeit, um zu entscheiden, ob sie das Angebot annehmen sollte.
    Elizabeth had little time to … .

§ 193

6 The infinitive after "for" + noun or pronoun

Fill each gap in the text by putting in the words given in brackets, together with any extra words that are necessary, e.g. "too", "enough". Be careful with the tenses.

Example: Turn the music down. It's too loud for people to chat. ....
(be – loud – people – chat)

Michael Grant is a 13-year-old British schoolboy. So perhaps it'll be ... (1. surprise – you – discover) that he's a member of a reggae group, called Musical Youth, that has already had a record at Number 1 in the hit parade. The group's most famous single so far has been "Pass The Dutchie". However, their recent LP was a big success, too, and they ... (2. not can – wait for – next one – reach) the shops in the autumn.

They've just returned from a trip to the U.S.A., though it ... (3. not be – easy – the boys – arrange) their eight-day visit, as it had to take place during their school holidays. It was a working trip, including a TV show and discussions with a record company, so there ... (4. not be – time – group – go sight-seeing). It was ... (5. possible – them – visit) Jamaica two months ago, however, and they ... (6. stay there – long – Michael – see) some of the sights on the island where his parents were born.

All five members of the group go to the same West Midlands school, and they consider their education to be very important. "It ... (7. make sense – me – think) about an alternative career," Michael admitted in a recent interview, "because it ... (8. be – soon – us – be) confident that the band's success will last."

Sometimes it must ... (9. be – difficult – five boys – concentrate) on an ordinary maths or history lesson. Equally, of course, it must ... (10. be – strange – their classmates – sit) next to their favourite pop stars in school every day!

§ 195 a/b

7 The infinitive after certain verbs + object

Complete the translations, using the verbs given in brackets.

1. Ben Down, ein Student, will, daß seine Eltern ihm mehr Geld geben.
   Ben Down, who's a student, ... (want)
2. Sie aber möchten, daß er weniger für Zigaretten und Kinobesuche ausgibt.
   But they ... . (would like)
3. Sie trugen ihm auf, er möge doch fleißiger arbeiten.
   They ... . (tell)
4. Sie wünschen sich, daß er Rechtsanwalt wird.
   They ... . (wish)
5. Ben möchte, daß sie seinen Standpunkt verstehen.
   Ben ... point of view. (would like)
6. Er meint, sie sollten es zulassen, daß er für ein Jahr nach Südamerika geht.
   He thinks they ... for a year. (allow)
7. Sie teilten ihm mit, daß er sich auf sein Studium konzentrieren möge.
   They ... his studies. (tell)
8. Sie erwarten, daß er nächsten Sommer sein Examen besteht.
   They ... next summer. (expect)

§ 196 a/b

The infinitive after certain verbs, "make" and "let"

8 Finish the sentences by putting in a suitable object from list A and a suitable infinitive from list B (with "to" if necessary).

Example: (the children – appreciate)
Mrs Hill would like *the children to appreciate* what she does for them.

A: the relationship, the strangers, the lorry driver, the Prime Minister, the viewers, the blacks, the sales assistant, the council
B: reject, share, continue, rush into, lose, leave, doubt, examine

1. Two of the people at the party hadn't been invited. So the hostess told ... her house immediately.
2. The high level of unemployment has made ... whether he'll win the next general election.
3. Marilyn's father doesn't like her new boy-friend. And he's told her he doesn't want ... any longer.
4. The Mayor dislikes the suggestion, so he's going to ask ... it.
5. Because of their racialist attitudes, the whites in South Africa won't let ... their facilities.
6. It was tiredness that caused ... control of his vehicle.
7. "Yes, it's an attractive commercial," the managing director told the team, "but will it make ... the shops and buy more of our products?"
8. The pickpocket waited nervously. He hadn't expected ... the stolen credit card so carefully.

§§ 196 a/b; 199; 200

9 Look at the verb that's underlined, then decide which of the following verbs means more or less the same: order, make (2 x), let (2 x). Re-write the sentences and put in the new verbs, but make other changes only if they are necessary.

Example: Who let the pupils leave school early? (permit)
Who permitted the pupils to leave school early?

1. Diana's unconventional clothes often <u>cause</u> people in the street to stop and stare at her.
2. The judge's neighbour was grateful to him for <u>permitting</u> her to use his telephone.
3. The police <u>told</u> the families living near the factory to evacuate their homes at once.
4. A laboratory technician <u>allowed</u> the journalist to enter the building before the experiment started.
5. According to Julia it was the pressure of work that finally <u>forced</u> her actress friend to take a holiday.

§ 196 b; 199; 200

•10 Mixed examples of the infinitive

Can you express the ideas in the following sentences in a different way, using infinitive constructions and only the number of words shown in brackets?

Example: My guest would be unhappy if you couldn't have a look at his car today.
My guest would like ..you...to..look..at..his..car.. today. (6)

1. A breakdown? Nobody knows more about repairing cars than my brother.
   If you need help with your car, my brother is … . (4)
2. You know, until you came, no Dane had ever stayed at this hotel.
   Actually, you're … at this hotel. (5)
3. If you stayed with us again, we'd be delighted.
   We'd like … again. (5)
4. You should visit Beaulieu. There's an excellent collection of old cars in the museum there.
   If you're interested in old cars, Beaulieu is … . (4)
5. It might be a good idea if you went to Beaulieu tomorrow.
   Why don't … tomorrow? (4)
6. It would help if you described the route to me.
   Could you explain … ? (4)
7. I can't come with you, I'm afraid. I'm really busy.
   Unfortunately, I'm too … . (5)
8. I'll show you. Would you mind if I borrowed your map?
   I'll show you. Would you let … ? (4)
9. It appears that you made your decision to come to Southampton six months ago.
   Your decision to come to Southampton seems … six months ago. (4)
10. I've forgotten so much English. I had to come here.
    It was the state of my English that made … . (3)
11. Now that I'm in England, my English should improve again.
    Now that I'm in England, I'm expecting … . (4)
12. My aunt has said I could stay with her in Toronto next year.
    My aunt has invited … in Toronto next year. (5)

§§ 189; 192; 193; 194; 196 a/b; 198; 199; 200

The gerund and gerund or infinitive

Test yourself

A **Gerund or infinitive?**

Fill in the gaps, using either a gerund or an infinitive. Sometimes a preposition is required as well.

1. Although he sings well, Al has a lot of trouble ... (remember) new songs.
* 2. Would you mind ... (lend) me £5? I'd like ... (buy) a record for my wife.
3. The guests apologized ... (arrive) late.
4. Kathy couldn't help ... (admit) that she had lost the car keys.
5. If you know one foreign language well, it's quite easy ... (learn) another one.
6. Mr Cooper avoided a head-on collision with another car ... (drive) into a field.
7. What about ... (the Mayers come) with us?
8. What's the advantage ... (have) a sports car if it breaks down so often?
* 9. We meant ... (take a bus), but as the baby wouldn't stop ... (cry) we decided to walk.
10. Diane used ... (stay up) late, but after the baby was born she got used ... (go to bed) early.
11. The band started ... (play) at once without ... (practise) first.
12. The pollution of the beaches made a lot of tourists ... (leave) the area.
* 13. What did you do when the microphone stopped ... (work)? – Well, I didn't go on ... (talk), anyway.

B Find suitable English equivalents for the German words or clauses given in brackets, using a gerund or infinitive construction. Sometimes a preposition is required as well.

14. Tom tried to avoid ... . (Marcia zu treffen)
15. In times like these ... to Australia. (ist es zwecklos auszuwandern)
16. ... about her husband's accident, Mrs Clark turned pale. (Als sie hörte)
17. The so-called sights of Detroit aren't worth ... . (gesehen zu werden)
18. ... such long distances. (Wir waren nicht daran gewöhnt, zu Fuß zu gehen)
19. Did you have any difficulty ... ? (das Haus zu finden)
* 20. The fans were disappointed ... . (daß die Kapelle so bald aufhörte)
21. He kept ... , but nobody wanted ... any more. (zu reden; zuhören)
* 22. We mustn't forget ... before we leave for Spain. (das Öl zu überprüfen)
23. After Don had begun ... long distances, he gave up ... . (zu laufen; zu rauchen)
24. Fred would like ... again, but she dislikes ... so early. (daß seine Frau arbeitet; aufzustehen)
* 25. Are you talking about the Whitakers? I'm so tired ... . (daß sie so viel über ihr neues Auto reden)
26. Dad says I should concentrate on my A-levels, ... (anstatt mit so vielen Jungen auszugehen)
27. ... that Mary is prettier and more interesting than me, but the way men run after her is crazy. (Die Tatsache läßt sich nicht bestreiten)

C Spot the mistakes.

There is one mistake in each of the following sentences. Spot the mistakes and write down what you think is the correct version. Be careful: three are not gerund or infinitive mistakes.

28. I'm looking forward to see you again.
29. Have you heard that Coopers used to live in France?
30. The captain made the passengers leaving the ship.
31. Tell Mr Wood that I would like speaking to him.
32. The new novel by Galetti isn't worth being read.
33. Kathy insisted to go to the Netherlands during their holidays.
34. The possibility to find him did not seem very great.
35. The crooks were arrested from the police for trying to smuggle heroin.
36. * We must remember paying our debts next week.
37. We had planned to go swimming but then Jill suggested to play table-tennis.
38. The most of the people standing at the gate were waiting for the exhibition to open.
39. We didn't want that the patients lie in the sun for too long.

"Frankly, Harold, you're beginning to bore everyone with your statistics."

Key

A

	1. ... trouble **remembering**	§ 205 b
*	2. ... mind **lending** ... ? I'd like **to buy**	§§ 205 c; 206 b
	3. ... apologized **for arriving** late.	§ 204 c
	4. ... couldn't help **admitting**	§ 205 a
	5. ... it's quite easy **to learn**	§ 191
	6. ... avoided a ... collision ... **by driving**	§ 204 a
	7. What about **the Mayers coming** with us?	§§ 205 a; 208
	8. What's the advantage **of (in) having** ... ?	§ 204 d
*	9. We meant **to take a bus**, but as the baby wouldn't stop **crying**	§ 206 c
	10. ... used **to stay up** late, but ... she got used **to going to bed** early.	§ 204 b
	11. The band started **playing/to play** at once without **practising** first.	§§ 206 a; 204 a
	12. ... made a lot of tourists **leave**	§ 199
*	13. ... when the microphone stopped **working? – Well, I** didn't go on **talking**	§ 206 c

B

	14. ... to avoid **meeting Marcia**.	§ 205 c
	15. ... **it's no use/no good emigrating** to Australia.	§ 205 a
	16. **On hearing** about	§ 204 a
	17. ... aren't worth **seeing**.	§ 205 b
	18. **We weren't used to walking**	§ 204 b
	19. Did you have any difficulty **finding/in finding the house?**	§§ 205 b; 204 d
*	20. ... were very disappointed **about/at the band/ the band('s) finishing so soon**.	§§ 204 b; 208; 209
	21. He kept **talking,** but nobody wanted **to listen** any more.	§§ 205 c; 196 a
*	22. We mustn't forget **to check** the oil	§ 206 c
	23. ... had begun **running/to run** ... he gave up **smoking**.	§§ 206 a; 205 c
	24. Fred would like **his wife to work** again, but she dislikes **getting up**	§§ 196 a; 205 c
*	25. ... I'm so tired **of them/their talking so much about their new car**.	§§ 204 b; 208; 209
	26. ... **instead of going out with so many boys**.	§ 204 a
	27. **There's no denying the fact** that Mary is prettier	§ 205 a

C

	28. I'm looking forward to **seeing** you	§ 204 c
	29. ... that **the** Coopers used to live	§ [25 a]
	30. The captain made the passengers **leave**	§ 199
	31. ... that I would like **to speak** to him.	§ 206 b
	32. ... isn't worth **reading**.	§ 205 b
	33. Kathy insisted **on going** to the Netherlands	§ 204 c
	34. The possibility **of finding** him	§ 204 d
	35. ... were arrested **by** the police for trying	§ [183]

* 36. We must remember **to pay** .... § 206 c
37. ... but then Jill suggested **playing/that we should play** .... §§ 205 c; [230 d]
38. **Most** of the people ... were waiting .... § [30 b]
39. ... want **the patients to lie** in the sun .... § 196 a

Exercise finder

Test yourself	ENGLISH G Grammatik	Exercises
1, 17, 19, 32	§ 205 b	4
2, 14, 21, 23, 24, 37	§ 205 c	6, •9
2, 31	§ 206 b	6
3, 28, 33	§ 204 c	2, 3, •9
4, 7, 15, 27	§ 205 a	•5, •9
6, 11, 16, 26	§ 204 a	1, •9
7, 20, 25	§ 208	8
8, 19, 34	§ 204 d	3, •9
9, 13, 22, 36	§ 206 c	7
10, 18, 20, 25	§ 204 b	2, 3, •9
11, 23	§ 206 a	•9
12, 30	§ 199	**8** : 8, 9, •10
20, 25	§ 209	8
21, 24, 39	§ 196 a	8
29	§ 25 a	**1** : 10
35	§ 183	**7** : 4, 10
37	§ 230 d	**11** : 11, •12, 13
38	§ 30 b	**1** : 13

Exercises

The gerund after prepositions

1 Complete the translations. Use the verbs in brackets as gerunds, preceded in each case by one of these prepositions: by, on, for (2x), in, instead of.

1. Liz wurden deshalb von ihren Eltern Vorwürfe gemacht, weil sie ihre Französischprüfung nicht bestanden hatte.
   Liz was criticized by her parents ... (not pass) ... .
2. Anstatt Französisch zu Hause zu lernen, arbeitete Liz drei Monate lang als Au-Pair-Mädchen bei einer Familie in Bordeaux.
   ... (learn) ... , Liz worked as an au pair for a family in Bordeaux for three months.
3. Liz wußte gleich bei der Ankunft, daß sie ihre „Arbeitgeber" mögen würde.
   Immediately ... (arrive) Liz knew she'd like her "employers".
4. Liz lernte neue Wörter dadurch, daß sie sie auf ein Stück Papier schrieb und dies an den Rand ihres Spiegels klebte.
   Liz learned new words ... (write) ... (stick) ... on the edge of her mirror.
5. Indem sie die neue Sprache lernte, lernte sie auch vieles über die Menschen und das Land.
   ... (learn) ... she also learned a lot about the people and the country.
6. Liz schrieb an ihre Französischlehrerin: Ich kann Ihnen nicht genug dafür danken, daß Sie mir diese Stelle als Au-Pair-Mädchen vermittelt haben.
   Liz wrote to her French teacher: I can't thank you enough ... (help) ... .

§ 204 a

2 Fill in the gaps in the story, using the verbs given in brackets together with other words where these are necessary. Remember that there are different forms of the gerund.

Examples: The pupils protested. They ...were... tired ...of being given... so much homework. (be – give)
The detective ran after the thief and ...prevented him from escaping... (prevent from – escape)

1. It was Saturday and a lot of the other foreign students at the language school in Bournemouth were going to the local football match. Jürgen, though, ... them. (decide against – go with)
2. He'd come to Bournemouth to learn English, and he felt it was silly to ... something he could do just as well back home in Bremen. (spend time and money on – do)
3. So, instead, he went to the station, where he easily ... , as his English was already fairly good. (cope with – buy)
4. He got off the train in Stratford. As he was leaving the station, he saw a text that someone had just sprayed on the wall. The paint was still wet. Unfortunately, before he'd finished reading it, a policeman spotted him there. And Jürgen ... public property. (arrest for – damage)

5. The text was in perfect idiomatic English, so at first Jürgen ... quite happy ... the author. (be – consider)
6. Then suddenly he began to feel afraid ... to leave the country. (tell)
7. Jürgen realized it was partly his own fault. He ... himself ... the text more quickly, before the policeman had arrived. (blame for – not read)
8. At the police-station Jürgen ... a crime. (accuse of – commit)
9. But he explained in great detail that it was all a mistake. And, fortunately, the policeman believed him. He even ... Jürgen's outing. (apologize for – spoil)
10. On the way back to Bournemouth Jürgen smiled to himself. He ... proud ... everything to the policeman in English. (can be – explain)

§ 204 b/c

3 Finish the sentences by putting in one of the following prepositions – on, for (2 x), from, of (3 x), about (2 x), to – followed by a gerund made from the verbs in brackets.

1. At a conference in London in 1983 Professor A. Breckenridge of Liverpool University said that doctors should visit primary schools regularly and check the blood pressure of every child above the age of four. He then explained his reasons ... (suggest) this.
2. Professor Breckenridge said he saw this as a way ... (reduce) the number of old people or middle-aged people who die of heart problems, although not all heart problems are caused by high blood pressure, of course.
3. According to his research, it is possible to look at very young children – from the age of two – and say which of them are in great danger ... (develop) high blood pressure later, as an adult, which could then be fatal.
4. Doctors made routine visits to schools anyway, he said, to check children's weights. He asked them to think ... (take) this opportunity to check blood pressures, too.
5. If it was discovered, for example, that an eight-year-old boy had comparatively high blood pressure, he could be advised to watch his weight. And he could probably be prevented ... (eat) too much salt.
6. Generally speaking, people at the conference recognized the advantage ... (know) about a child's blood pressure at an early age.
7. However, school doctors had their doubts ... (introduce) tests of this kind.
8. Regular tests might themselves cause a lot of children to worry ... (have) an illness which, in their case, was most unlikely.
9. In addition, the doctors said, they didn't know where the funds might come from to pay ... (organize) such a large programme.
10. Moreover, they stressed, if more parents got used ... (take) their children to see their own family doctor regularly, every six months, for example, it wouldn't be so difficult to spot cases that required special advice or treatment.

§ 204 b/c/d

4 The gerund after the adjective "worth"

Finish the translations, using the word "worth" and the verbs in brackets.

1. „Ich frage mich, ob es sich lohnt, den neuen Film zu sehen," sagte Mrs MacTavish.
   "I wonder if the ... ," Mrs MacTavish said. (see)
2. „Es lohnt sich nicht, diese alte Lampe aufzuheben," sagte Ellen.
   "This ... ," Ellen said. (keep)
3. „Die Äpfel sind zu klein," sagte der Gärtner. „Sie sind nicht wert, geerntet zu werden."
   "The apples aren't big enough," the gardener said. "They ... ." (pick)
4. „Der Bürgermeister hat Einfluß. Es lohnt sich, ihn kennenzulernen," sagte der Rechtsanwalt.
   "The Mayor is influential. ... ," the lawyer said. (know)
5. Wenn es sich lohnt, daß man eine Sache überhaupt macht, so lohnt es sich, daß man sie gut macht.
   If a thing ... , then ... well. (do) (2 x) § 205 b

Gerund or infinitive?

•5 Read the text. Then complete the sentences, using a gerund or infinitive.

When Martina stayed with her pen-friend in Hatfield, near London, last summer, she made a lot of new friends. But they often had very long discussions before deciding how to spend their time together.

One Friday, for example, Martina mentioned an exhibition of local history at the town hall which sounded interesting. But Christine, her pen-friend, had been looking forward to a visit to the new indoor swimming-pool. And Anthony, Christine's boy-friend, thought that a trip to the coast – to Bournemouth, say – would be more interesting for a change. He also pointed out that the weather might not be as good again for a long time.

Christine's younger brother had an idea of his own. He suggested a boat trip on the Thames, and he thought it would be a nice idea if they invited their parents to go with them. However, Christine said her father and mother were likely to be too busy that weekend.

"Are you sure?" asked Martina, who thought it might be a good thing if they asked them at least. So Christine agreed to do this, though she felt it would be a waste of time.

1. Martina said, "How about ... ?"
2. Her pen-friend, on the other hand, said, "Why not ... ?"
3. "Oh, not indoors, not today, not in this weather. Let's ... ," Christine's boy-friend said.
4. "There's no ... as good as this again," he added.
5. Christine's younger brother said, "What about ... ?"
6. "And why don't ... ?" he went on.
7. His sister said, "Oh, Alan, you know it's no good ... . They're much too busy this weekend."
8. Martina said, "Are you sure, Christine? I mean, you know, it might be worth ... ."
9. "Okay," Christine said, "though I can't help ... ." §§ 205 a, 198, 200

6 Complete the text by putting in the verbs given in brackets either in the form of a gerund or an infinitive with "to".

When Ron Johnson told his wife and two children that he was considering ... (1. take) a job in London, he thought they would be delighted. In fact, they asked him to delay ... (2. make) a decision until they'd all had a chance to think about it.

His daughter admitted ... (3. complain about) the fact that there wasn't a disco in their village – the nearest one was fifteen miles away – but said she wouldn't like ... (4. change) schools, at least not until she'd finished her O-levels.

"If we lived in London," her brother said, "I wouldn't mind ... (5. watch) some of the top football teams, instead of our local rubbish. But I'd really miss ... (6. help) Uncle Albert on the farm, Dad, and that includes ... (7. clean) the stables!"

Mrs Johnson denied ... (8. tell) her husband that life in the village was dull. "But at the same time I think I might appreciate ... (9. live) in a big city in some ways, particularly if we had a house with a garden. As you all know, I enjoy ... (10. grow) my own vegetables and flowers."

§§ 205 c; 206 b

7 Choose the right form to complete the sentences.

1. Enjoy your trip, Mark. – Thanks. But don't forget (feeding/to feed) my budgie.
2. Do you know how many goals you've scored in your career so far? – Certainly. And I'll never forget (scoring/to score) my first one.
3. You must be pleased about your wife's promotion? – Yes, of course, but unfortunately it means (moving/to move) to Birmingham.
4. How can you say such a terrible thing? – I'm sorry, Mrs Robinson. I didn't mean (hurting/to hurt) you.
5. It's very late, you know. – I'm sorry. I tried (ringing/to ring) you up earlier, but you were out.
6. We haven't found anybody to help us with our baby-sitting problem. – Have you tried (advertising/to advertise)?
7. You will write, won't you? – Sure. But remember (giving/to give) us your new address.
8. You know, I didn't like you at first. – That's funny. I remember (thinking/to think) you were pretty boring.
9. How's your pen-friend in Miami? – I don't know. Six months ago she suddenly stopped (writing/to write) to me.
10. Watch out, Karl-Heinz. The traffic drives on the left in England, remember. – Oh, really! Stop (treating/to treat) me like a child!
11. Have you managed to get a job yet? – No, I haven't. But I'm going to go on (applying/to apply) for one.
12. What happened to Henry after he left university? – He became a lawyer. Then after a while he went on (becoming/ to become) a judge, I believe.
13. Has your aunt retired yet? – No, she hasn't, though she's old enough to, of course. No, she prefers to go on (working/to work).

§ 206 c

8 Sabine Hamann from Freiburg, who is teaching German at a school in Wales for a year, is telling some other teachers about last night's parents' evening. Complete her sentences with the help of the words in brackets and other words where necessary. Use one of the following patterns: verb + object + gerund or verb + object + infinitive with "to".

Examples: We can sit in this room. The head ...*won't mind us using*... it. (not mind – use)
This letter is for you. A teacher ...*told me to give it*... to you. (tell – give)

Sabine: Barbara's father thinks I should make the pupils work harder. He ... them too little homework. (1. complain about – give)
Mrs Rix: Really?
Sabine: Yes. He feels I should make them do more written work. He said he ... the pupils how to write German as well as how to speak it. (2. expect – teach)
Mrs Rix: Is Barbara good at German?
Sabine: No, she isn't, I'm afraid. That's why her parents ... the exam next summer. (3. be worried about – fail)
Mr Baum: Well, the new timetable won't help. I mean, next term her class will only be having 3 German lessons a week instead of 4.
Sabine: That's right. That's what Barbara's father said. He ... after Christmas. (4. not be happy about – be reduced)
Mr Pegg: What did Peter's parents say? Peter's very good at languages, isn't he? He wants to study German at university, doesn't he?
Sabine: Well, his mother ... a foreign language, I'm afraid. (5. not be keen on – study)
Mr Pegg: Why ever not?
Sabine: She ... an electronics engineer, like his father. (6. would like – become)
Mrs Rix: Well, of course, he's good at the science subjects too, isn't he? Like Lucy. They're good at most subjects.
Mr Baum: Did Lucy's parents say anything about the trouble last week?
Sabine: Yes, they felt the head shouldn't have punished her. According to them, what she'd done hardly ... that sort of punishment. (7. justify – be given)
Mr Baum: Have they spoken to the head about it?
Sabine: No. I suggested it to them. But they felt it ... now. (8. be no use – talk to)
Mr Pegg: You seem to have had a tough evening. Did nobody say anything nice to you? What about that trip to Freiburg that you're organizing, for example?
Sabine: Oh, Pamela's mother emphasized how much she ... . (9. appreciate – organize)
Mr Baum: She comes from Berlin herself, doesn't she? Did she ask you why you weren't taking the pupils there instead?
Sabine: Well, yes, she did say she ... if possible. Not like Robert's parents. (10. would like – visit)
Mr Baum: Why? What did they say?
Sabine: They said the school always wanted money for something. They ... money for unnecessary outings. (11. be tired of – be asked for)
Mr Pegg: Oh dear.
Sabine: Yes, and I'm afraid they said they ... with us. (12. not allow – come)

Mrs Rix: Poor Robert. I think he'd enjoy a trip to Freiburg.
Sabine: They don't think he can afford the time. They ... his ordinary lessons for ten days. (13. not like the idea of – miss)
Mrs Rix: Well, I think it's a pity.

§§ 208; 209; 196 a/b

•9 Put in the verbs in brackets, either as an infinitive – where necessary with "to" – or as a gerund, preceded where suitable by one of the following prepositions: against, from, for, in, of. If you think there are two possible answers in some cases, write down both forms.

PROTESTS AT DEATH ON WELSH MOUNTAIN

Two teenage members of a West Midlands youth group, who had been enjoying ... (1. take part in) a route-finding exercise in the mountains of South Wales at the weekend, became separated from the main group – because of the terrible weather conditions – and fell 100 metres down Pen-y-Fant mountain. Unfortunately, ... (2. hurt) themselves in this way, they played a part ... (3. cause) the death of a 36-year-old man. And the local police feel this was a tragedy that needn't ... (4. happen)

One of the two boys, 17-year-old Peter Hughes from Birmingham, wasn't injured as badly as the other, 16-year-old Martin Leather. And somehow Peter managed ... (5. walk) three miles through snow, wind and rain in the hope ... (6. get) help for his friend. Immediately, a helicopter and about 50 men on the ground, consisting of four local teams that specialize ... (7. help) in cases like this, started ... (8. search) for Martin.

It was dangerous work. But the teams kept ... (9. look). As long as there was the slightest chance ... (10. find) the boy, nobody wanted to give up.

Hours later it was Mr Michael Rudall, a married man from Bridgend, who finally came across the injured boy. But the weather hadn't improved. And Mr Rudall decided it wasn't worth ... (11. set off) back down the mountain in such conditions. As an experienced mountain expert, he couldn't help ... (12. feel) it would be better to wait until the following morning, when the helicopter would be able ... (13. spot) them more easily.

Unfortunately, during the night some rocks began ... (14. fall) towards them. Mr Rudall – whom the press have described as a hero – used his body to prevent the rocks ... (15. hit) Martin. But he himself was hit on the head and killed.

Later the local police condemned the leaders of the youth group ... (16. allow) the teenagers ... (17. go up) the mountain when the weather was obviously turning worse. They accused them ... (18. take) unnecessary risks and said they ought to have decided ... (19. let) the group ... (20. set off).

However, Mr Ian Powney, one of the leaders of the group, denied ... (21. make) a bad decision. He pointed out that the group was well trained and had all the equipment necessary ... (22. cope with) bad weather. He said he wouldn't think ... (23. cancel) a future outing of this kind if the conditions were similar.

"Obviously we are deeply sorry that this terrible fatal accident happened", he said. And he stressed that he was extremely grateful to everybody ... (24. help) to find the injured boy. But at the same time Mr Powney said he had great difficulty ... (25. accept) that young people should always stay off mountains in bad weather.

§§ 204 a/b/c/d; 205 a/c; 206 a; 189 a; 196 b; 198

The participle

Test yourself

A **Present participle, past participle or infinitive?**

Fill in the gaps, using either a present participle, a past participle or an infinitive. Sometimes they must be preceded by another word (e.g. an adverb or a conjunction).

1. I'd like to have a word with the gentleman ...(stand) next to the book-shelf.
2. This isn't just badly ...(play) music – it's pure noise!
3. David decided not to go to the show, ...(see) its star twice before.
4. Though ...(wake up) early by his mother, Tim didn't feel a bit tired that afternoon.
5. Diana remained ...(lie) in bed throughout the day.
6. When Bill looked out of the window, he noticed an ambulance ...(approach) the factory gate.
7. What I don't like about my job are all the ...(waste time) meetings we have.
8. Mr Wallace is having his car ...(repair) at the moment.
9. The police have found the pictures ...(steal) from the museum.
10. It will be dangerous to drive by the river with the water ...(rise) so quickly.
11. Always try to be polite ...(ask) a question, however stupid it may be.
12. Mr Sawyer is going to have his front door ...(paint) red.
13. Mike was a bit worried when a ...(eat; man) tiger suddenly appeared from behind some bushes.
14. He felt quite sick when he saw the tiger ...(move) towards him.
15. The two stood ...(look) at each other for a few minutes before the tiger turned and walked away.

B Find suitable English equivalents for the German words or clauses given in brackets, using present or past participles wherever possible.

16. Joan picked up the coins ... . (die auf dem Fußboden lagen)
17. ... belongs to Diana. (Der im Bus gefundene Geldbeutel)
18. The owner of the house ... . (ließ letztes Jahr neue Heizkörper einbauen)
19. The patient stood at the window of the hospital ... . (und lächelte traurig)
20. ... by everyone, this suggestion will save the firm a lot of money. (Wenn er ernst genommen wird)
21. Don's mother was shocked ... . (als er plötzlich über die Straße gerannt kam)
22. Lots of people are buying ... . (zeitsparende Maschinen für ihre Küche)
23. ... Cliff practised from morning till night. (Da er durch den Erfolg seines ersten Konzerts ermutigt war)
24. He saw ... . (wie das Mädchen auf das Boot zuschwamm)
25. Sorry, but I can't sleep ... . (wenn du immer so im Zimmer herumrennst)
26. ... Jean went to the hairdresser's. (Nachdem sie das Büro verlassen hatte)
27. Jim Daniels is the author ... . (mehrerer gutgeschriebener Artikel)
28. I can't say I'm enjoying this dance ... . (wenn du die ganze Zeit auf meinen Füßen stehst)
29. What? You say my dog bit you? That's impossible – he never does anything ... . (außer, wenn man es ihm sagt)

C Spot the mistakes.

There is one mistake in each of the following sentences. Spot the mistakes and write down what you think is the correct version. Be careful: two are not participle mistakes.

* 30. Carl noticed a new tree driving past his sister's garden.
31. Fiona has held several high-paid jobs over the last few years.
32. When the telephone rang, Jim forgot the on their doorstep waiting man.
33. Old Mrs Taylor watched the thief opening the window, climbing into the room, unlocking the desk and taking out her daughter's jewellery.
34. Being a teenager isn't easy when people treating you sometimes as an adult and sometimes as a child.
35. A bird came flown into the room.
36. When are you going to let your hair cut?
37. Hand-made pullovers are nicer than machine-made.
38. Having worked in the firm for several years, he became involved in the decision-made process.
39. Do you like books writing by Dick Francis?
40. Having had drunk half a bottle of whisky, Peter started a quarrel with the bar-keeper.
41. Having saved money for many years, they could now afford an own house.

Key

A

1. … gentleman **standing** next to … . § 211
2. … badly **played** music … ! § 216 a
3. … show, **having seen** its star … . § 220 b
4. Though **woken up** early … . § 221
5. Diana remained **lying** in bed … . § 215 a
6. … he noticed an ambulance **approaching** … . § 214
7. … **time-wasting** meetings … . § 212 b
8. … is having his car **repaired** … . § 218 a
9. … pictures **stolen** from … . § 217
10. … with the water **rising** … . § 222 a
11. … **when/if asked** a question … . § 221
12. … is going to have his front door **painted** red. § 218 a
13. … when a **man-eating** tiger suddenly appeared … . § 212 b
14. … he saw the tiger **moving** … . § 214
15. The two stood **looking** at each other … . § 215 a

B

16. … coins **lying on the floor**. § 211
17. **The purse found on/in the bus** … . § 217
18. … house **had new radiators put in last year**. § 218 a
19. … hospital **smiling sadly**. § 220 b
20. **If taken seriously** by everyone … . § 221
21. … shocked **when he suddenly came running across the street**. § 215 a
22. … are buying **time-saving machines for their kitchens**. § 212 b
23. **Encouraged by the success of his first concert,** Cliff … . § 220 b
24. He saw **the girl swimming towards the boat**. § 214
25. … sleep **with you running around the room like that**. § 222 a
26. **Having left (After leaving) the office,** Jean went … . § 220 a
27. … author **of several well-written articles**. § 216 a
28. … **with you standing on my feet the whole time**. § 222 a
29. … he never does anything **unless/except/if told to**. § 221

C

30. … tree **when/while** driving/**(when he drove)** past … . § 220 a
31. … several **highly-paid** jobs … . § 216 a
32. … forgot **the man waiting on their doorstep**. § 211
33. … watched the thief **open** the window, **climb** … , **unlock** … and **take out** … . § 214
34. Being a teenager isn't easy **with** people treating you/**(when people treat you)** … . § 222 a
35. A bird came **flying** … . § 215 a
36. … **have/get** your hair cut? §§ 218 a; [200]
37. … than machine-made **ones**. § [39]
38. … involved in the decision-**making** process. § 212 b
39. Do you like books **written** … ? § 217
40. **Having drunk** half a bottle … . § 220 a
41. … afford **a house of their own/their own house**. § [45]

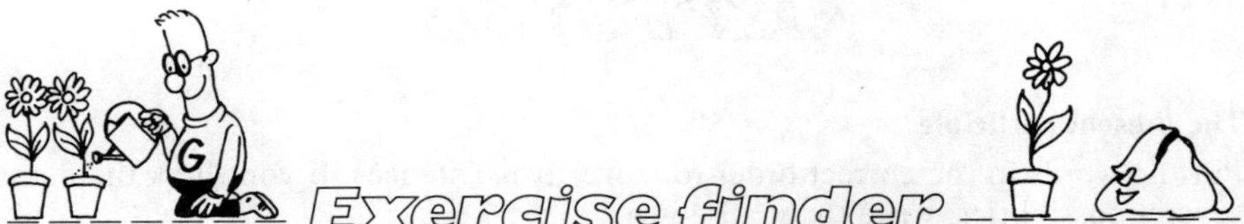

Exercise finder

Test yourself	ENGLISH G Grammatik	Exercises
1, 16, 32	§ 211	1, 2, 3, 4, 5, 14, •15
2, 27, 31	§ 216 a	10, 14
3, 19, 23, 26	§ 220 b	14, •15
4, 11, 20, 29	§ 221	12, 14, •15
5, 15, 21, 35	§ 215 a	8, 14, •15
6, 14, 24, 33	§ 214	•6, •7, 14, •15
7, 13, 22, 38	§ 212 b	5, 14, •15
8, 12, 18, 36	§ 218 a	9
9, 17, 39	§ 217	10, 14, •15
10, 25, 28, 34	§ 222 a	13, •15
23, 30, 40	§ 220 a	11, 14
36	§ 200 **8**	8, 9, •10
37	§ 39 **1**	:8; 2 : 3
41	§ 45 **2**	: 7

Exercises

The present participle

1 Put the words in the correct order to make five sentences. If you think there are several possiblities, write them all down.

1. runs an – Lucy's aunt – offering bed and breakfast – guesthouse – old-fashioned –.
2. part-time – there – serving breakfast – job – has got a – Lucy –.
3. some toast – to a – just taken – reading – a daily newspaper – man – she's –.
4. has just ordered – low-cut – some more coffee – a – wearing a – summer dress – woman –.
5. aggressively – sitting near her feet – black dog – is barking – the little –.

§ 211

2 University students often take holiday jobs in the summer if they're short of money. Read the following information, then work out what each of these students might say if they discussed the subject.

Last year Carol had a job in a big department store; she sold sports equipment and quite enjoyed it.

Gopal worked for a company that makes automatic barriers for car parks.

Philippa visited old people who needed help with things such as shopping and washing.

Al had a job in the personnel department of a firm that produces frozen food.

Howard interviewed unemployed people who hoped to work on his uncle's farm for a few weeks.

Shirley had a job with a big American electronics company in which she programmed computers.

Roy, who would like to be a vet, had a job on a sheep farm in Wales; he helped to check the condition of the animals.

Go on from here, using nouns followed by present participles:

Carol: Last year I had ... a job selling sports equipment ... in a big department store, and I quite enjoyed it.

§ 211

3 Complete the text with the help of the words in brackets. But leave out the relative pronoun and replace the finite form of the verb with a present participle.

Example: Diana is on the train leaving the station now. (the train that is leaving)

There has been growing criticism of the Government's ... (1. new law that allows lorries to have) a bigger total weight of up to 38 tonnes. Some experts are worried about the extra traffic problems on ... (2. routes that lead through) small villages. In a lot of cases the new lorries may be no longer than the majority of ... (3. the older, lighter vehicles that are moving along) our roads now. However, their extra weight could damage thousands of ... (4. old bridges that already find it hard) to cope with modern traffic. In addition, several groups – including the Council for the Protection of Rural England – point to the added pollution and greater accident risks for ... (5. people who live in the country).

§ 211

4 Complete the translations. Use present participles.

1. Die Verwaltung der Stadt London wurde 1982 gezwungen, ihre neue Politik der billigeren Fahrpreise für Leute, die mit den städtischen Bussen und U-Bahnzügen fahren, aufzugeben.
   In 1982 the Greater London Council was forced to give up its new policy of lower fares for ... .
2. Die Anzahl der Fahrgäste, die öffentliche Verkehrsmittel benutzen, nahm sofort ab.
   The number of ... went down at once.
3. Die Verwaltung der Stadt London veröffentlichte 1983 einen Bericht, der die Folgen der höheren Fahrpreise detailliert darstellte.
   In 1983 the GLC published ... in detail.
4. Die Anzahl der Fahrgäste, die mit der U-Bahn fahren, hatte sich um 13,5 % reduziert.
   The ... had been reduced by 13.5 per cent.
5. Darüber hinaus war die Anzahl der sich täglich ereignenden Verkehrsunfälle enorm gestiegen. In dem einen Jahr wurden zusätzlich 3.700 Menschen verletzt oder getötet.
   Moreover, the ... had gone up enormously. During that one year an extra 3,700 people had been injured or killed.

§ 211

5 **The present participle before or after a noun**

Replace the relative clauses. Use a present participle each time either in front of the noun (as a compound adjective) or after the noun, as in the second example.

Examples: Fiona's brother is a professional rugby player who likes drinking beer.

Fiona's brother is a ...beer-drinking professional rugby player...

Her father is the man who's wearing a red pullover.

Her father is ...the man wearing a red pullover.....

1. What sort of work do you do, Fiona? – I'm with a firm that produces home computers and video equipment.
2. What's business like? – Very good. I'm lucky to be in an industry that's growing fast.
3. Do you enjoy it? – Yes, I do. Last month I was even mentioned in the company's magazine, because I'd had an idea that made money.
4. Have you got any children? – We've got a daughter who's studying French.
5. Tell me, who's the man who's talking to our hostess?
6. Do you mean the man who looks attractive or the other one?
7. The handsome one. – It seems he's married to that girl who's sitting on her own in the corner near the window.
8. What about the other one? – Oh, he's quite famous. I've forgotten his name, but he's a concert pianist who's won several prizes.

§§ 211; 212 b

The present participle or the infinitive after verbs of perception

•6 Complete the text, using the words given in brackets. You must decide whether to use the verbs as present participles or infinitives.

Example: The pilot ..spotted...the..farmer.....working in his field. (spot – farmer – work)

After an Air Force jet, a Jaguar XX-113, had crashed into open country in Herefordshire last July, several people were interviewed by a reporter from the 'Western Star'.

"As soon as I ... (1. feel – aircraft – roll) to the left, I knew something was wrong," the pilot said, "but there was nothing much I could do."

"I happened to be looking out of the window at the time," the local vet's au pair girl said, "so I saw the whole thing. I ... (2. saw – plane – spin) a full 360° twice, then ... (3. go) out of control completely. I was very worried. It was a great relief ... (4. see – parachute – open)."

"I was driving my old tractor," a local farmer explained, "when I ... (5. hear – something – crash) in the next field. It gave me quite a shock, I can tell you."

"The pilot came down in those trees over there," the farmer went on, "and broke his leg. We weren't able to find him at first. But in the end we ... (6. hear – poor fellow – shout for) help."

§ 214

•7 Make up sensible replies. In each case use a verb of perception, e.g. "see", "hear", followed by a suitable object and the verb given in brackets. You must decide whether to use this verb as a present participle or as an infinitive.

Examples: Didn't you switch the cooker off? – Why? Can you smell.something ...burning.... ? (burn)

How did the air traffic controllers feel? – Well, they felt okay after they'd ...seen.the.plane.land..... safely. (land)

1. I'm fed up with waiting at this bus stop. – Oh, listen. I think I can .... (come)
2. When did the scientists realize there might be an explosion? – As soon as they ... out of the laboratory. (come out)
3. Are you sure this is Angela's signature on the cheque? – Yes, definitely I .... (write)
4. Did you say Karen has got a motor-bike? – Yes, I .... (ride)
5. How do you know it was Mrs Wilkinson's little boy who broke the window? – Because I .... (throw)
6. Is the driver dead or just unconscious? – Well, she's badly injured, I'm afraid, but she isn't dead. I can .... (beat)
7. Are you sure this woman is the thief, Mr Drummond? – No question about it. I .... (pick up; put in)
8. What makes you think that it's Helmut's birthday today, Michael? – Well his office door was open and as I walked past I .... (wish)
9. Didn't Franz Beckenbauer use to play football for Hamburg FC? – Yes, of course. In fact, my uncle .... (play)
10. Does your grandfather like whisky? – Not as far as I know. At least I .... (drink)

§ 214

8 The present participle after certain verbs

Finish the translations, using the pairs of verbs given in brackets. Where possible, put in the second verb as a present participle. If this isn't possible, join the two verbs with "and" or "to".

Examples: Der Detektiv und der Dieb standen da und sahen einander an.
The detective and the thief *stood there looking at each other*. (stand + look)
Lynn ging fort und kaufte einen neuen Fernseher.
Lynn *went out and bought* a new TV set. (go out + buy)

1. Helen lag am Strand und beobachtete die kleinen Boote.
   Helen ... the little boats. (lie + watch)
2. Ihr Freund saß neben ihr und las die Zeitung.
   Her boy-friend ... the paper. (sit + read)
3. Nach einer Weile ging sie zum Hotel und holte ihre Sonnenbrille.
   After a while she ... her sun-glasses. (go + fetch)
4. Auf einmal kam ein Kellner vom Hotel auf sie zugelaufen.
   Suddenly a waiter from the hotel ... towards her. (come + run)
5. Er stand ein paar Sekunden vor ihr und atmete tief.
   For a few seconds he ... deeply. (stand + breathe)
6. „Ein Polizist sitzt im Hotel und wartet auf Sie," sagte er.
   "A policeman ... ," he said. (sit + wait for)
7. „Er möchte, daß Sie kommen und mit ihm Tee trinken."
   "He'd like ... a cup of tea with him." (come + have)
8. Helen stand auf und lächelte. „Das wird mein Vater sein," sagte sie.
   Helen ... . "It'll be my father," she said. (get up + smile)

§ 215 a

9 "Have" + object + past participle

Bob and Linda have just taken over a country hotel in Cornwall. But there's a lot that has to be done before their first guests arrive. Read Bob's comments, then work out Linda's responses. Use "have" + object + the past participle of one of the following verbs: design, extend, re-plant, re-decorate, repair.

1. This bedroom looks really grotty, Linda. I mean, look at that wallpaper. – You're right, Bob. We should ... as soon as possible.
2. This old clock doesn't seem to be working. Shall we get rid of it? – Oh, no. Not yet anyway. It's nice, Bob. Why don't we try ... ?
3. Is the kitchen really big enough, Linda? – No, of course it isn't. We'll have to ... before we can open the restaurant.
4. If we make the kitchen bigger, that little apple tree can't stay where it is now. – True. We'll have to ... .
5. The previous owner's hotel brochure isn't very attractive, Linda, is it? – It's awful. Let's ... by a professional advertising agency.

§ 218 a

10 The past participle before or after a noun

Re-write the underlined words by leaving out the relative pronouns and changing the verbs into past participles.

Examples: a picture that somebody stole → a stolen picture
a photo that someone took last week → a photo taken last week

1. To turn on the video cassette recorder (VCR) you press the "ON/OFF" switch that you usually find at the back or the side of the machine.
2. To put a cassette into a top-loading VCR, you open a little door by pressing a button that is labelled "EJECT".
3. The numbers that are shown in this "window" tell you the amount of space on the cassette that you haven't used yet.
4. Press the "SELECT" button to obtain the TV channel that you require.
5. The "TIMER" operates like an alarm clock. If you programme it, it will automatically begin to record a TV programme at a time that you have chosen.
6. The "TV/VCR" switch allows you to watch one TV channel "live" and, the same time, record a programme that is being transmitted on a second channel.
7. The "TRACKING" knob will improve the quality if you re-play a cassette that you have borrowed, i.e. a recording that was made on somebody else's machine.
8. The "DEW LAMP", a safety control that you don't see on a lot of VCRs is a warning light that tells you if the tape heads are slightly wet e.g. because the air is too humid.

§§ 216 a; 217

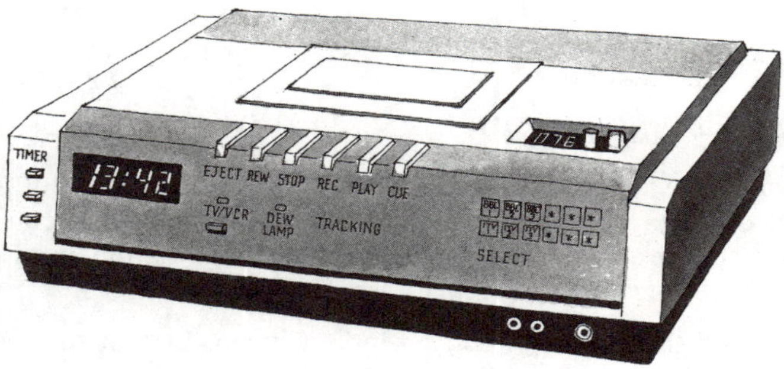

11 Participles instead of adverbial clauses of time or reason

Put in either a present participle or "having" + past participle.

1. Finding. it hard to look after her three children and do her office job at the same time, but ... to give up her job, Mrs Wagner decided to advertise for a German au pair girl. (find; not want)
2. ... her English exam, Ulrike wondered how she would ever be able to get the job she'd always wanted. (fail)
3. ... to improve her English this way, Ulrike applied for the job in Philadelphia that Mrs Wagner had advertised. (hope)
4. ... to such a big city before, Ulrike felt rather lost at first. (never go)
5. ... out of the house at work most of the day, Mrs Wagner always had to give Ulrike a list of jobs to do before she set off for the office. (be)
6. ... how busy she would be, Ulrike was surprised how little free time she had during her year abroad. (not realize)
7. ... to be paid \$35 a week, she was disappointed to be offered only \$25 at the end of her first week. (expect)
8. ... the question with her mother on the phone, Mrs Wagner agreed to give Ulrike \$35 a week after all. (discuss)
9. ... her stay, Ulrike didn't really want to go home when the time came. (enjoy)
10. ... her English so much, she was sure, however, that now she'd be able to get the job she wanted. (improve)

§ 220 a/b

12 Participle clauses introduced by conjunctions

Put in either the present participle or the past participle of the verbs given in brackets, preceded by a suitable conjunction from the following list: until, unless, if (4 x), before (2 x), whether, whenever (2 x), as if.

SOME WORDS OF WARNING TO GARDENERS

- All chemicals are safer ... (1. keep) in a locked cupboard in a garden shed.
- ... (2. use) electrical equipment in the garden, e.g. to cut the grass, always remember to turn off the electricity at its source ... (3. take a break), ... (4. intend) to go on again afterwards or not.
- ... (5. switch off) at the source of its electrical power, a machine might be started by a young child.
- Some modern machines used for cutting grass are based on the hovercraft principle. ... (6. operate) a machine of the type, move it from side to side, not backwards and forwards ... (7. clean) a carpet with a vacuum cleaner. ... (8. pull) backwards towards you, a machine of this type could easily swing over your feet and cut them badly.
- ... (9. start) a fire in the garden, always make sure that any young children are standing far enough away.
- A fire will burn more quickly ... (10. start) with petrol or other fuel but it might start too quickly. Use a safer method.
- Remember that old cans, especially aerosol sprays, will explode like bombs ... (11. put) onto a fire.
- And don't ever leave a fire ... (12. convince) that it's gone out.

§ 221

13 Participle clauses introduced by "with"

You might hear sentences like the following on the news. Finish the sentences by putting in a participle clause introduced by "With ...". Use the nouns and verbs given in brackets. But be careful to choose the right kind of participle (present or past).

Example: ..With his arms held.. behind him by two policemen, bank robber Donald Briggs was taken to court early this morning. (arms – hold)

1. ... brightly, the U.S. space shuttle Discovery made a perfect landing at Cape Canaveral this afternoon. (sun – shine)
2. ... from midnight tonight, motorists throughout the country were queueing up today to fill up for the last time at the old prices. (petrol – go up)
3. ... down his face, Joe Buggins surprised everyone by going on to win the European Heavyweight Boxing Championship. (blood – pour)
4. ... because of the continuing strike by bank clerks, thousands of tourists were faced with the problem of how to cash their traveller's cheques today. (banks – close)
5. ... across the North Sea, a period of rain followed by some sunshine can be expected. (area of high pressure – move away)
6. ... already, the organizers are confident of making a big profit. (most of the tickets for tomorrow's big concert – sell)
7. ..., athletics star Daley Thompson had plenty of time to look back at the rest of the runners before crossing the line. (race – win)
8. ... at the factory gates, at least one lorry driver decided not to deliver his goods. (large group of strikers – stand)

§ 222 a

Present participle or past participle?

14 Decide whether the verbs in brackets should be put in as present participles or as past participles.

Some new rules ... (1. introduce) by the Minister of Transport will affect all motorbike owners who haven't yet passed their driving test. The rules say that from February 1984 a learner will not be allowed on public roads with a bike over 125 cc, and the driving test itself will be in two parts, the first part on a special track. Only riders ... (2. complete) the first part of the test successfully will be allowed to take their practical test on the roads.

In a recent interview Mick Hockley, an instructor with the largest organization ... (3. run) training programmes for learners, welcomed the changes, ... (4. point out) that today's 125 cc machines are as powerful as the 250 cc machines of twenty years ago. In fact, with some of today's small but powerful bikes easily ... (5. reach) maximum speeds above the legal speed limit, some critics say that even the new laws will not be strict enough.

Young riders on the courses ... (6. run) by Mick Hockley learn to look after their bikes, because if ... (7. keep) properly a machine is less likely to cause an accident. Even if ... (8. intend) to let a garage do any repairs, all riders should understand certain basic things about their bikes. For example, unless ... (9. replace) whenever necessary, a front tyre can easily get a puncture or start to skid. And then, according to Mick, the rider will go ... (10. fly) and "will end as part of the decorations."

In traffic there are always a number of things ... (11. happen) at the same time. So, as a rider, you must be conscious of cars behind you ... (12. try) to overtake you. And you must learn to watch people ahead of you ... (13. get ready) to rush out onto a zebra crossing as soon as you get nearer.

Bad roads, with lots of bone- ... (14. shake) holes in them, though possibly ... (15. provide) a few moments of excitement, should be avoided by riders who want to go on living. Similarly, in a recently ... (16. publish) book ... (17. offer) advice to the average learner – called 'Sorry, mate, I didn't see you', Tim Monaghan stresses that when ... (18. buy) gloves, jackets, boots, helmets, etc., riders should make sure they choose items that might give some protection in an accident.

§§ 211; 212 b; 214; 215 a; 216 a; 217; 220 a/b; 221; 222 a

•15 Complete the translation. Make use of the verbs in brackets, putting them in each time in the form of a present or past participle (active or passive). Add extra words if necessary.

1. Weil er dabei beobachtet worden war, wie er in der Nähe seines Zuhauses Motorrad fuhr, mußte Großbritanniens Rekorde aufstellender 26jähriger Motorradstar Ron Haslam gestern £130 Strafe zahlen; denn, er besitzt keinen Führerschein, um auf öffentlichen Straßen Motorrad fahren zu dürfen, da er die entsprechende Fahrprüfung noch nicht abgelegt hat.

   Having been spotted (spot) ... (1. ride) a motor-bike near his home, Britain's ... (2. break) 26-year-old motor-bike star, Ron Haslam, had to pay a £130 fine yesterday, because ... (3. not take) the relevant test yet, he doesn't possess a licence to ride motor-bikes on public roads.
2. Dem Gericht in Ilkeston, Derbyshire, wurde mitgeteilt, daß Haslam, der dabei gesehen wurde, wie er die Straße entlangfuhr und die Maschine eines Freundes testete, weder L-Schilder noch Sturzhelm noch Versicherungsschein gehabt habe.

   The court in Ilkeston, Derbyshire, was told that Haslam, who had been seen ... (14. ride) ... (5. test), had no L-plates, no crash helmet and no insurance.
3. Obwohl er zugab, daß ein Gesetzesverstoß vorliege, betonte der Rechtsanwalt, der Haslam verteidigte, daß Haslam nicht zu der Art von jungen Menschen gehöre, die sich ständig herumtrieben und verantwortungslos benähmen.

   Though ... (6. admit) that the law had been broken, the ... (7. defend) stressed that Haslam wasn't the sort of young man who regularly went around ... (8. behave) irresponsibly.
4. Dies sei eine Gefälligkeit, die erwiesen worden sei, um einem Freund der Familie zu helfen.

   It was a favour ... (9. do) to help a friend of the family.
5. Der Rechtsanwalt wies ferner darauf hin, daß dies für Haslam, der ein sehr talentierter Profi-Motorradfahrer sei, der im In- und Ausland an Wettrennen teilnehme und dabei häufig die britische Mannschaft vertrete, eine ziemlich paradoxe Situation sei.

   The lawyer continued his defence, ... (10. point out) that, with Haslam ... (11. be) a professional motorcyclist of great talent who raced in this country and abroad, frequently ... (12. represent), it was a rather paradoxical situation.

§§ 211; 212 b; 214; 215 a; 217; 220 b; 221; 222 a

Reported speech

Test yourself

A Change direct speech into reported speech and fill in the missing forms.

1. *John:* "I play tennis once a week."
   A few minutes ago John said that … played tennis once a week.
2. *Jill:* "I haven't seen my brother for ten months."
   Jill mentioned that she … her brother for ten months.
3. *David:* "The journey may be very dangerous."
   David remarked that the journey … very dangerous.
4. "Do you like swimming?" Bob asked the girl.
   Bob asked the girl … swimming.
5. *Mrs Dawson to Jean:* "Call a doctor quickly."
   Mrs Dawson told Jean … a doctor quickly.
6. *Debbie (on Tuesday):* "I bought a new bike yesterday."
   Liz (on the following Wednesday): "Debbie told me yesterday that she'd bought a new bike … ."
7. *Tom:* "Fred should sell his tent if he can."
   Tom said that Fred … his tent if he …
8. *Mr Miller:* "You'd better do your homework at once, Bob."
   Mr Miller … Bob … his homework at once.
9. *Bill:* "I wash my car every week."
   Bill (a little later): "A short time ago … said that … washed … car every week."
10. *Caroline:* "Where did you stay after you came back from Australia, Lucy?"
    Caroline asked Lucy … after she … back from Australia.
11. *Martina:* "I can't do this question, so I might have a look at the answers on the next page."
    Martina admitted that she … the question and that she … have a look at the answers on the next page.

B Find suitable English equivalents for the German words or clauses given in brackets.

12. Terry said … . (daß er müde sei)
13. Mrs Hedley wanted to know … . (ob ich Geschwister habe)
14. Dave suggested … . (daß wir all unseren Freunden eine Postkarte schrieben)
15. *Harry:* "I met Tony last week and he mentioned … ." (daß er drei Tage zuvor in Paris gewesen sei)
16. Susan asked her friend … . (ob sie nicht ihren Cousin kenne)
17. Mr Brown wanted to know … . (wann er kommen solle)
18. Mrs Haines told her son … . (das Geld zu holen und nicht die Reiseschecks zu vergessen)
19. Tom thought … . (daß seine Tante in ein Altersheim gehen solle)
20. Uncle Henry told us … . (daß das das letzte Weihnachtsfest sei, das er bei uns verbringen würde)
21. Then Katy asked him … . (ob er nicht mehr kommen wolle, weil ihre Mäuse an dem Morgen in seinem Zimmer gewesen waren)

C Spot the mistakes.

There is one mistake in each of the following sentences. Spot the mistakes and write down what you think is the correct version.

22. *Francis:* "Bob, you're my best friend."
    Francis remarked to Bob that you're my best friend.
23. Liz asked him whether his mother is dead.
24. Yesterday morning Debbie told the police that her handbag was missing. She said she might have left it at the pub last night.
25. The mechanic promised that he will repair the TV set the next day.
26. Pete asked Susan did she meet John Webb the previous week.
27. The children were bored, so their mother suggested to go to the zoo.
28. Clare advised Joe that he better take a good map of the area.
29. Mrs Gallion asked her husband to come home soon and don't go to the pub.

A man was given a job as a bus driver. When he reported for work on his first morning he asked where his conductor was.

"You don't have a conductor," replied the inspector. "These are one-man buses."

So the man boarded his bus and drove off, while the inspector went to have a cup of tea. Five minutes later the man telephoned the inspector from the High Street to tell him that he'd had a crash.

"What happened?" asked the inspector.

"How should I know?" replied the man. "I was upstairs collecting fares at the time!"

Key

A

1. ... John said that **he** played ... . § 225
2. ... that she **hadn't seen** ... . § 226 a
3. ... the journey **might be** ... . § 228 a
4. ... **if/whether she liked** swimming. § 226 b
5. ... told Jean **to call** ... . § 230 b
6. ... a new bike **on Monday/the day before/the previous day**. § 231
7. ... Fred **should sell** his tent if he **could**. §§ 228 b; 228 a
8. Mr Miller **advised** Bob **to do/told** Bob **that he'd better do** ... . § 230 c
9. ... **I** said that **I** washed **my** car ... . § 225
10. ... asked Lucy **where she'd stayed** after she**'d come** back ... . § 226 b
11. ... she **couldn't do** ... she **might** have a look ... . §§ 228 a; 228 b

B

12. ... said **(that) he was tired**. § 226 a
13. ... know **if/whether I had a brother or (a) sister/ any brothers or sisters**. § 226 b
14. ... suggested **writing/that we should write postcards/ a postcard to all our friends**. § 230 d
15. ... mentioned **that he'd been in Paris three days before**. § 231
16. ... friend **if/whether she didn't know her cousin**. § 226 b
17. ... wanted to know **when he should come/when he was to come (when to come)**. §§ 228 a; 226 b; [193]
18. ... son **to get the money and not to forget the traveller's cheques**. § 230 b
19. ... **that his aunt ought to/should go to an old people's home.** § 228 b
20. ... **that it was the last Christmas he would spend with us.** § 226 a
21. ... **whether he didn't want to come again because her mice had been in his room that morning**. §§ 226 a; 231

C

22. Francis remarked to Bob that **he was his** best friend. §§ 225; 226 a
23. ... whether his mother **was** dead. §§ 226 a; 226 b
24. ... might have left it at the pub **the night before**. § 231
25. ... that he **would** repair ... . § 228 a
26. ... asked Susan **if/whether she'd met** John Webb ... . §§ 226 b; 226 a
27. ... suggested **going/that they should go** ... . § 230 d
28. ... that he**'d** better take **(to take)** ... . § 230 c
29. ... to come home soon and **not to** go ... . § 230 b

Exercise finder

Test yourself	ENGLISH G Grammatik	Exercises
1, 9, 22	§ 225	1, 2, 4, •7, •8, 10, 13, 14
2, 12, 20, 21, 22, 23, 26	§ 226 a	1, 2, 4, 5, •7, •8, 9, 10, 13, 14
3, 7, 11, 17, 25	§ 228 a	5, 6, •7, •8, 9, 13, 14
4, 10, 13, 16, 17, 23, 26	§ 226 b	3, 4, 6, •7, 9, 13, 14
5, 18, 29	§ 230 b	•12, 13, 14
6, 15, 21, 24	§ 231	13, 14
7, 11, 19	§ 228 b	•7, •8, 9, 10, 13, 14
8, 28	§ 230 c	11, •12, 13, 14
14, 27	§ 230 d	11, •12, 13
17	§ 193	**8** : 5, •10

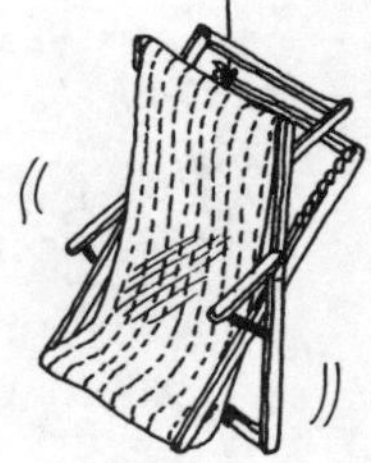

Exercises

1 A by-election is being held in Pudley, and yesterday afternoon two Liberal activists, Shirley Thorpe and Cyril Meadowcroft, did some canvassing in Middle Way. They went from house to house, knocking on every door and trying to persuade everybody to vote for the Liberal candidate.

This is what the voters said:

Mr Anderson: "I always vote Labour."
Mrs Woodward: "I'm not interested in politics."
Mr Ferguson: "I'm definitely voting Liberal."
Mrs Parkinson: "I'm considering voting for the Socialists this time."
Mr McAllister: "Your party has never helped the working class."
Mrs Sherwood: "I've just joined the Conservative Party, young lady."
Mrs Holliday: "I've voted Labour since 1945 and I'm not going to change now."
Mr Woodhouse: "I've been looking forward to asking you some questions about your policies."
Mr Pym: "I've been thinking about voting for your party for some time."
Mrs Lawson: "I voted for the SDP at the last election, you know."
Mrs Hitchcock: "Election? What election? Is there going to be one?"
Mr Ainsworth: "I voted for your party last time, but the Conservative candidate won."
Mr Hoolihan: "I read your leaflet recently and I agree with your policies."
Mr Jenkinson: "I knew your candidate's grandfather, my dear."
Mrs Patterson: "I'm going to vote Conservative."
Mr Armstrong: "My wife and I are going to vote Labour."
Mrs Townsend: "The Conservative candidate will win."
Mr Bradbury: "Yes, I'll vote for your candidate."
Mrs Thompson: "I'm sure your candidate will be elected."

Now put the voters' comments into reported speech. Begin like this:
Mr Anderson told Cyril and Shirley that he always voted Labour.

§§ 225; 226 a

2 Sir Richard Attenborough, who made a film about the life of Mahatma Gandhi, was invited to go to South Africa in 1983 when the film first came out. The film shows very clearly how Gandhi campaigned against racial and religious discrimination. So some people were shocked when Sir Richard agreed to attend a premiere of the film at which the audience would be all-white.

In the end Sir Richard was persuaded not to go. This is how different people reacted to the news.

1. A non-white leader in South Africa: "I'm delighted at Sir Richard's change of heart."
2. Dr Essop Jassai, head of the Indian Anti-Apartheid Movement in the Transvaal: "I'm pleased about his decision."
3. Dr Jassai: "They've been trying to claim that apartheid is no longer so bad, but this discussion has made it clear that all the hurtful things still exist in South Africa."
4. Mr S. Kotze, the South African Minister of Community Development: "My Government is against people trying to gain political advantage from the way the film is shown."
5. Mr Kotze: "We have not stopped people from seeing the film and, in general, there are adequate facilities in each separate community."
6. Sir Richard Attenborough: "I have decided not to go to South Africa unless my film is allowed to be shown to mixed audiences in every cinema."
7. Sir Richard: "All my personal profits from showings of the film in South Africa will be given to multi-racial organizations in South Africa."
8. Mr Cassin Saloojee of the Gandhi centenary council: "I'm very, very happy to hear about Sir Richard's attitude."
9. Mr Saloojee: "His decision makes sense when you consider Gandhi's principles and values."
10. The group organizing the showing of the film in South Africa: "We're sorry that Sir Richard won't be coming to our country, but we hope he'll visit us in the future in more encouraging circumstances."

Write about these reactions, using reported speech. Go on from here:
Reactions to Sir Richard's announcement have been mixed. A non-white leader in South Africa said he … .

§§ 225; 226 a

3 Find the correct word order for each sentence.

1. how long – had – Colin asked – her motor-bike – owned – Sue – she – .
2. if – it – let him – she – he wondered – ride – would – .
3. his machine – when – had – Colin – Sue asked – bought – he – .
4. to know – who – were – she wanted – his repairs – done – by – .
5. how – did – many miles – she asked – his bike – per gallon – him – .

§ 226 b

4 Lesley Stephens was standing outside the supermarket, talking to her friend Kathy Torrance, when they spotted one of their friends. It was Andrew Rainbird and he was riding a most unusual bike.

Kathy: Hallo, Andrew. How are you?
Andrew: Hallo, Kathy. Hallo, Lesley. Fine, thank you.
Lesley: What's that you're riding? I haven't seen a bike like that before.
Andrew: No, well, I'm probably the first person in the county to buy one.
Kathy: How does it work?
Andrew: Well, it's got a small motor that's driven by a battery, and it's also got ordinary bike pedals. It's up to the rider how he or she operates it. It's possible to use either just the pedals or just the battery-drive motor. It's possible to use both at the same time, too.
Lesley: Can it go very fast?
Andrew: No. But it travels at up to 15 mph.
Kathy: How did you find out about it, Andrew?
Andrew: I read an article in a Sunday newspaper. I liked the idea and decided to buy it at once.
Lesley: Why?
Kathy: Yes, why?
Andrew: It's just what I need. I've managed to get a job at last, you see. But it's in the hospital at the top of Jordan Hill – and if you ride a normal bike, you have to get off and push.
Lesley: It is a steep hill, I agree. But why not take a bus to work?
Andrew: Oh, I enjoy the exercise. I just need something to help me to get up that hill, that's all. I don't want to be late for work every day.
Kathy: What's wrong with ordinary motor-bikes or proper mopeds?
Andrew: This is better, because I don't have to have insurance or pay road tax and I don't even have to wear a crash helmet. This bike won't cause any pollution, either.
Lesley: You know this will interest my Dad.

That same evening Lesley told her father about the conversation. Go on from here, using reported speech:
Listen, Dad, Kathy and I saw Andrew this morning – on a funny sort of bike. Of course, I asked him what it was that he was riding, as I . . . .

§§ 225; 226 a/b

5 A discussion took place recently between Mrs Jones, the head of a private language school in Pudley and two members of the town council, Simon Walker and Ray Bell. Use these notes to make a report of the discussion.

Example: Mrs Jones – say – school – want – build – clubroom – corner – underground car park.
Mrs Jones said that the school wanted to build a clubroom in a corner of their underground car park.

1. The head – explain – school – need – place – where – teachers – students – can meet.
2. Councillor Walker – say – he – think – car park – be – too small already.
3. He – tell – Mrs Jones – school – need – all – space in the car park – cars.
4. Councillor Bell – tell – Mrs Jones – neighbours – already – complain – students' cars – cause – problems – in the street outside the school.
5. He – stress – council – receive – a large number – protests – school.
6. The head – point out – corner – car park – which – school – want – use – be – inconvenient – cars.
7. She – explain – school – use – this corner – bicycles – not cars.
8. She – emphasize – same number – cars – can park – car park – after – clubroom – be built.
9. Councillor Walker – repeat – car park – not have – enough space – cars – if – school – be allowed – build – clubroom.
10. The head – ask – councillors – if – all the members of the council – visit – school – following week – look at – corner – car park – which – school – want – use.

§§ 226 a; 228 a

6 Some visitors are looking round a carpet factory near Salisbury. As some of the machines are rather noisy, they've got to keep repeating their questions.

Example: (Visitor) This is the biggest factory of its kind, isn't it? – (Guide) Sorry? Could you repeat that? – (Visitor) I asked you if this was the biggest factory of its kind.

1. How old are these machines? – Sorry? – I asked you … .
2. Do you sell a lot of carpets abroad? – What was that? – I wondered … .
3. Have you got more male or female employees? – Pardon? – I wanted to know … .
4. Will we get a chance to talk to some of your employees? – I beg your pardon? – I … .
5. Do your employees get a company pension when they retire? – Would you mind repeating that? – I … .
6. How long have you yourself worked here? – Could you say that again? – I … .
7. Will we be able to buy some of your company's products at a special price at the end of the tour? – Sorry? – I … .
8. Shall I close this door? – I beg your pardon? – I … .
9. May I touch this wool? – Could you repeat that, please? – I … .
10. Can we go to a quieter room now? – I'm sorry, I can't hear you very well. It's so noisy in here. – I know it is. That's why I … .

§§ 226 b; 228 a

•7 Nancy Wagner, a clerk at a bank in South Dakota, was visited by a customer called Jerry Kowalski last month.

Jerry Kowalski: I'm worried about the security of the money in my bank account.
Nancy Wagner: Why's that, Mr. Kowalski?
Jerry Kowalski: It's because you're starting to allow your customers to take money out of their accounts via these new machines outside your banks, these ATMs.
Nancy Wagner: Most customers find the Automated Teller Machines a useful service.
Jerry Kowalski: Well, last week I read about a court case in Japan. An employee of the national telephone company used his knowledge of communications systems to steal money from accounts at three different banks. You see, the police can listen to private telephone conversations. Well, similarly, it's possible for crooks to "listen" to an electronic message sent from an ATM outside a bank to the bank's central computer.
Nancy Wagner: How could this help a crook?
Jerry Kowalski: If I use an ATM to get some money out of my account one day, a crook may be using a cassette recorder at that moment to record the message that the ATM is sending to the central computer. Then, after I've been given my money and have gone away, the crook can re-play the message he recorded – and the central computer will think I've asked it to pay out the same sum of money again. This worries me.
Nancy Wagner: I'll find out more about this, Mr Kowalski.

Imagine you're Nancy Wagner. Tell the manager of your bank, Mr Gomez, about the conversation. Go on from here, using reported speech:
A customer came into the bank this morning, Mr Gomez, and said he ..*was*... ..*worried about*..... the security of the money in his bank account. When I asked … .

§§ 225; 226 a/b; 228 a/b

•8 The bank manager did some research (see Exercise 7). Then he gave Nancy some notes explaining what several experts had to say on the subject.

1. Gerry Ely, director of technology planning at Merrill Lynch & Co: "Almost any system is open to attack if someone tries hard enough." (admit)
2. Boris Melnikoff, director of security at First Atlanta Corp: "For every three or four hours we put into designing a system, there is someone who will stay up an extra hour to defeat it." (point out)
3. Michael Strada, technical specialist at PLUS SYSTEM Corp: "It would have to be an educated crook, though it could be done. However, we're introducing special codes now that will help to protect ATM systems." (stress; point out)
4. Another expert: "It will be five years before all the nation's ATM networks are adequately protected from crimes of this kind." (predict)
5. A banker in New York: "I don't think there's a very great risk. If a crook wants to do this, he'll need very expensive equipment. But an ATM usually only pays out small sums, say $50 or $100. For $50 or $100 it's probably easier just to mug people after they've used an ATM." (doubt; emphasize; point out; say)

Imagine you're Nancy Wagner. Tell Mr Kowalski about the experts' opinions. Use reported speech, introduced by the verbs given in brackets. Go on from here:
I've got some good news and some bad news for you, Mr Kowalski. Several experts have been asked about this problem recently. One of them, Gerry Ely of Merrill Lynch, ...*admitted*... that almost any system ... to attack. And Boris Melnikoff ... . However, ...

§§ 225; 226 a; 228 a/b

9 Complete the translations. Be careful with the tenses.

1. Der Mann im Auskunftsbüro fragte die alte Dame, ob er ihr helfen könne.
   The man in the information bureau ... .
2. Sie fragte ihn, ob es ihm etwas ausmachen würde, für sie ein Hotel für zwei Nächte ausfindig zu machen.
   ... finding her a hotel for two nights.
3. Der Mann fragte sie, wieviel sie zahlen wolle.
   The man ... .
4. Der Preis sei nicht so wichtig, erklärte sie ihm, aber das Zimmer müsse sehr ruhig sein.
   The price ... very quiet.
5. Der Mann sagte ihr, daß sie müde aussehe.
   The man ... .
6. Die alte Dame sagte ihm, daß sie ihre Wohnung in Salzgitter um fünf Uhr früh habe verlassen müssen.
   The old lady ... .
7. Sie sagte ihm, daß sie an einer Konferenz zum Thema „Inflation" teilnehme.
   ... a conference on the subject of inflation.
8. Sie sei gerade vom Flughafen gekommen, fügte sie hinzu.
   She ... , she added.

§§ 226 a/b; 228 a/b

10 Read the text, then take over the role of the reporter who interviewed the people mentioned.

When a lioness called Hagar escaped from a travelling circus in the middle of a show in Didcot last year, she made her way towards the centre of the town.

Later, Mrs Eileen Hodges told a reporter what she'd seen. "I was in the audience with my son and my mother-in-law when Hagar escaped," she said. "It's strange," she added, "there was no panic, no screams. Everyone was very calm."

Philip Cox said, "I was in Norry's Road with Dave Stacey at the time. We were in the middle of discussing the state of my car. Suddenly we looked up and saw this great lioness standing 20 yards away looking at us."

"At first we just couldn't believe it," Mr Stacey explained. "We were more shocked than frightened. It's the last thing we expected to see."

"The lioness disappeared down the garden path of Number 58," Mr Cox went on, "so we followed her. We had a look to see where she'd gone. We saw her in the garage, so then we went to call the police."

A circus employee said, "I arrived on the scene before the police, and I managed to shut the garage door. I saw the lioness inside the garage, sitting on top of an old fridge."

Mr Norman Boast said, "I live at Number 58, but I only learned about the drama from a neighbour. I myself stayed indoors."

Another circus worker said, "We put up a huge cage around the mouth of the garage. Then Dick Chipperfield, a lion tamer, arrived."

"I crept into the garage," Mr Chipperfield explained, "and made some special lion sounds. Hagar felt lost. She made some aggressive noises. But I showed her the way to the cage, and after that she was okay. A good night's sleep and I'm sure she'll be fine."

Go on from here, using reported speech:
I talked to several people afterwards. Mrs Eileen Hodges told me that she'd been in the audience with … .

§§ 225; 226 a; 228 b

11 Reported invitations, requests, advice, suggestions

Finish the sentences, using the verbs given in brackets and adding any extra words that are necessary.

Example: Marilyn's parents agreed to let her invite her boy-friend to dinner at their house last Sunday. So she ..asked him if he would.. ..like to be there. at 7 o'clock. (ask – would like – be)

1. Marilyn thought somebody might steal or damage Graham's motor-bike if he parked it in the street outside their house. She knew there was plenty of room in the garage, though. So she .... (suggest – should – put)
2. There was a lot of oil on Graham's hands. So Marilyn .... (tell – had better – wash)
3. As Marilyn led Graham past the dining-room, she realized that the table wasn't ready. So she .... (ask – would mind – help – lay)
4. The main dish was curry. As Marilyn knew her mother usually made it very hot, she .... (tell – had better – not take)
5. Marilyn couldn't reach the salad, because it was on the other side of Graham. So, naturally, she .... (ask – would mind – pass)
6. Graham's cup was empty and Marilyn had the coffee-pot in her hand. So she .... (ask – would like – have)
7. Marilyn had baked a cake. As Graham had obviously enjoyed his first piece of it, she .... (ask – want – have)
8. When it was time to do the washing up, Marilyn smiled at Graham and .... (suggest – should help – do) § 230 c/d

•12 Reported commands, invitations, requests, advice, suggestions

Neil Sinclair, who keeps a diary, is making a note of some of the things people said to him yesterday. Imagine you are Neil. Write the diary entries, using reported speech. Make use of the verbs in brackets.

Example: Our neighbours: "Won't you and Clare come to dinner on Friday?" (invite – have)
Our neighbours invited Clare and me to have dinner with them on Friday......

1. My assistant: "There's an article in the 'Financial Times' that I think you should look at, Neil." (advise – read)
2. The Managing Director: "Bring me the new plans as soon as possible, Neil." (tell – show)
3. The Sales Manager: "Shall we talk about the new advertising campaign over lunch?" (suggest – discuss)
4. The Marketing Director: "There's an exhibition in Detroit and I'd like you to be there." (ask – attend)
5. The Export Manager: "Could you call in at our Chicago office while you're in the States? Would that be OK?" (ask – would mind – visit – be)
6. The Personnel Manager: "Would you like a bigger desk?" (offer)
7. My secretary: "You'd better ring up the architect at once." (advise – had better-phone)
8. My doctor: "Get more exercise, Neil." (order – get)
9. He: "Don't work such long hours." (tell – not work) § 230 b/c/d

Changes in adverbial expressions of time and place

13 a) The following conversation took place two days ago, i.e. on Wednesday:

John: Would you like to go to the Odeon with me on Friday?
Sandra: Yes. But I've got an orchestra practice after school on Friday. I have them every week.
John: How long will it last?
Sandra: I don't know. It usually lasts about an hour. But we had one yesterday and it went on for over two hours. We're giving a concert at the town hall on Saturday, you see.
John: Well, I don't really want to miss the start of the film.
Sandra: What time does it start?
John: At 7.15.
Sandra: Oh, I'll be there by then, John, even if I have to miss my tea.

It's Friday evening now and John is standing outside the Odeon with Bob and Linda. Imagine you're John. Go on from here, using reported speech:

Linda: It's 7.15., John. Why don't you forget Sandra and come in with us? She must have forgotten you.
John: No, she might still come. You see, when I spoke to her on Wednesday, and asked her ... .

b) This telephone conversation took place on Thursday, i.e. yesterday:

Mrs Pegg: Listen, we ordered some textbooks from you last Thursday and they haven't arrived.
Mr Lind: Yes, I can remember you doing that, Mrs Pegg, because you came here personally.
Mrs Pegg: Well, where are they?
Mr Lind: I don't know. But they aren't here. I sent them to you on Friday.
Mrs Pegg: Are you sure?
Mr Lind: Why don't you come to the bookshop and have a look?
Mrs Pegg: Don't be silly, Mr Lind.
Mr Lind: Look, I took the parcel to the post-office myself. I've got no idea why it hasn't got there. But it isn't my fault.

It's Friday today and Mrs Pegg has just told the headmaster, Mr Roberts, about the phone call. Go on from here, using reported speech:

Mr Roberts: Did you phone old Lind yesterday about those textbooks?
Mrs Pegg: Yes, of course. I said we weren't very pleased. I pointed out that we ... .

§§ 225; 226 a/b; 228 a/b; 230 b/c/d; 231

14 Here is a telephone conversation between Mrs Fenton and a town councillor:

Mrs Fenton: I'd like to speak to you about the lovely 15-foot-high hedge that separated my back garden and my neighbour's back garden from the railway line – until 10 o'clock this morning.
Town councillor: I don't know what you mean.
Mrs Fenton: A new road is going to be built in this part of town to link the new housing project at Fairfield Farm with the main road.

Town councillor:	I know that. Why don't you tell me what your problem is?
Mrs Fenton:	The new road is to run between the end of my back garden, where the hedge was, and the railway line. And between my neighbour's back garden and the railway line, too, of course.
Town councillor:	Surely you've known for two months that this road would be built?
Mrs Fenton:	Yes, I knew that. And my neighbour, Mrs Silver, knew it, too. But some workers arrived here with a bulldozer half an hour ago and the whole hedge has been torn up. It's terrible. We were given no warning. It was a complete surprise. So we could do nothing to stop it. Do you realize that we were promised only two days ago that the hedge would be saved?
Town councillor:	Yes, that is terrible. It's most unfortunate. I'm very sorry this has happened.
Mrs Fenton:	What about the conditions you made when you gave the building company permission to develop the site?
Town councillor:	As far as I can remember, we told them the hedge should be kept if possible. It seems it wasn't possible. I imagine the hedge was too wide.
Mrs Fenton:	Well, I think my neighbour and I have been misled. And I'd like you to do two things for me.
Town councillor:	Oh? What's the first thing?
Mrs Fenton:	Make the building company plant a new hedge immediately.
Town councillor:	I can try. What else?
Mrs Fenton:	Don't ask me to vote for you in the next council elections!

The next day Mrs Fenton told her next-door neighbour, Mrs Silver, about the conversation. Go on from here, using reported speech:
I rang up someone on the town council yesterday, as I'd told you I would. I said I'd like to speak to … .

§§ 225; 226 a/b; 228 a/b; 230 b/c; 231

Clauses

Test yourself

A If-clauses

Fill in the correct forms of the verbs in brackets.

1. If you visit London, you ... certainly ... (want) to see the Tower.
2. I'd have a car of my own if I ... (be) ten years older.
3. If there hadn't been an energy crisis, people ... (not save) so much oil last year.
4. I'll just have to wait if the office ... (not be) open.
5. I go to Edinburgh every year. If the weather is bad, I ... (go) to the museums and art galleries.
6. I would apply for the job if I ... (be) you.
7. If John ... (not buy) his season ticket yet, he ought to do so immediately.
8. We might have arrived on time if the bus ... (not have) a breakdown.
9. Mrs Robinson always gets upset if people ... (not like) her terrible cat.
10. I'm not really expecting Lulu to call, but if she ... (call), tell her I ... (have) a bath.

B Put in either a conjunction or a relative pronoun (but leave out the relative pronoun where possible).

11. Do you know the boy ... bike was stolen yesterday?
12. ... Raymond didn't like meat, he became a vegetarian.
13. Is there anything ... ought to be discussed now?
14. Please do call me this evening, ... late it may be.
15. Jane came to see me on Sunday, ... was very nice.
16. Nobody has met the people ... have moved in next door.
17. I always take my dog with me ... I go.
18. Don't forget the book ... you wanted to take to Grandma.
19. My boss thinks I earn enough money, ... I think I'm completely underpaid.

C Find suitable English equivalents for the German words or clauses given in brackets.

20. Jean could save a lot of time .... (wenn sie ein Moped hätte)
21. This is the boy .... (mit dem ich zur Schule ging)
22. If Bruce sets off at once, ... (erreicht er das Flugzeug noch)
23. We'll unload the car .... (sobald Bob eingetroffen ist)
24. This exhibition is a 'must' .... (auch wenn du nicht viel Geld hast)
25. If Mr Dawson hadn't sold his car, ... (müßte er jetzt nicht zu Fuß gehen)
26. After the tiring trip we had a swim in the Clarks' swimming-pool, ... (was den Kindern großen Spaß machte)
27. We asked him .... (wohin er fahren wolle)
28. This is all .... (was im Augenblick getan werden kann)
29. We spent all our money on food .... (da wir großen Hunger hatten)

D Spot the mistakes.

There is one mistake in each of the following sentences. Spot the mistakes and write down what you think is the correct version.

30. What would you do if somebody would give you a sports car?
31. Why don't we invite the people which have moved in next door?
32. Since the Coopers have been in Spain, they didn't hear about the terrible accident in Bond Street.
33. If Jerry hadn't forgotten his map, they had reached their destination in time.
34. We can wait at the entrance till you'll come back.
35. So this was the famous sight about that we had heard so much in the past!
36. Mrs Bloom went to a restaurant while it was too late to buy something to cook herself.
37. All what I know is that old Peter Duke is not guilty.
38. Please tell Miss Bews that if she should decide to sell her piano I take it.
39. We were able to make photocopies, what saved a lot of time.

"If you only knew what it cost!"

Key

A

1. If you visit ... you'**ll** certainly **want** to see ... . § 232 a
2. ... if I **was** ten years older. .... § 233
3. If there hadn't been ..., people **wouldn't have saved** ... . § 234
4. ... if the office **isn't** open. .... § 232 a
5. If the weather is bad, I **go** ... . § 232 c
6. I would apply ... if I **were** you. .... § 233
7. If John **hasn't bought** ... . § 232 a
8. We might have arrived ... if the bus **hadn't had** ... . § 234
9. ... always gets upset if people **don't like** ... . § 232 c
10. ... if she **should call,** ... I **am having** a bath. .... § 232 b

B

11. ... boy **whose** bike was stolen ... ? .... § 238 e
12. **Since/As (Because)** Raymond didn't like ... . § 245
13. Is there anything **that** ... ? .... § 238 b
14. ... **however** late it may be. .... § 246
15. Jane came to see me on Sunday, **which** was ... . § 237
16. ... the people **who/that** have moved in ... . § 238 b
17. I always take my dog with me **wherever/when/if** I go. § 244
18. Don't forget the book **(that/which)** you ... . §§ 239; 238 c
19. My boss thinks ... **whereas/while (but)** I think ... . .. §§ 246

C

20. Jean could save ... **if she had a moped**. .... § 233
21. ... the boy **(who/that) I went to school with/(with whom I went to school)**. .... §§ 239; 238 d
22. If Bruce sets off ... , **he'll still catch the plane**. ...... § 232 a
23. We'll unload ... **as soon as Bob arrives**. .... §§ 243; [129]
24. ... **even if you haven't got/don't have much money**. ... § 246
25. If Mr Dawson hadn't sold ... **he wouldn't have to walk now**. .... § 234
26. ... we had a swim ... , **which was great fun for the children**. .... § 237
27. We asked him **where he wanted to go (to)**. .... § 244
28. ... all **that can be done at the moment**. .... § 238 b
29. **as/since (because) we were very hungry**. .... § 245

D

30. ... if somebody **gave** you ... ? .... § 233
31. ... the people **who/that** ... ? .... § 238 b
32. Since the Coopers **were** ... ./... they **haven't heard** ... . §§ 245; [146]; [139]
33. ... they **would have reached** ... . § 234
34. ... till you **come** back. .... §§ 243; [129]
35. ... sight **(that/which)** we had heard so much **about/ about which** we had heard so much. .... §§ 239; 238 d
36. ... **because** it was too late ... . § 245
37. All **(that)** I know ... . § 238 b
38. ... **I'll** take it. .... § 232 b
39. ... **which** saved ... . § 237

Exercise finder

Test yourself	ENGLISH G Grammatik	Exercises
1, 4, 7, 22	§ 232 a	1, 2, 8
2, 6, 20, 30	§ 233	3, 4, 8
3, 8, 25, 33	§ 234	5, •6, 7, 8
5, 9	§ 232 c	2
10, 38	§ 232 b	2, 8
11	§ 238 e	10, 11
12, 29, 32, 36	§ 245	14
13, 16, 28, 31, 37	§ 238 b	9, 10, 11, 12
14, 19, 24	§ 246	14
15, 26, 39	§ 237	11
17, 27	§ 244	14
18	§ 238 c	10, 11, 12
18, 21, 35	§ 239	12, •13
21, 35	§ 238 d	11, 12, •13
23, 34	§ 243	14
23, 34	§ 129	**5** : •11, 12
32	§ 146	**5** : 3, 4, 5, 6, 7, 8, •9, 10, •14
	§ 139	**5** : 2, 4, 5, 6, 7, 10, •14
34	§ 129	**5** : •14

Exercises

If-clauses

1 Read the text, then complete the sentences that follow it. Put in the verbs given in brackets, using the simple present, present progressive, present perfect or "will" + infinitive.

Last month the Government announced plans to build a new prison for 600 men on the outskirts of the village of Arnsley, about a mile from the villages of Gunning Newell and Piddington. When they heard the news, a lot of local people were angry.

"It's dangerous to put a prison so close to a village with so many children," said Mrs Cheryl Blackthorn. "We'll be frightened to let the kids play outside. They like to play in the woods, and they can do that now, because it's safe. But what about the future?"

Another mother, Mrs Maisie Bell, agreed. "This is an attractive village now and old people like to retire here. But places with prisons often have bad reputations, don't they? Old people looking for a quiet place to retire to won't want to come and live next to a prison. And that will definitely bring down the value of our houses."

"I don't expect we can do anything to prevent it. They seem to have made up their minds. But I'm going to protest," Mrs Florrie Taylor said. "The officials probably think this is a quiet area, but I'm going to make a lot of noise. There's a prison in Grendon Underwood already, we don't want to have two in the neighbourhood."

However, Mrs Betty Walker disagreed. "Personally, I'm glad to see they've decided to use that piece of land at last. I can't understand why other people around here aren't equally delighted."

Mr Martin Chapman agreed. "They've got to put the prison somewhere, so why not here? We've got plenty of space around here, so I'm all for it. It'll make work for local people."

1. If they go ahead and build a prison in Arnsley in 1987, a lot of local people ... very upset. (go ahead; be)
2. "If we ... a prison so close to the village, the children ... play in safety." (have; not be able to)
3. "People ... come and live here if they ... that there's a prison here." (not want to; find out)
4. "People ... houses here if they ... a quiet place to retire to." (not buy; look for)
5. "If the number of people wanting to buy houses here ..., anyone wanting to move home ... sell their homes very cheaply." (go down; have to)
6. "If the officials ... their minds, which seems to be the case, we ... do anything to stop them." (make up; not be able to)
7. "If they ... our village because they think nobody will complain, we ... surprise them by making a lot of noise!" (choose; have to)
8. "We ... two prisons in the neighbourhood if they ... their plans, because there's already one in Grendon Underwood." (have; not change)
9. "If they ... to do something useful with that piece of land at last, everybody ... delighted." (decide; be)
10. "I welcome the idea. If they ... the prison here, it ... work for the local people." (put; provide)

§ 232 a

2 Complete the translations, using the verbs in brackets.

1. Wenn unsere Preise weiter steigen, kaufen unsere Kunden billigere Produkte aus dem Ausland.
   If our ... go up, our ... products from abroad. (continue; buy)
2. Wenn du jetzt gerade beim Briefschreiben bist, komme ich nachher wieder.
   If ... a letter, I ... later. (write; come back)
3. Wenn die Lebenshaltungskosten steigen, steigen normalerweise auch die Löhne.
   If the cost ..., wages ..., too. (go up; go up)
4. Du brauchst keinen Paß, wenn du einen Staat innerhalb der EG besuchst, ein Ausweis genügt.
   You ... if you ... within the EEC, an identity card ... good enough. (not need; visit; be)
5. Ich rufe dich sofort an, falls ich die Stelle bekommen sollte.
   I ... if ... the job. (ring up; get)
6. Wenn du dein Visum noch nicht beantragt hast, solltest du es jetzt tun.
   If you ... your visa yet, ... (not apply for; do)

§ 232 a/b/c

3 After an extremely dry summer there weren't so many vegetables on the market as usual and the price of tomatoes, potatoes, etc. began to go up. A reporter asked some shoppers how this might affect them. Complete the translation of the shoppers' replies.

1. *Mr Lear:* „Ich esse Tomaten für mein Leben gerne. Ich würde sie weiterhin kaufen, auch wenn sie £1 pro Pfund kosten würden."
   Mr Lear: "I love tomatoes. I ... even if ... £1 a pound." (continue + buy; cost)
2. *Mrs Maple:* „Ich müßte einfach aufhören, Tomaten zu kaufen, wenn die Preise zu hoch stiegen."
   Mrs Maple: "I ... just ... if ... too much." (have to + stop + buy; go up)
3. *Mrs Brownshill:* „Ich könnte auf Kartoffeln nicht verzichten. Mein Ehemann würde meckern, wenn er keine kriegte."
   Mrs Brownshill: "I couldn't manage without potatoes. My husband ... if ... any." (complain; not get)
4. *Mrs Brown:* „Wenn sie zu teuer würden, würde ich vielleicht weniger kaufen."
   Mrs Brown: "If ... less." (become; may + buy)
5. *Mrs Pyle:* „Wenn man mich auffordern würde, für einen Salatkopf 40p zu zahlen, würde ich mich weigern."
   Mrs Pyle: "If I ... 40p for a lettuce, I ... ." (be asked + pay; refuse)
6. *Mr Lock:* „Wenn Salat pro Kopf mehr als 30p kosten würde, würde ich keinen mehr kaufen."
   Mr Lock: "If lettuces ... 30p each, I ... ." (cost; stop + buy)
7. *Mrs MacGregor:* „Wenn ich Salat brauchte, um zum Beispiel einen gemischten Salat zu machen, würde ich jeden Preis bezahlen, den sie verlangten."
   Mrs MacGregor: "If I ..., say for a salad, I ... whatever price ... ." (need; pay; ask)

§ 233

4 Instead of the answer given, make a new answer using "if" with the simple past.

Example: Are you going to watch the French film on TV tonight? – No, it's on too late.
I'd watch it (I might watch it) if it wasn't on so late.

1. Are you going to Miriam's party? – I'd like to, but I don't know any of the other people she's invited.
   Well, I'd go if ... .
2. Can you lend me £5? – I'd like to, but I can't.
   Well, I ... if ... .
3. Any chance of a lift home in your car? – I'm sorry, but I haven't come in my car tonight. No problem otherwise, of course.
4. How about coming to the West Indies with Nancy and me next year? – What a super idea! But I can't afford it, I'm afraid.
5. Will Genevieve pass her exam? – Well, she's clever enough, but she isn't working hard enough at the moment.
6. Will Christopher pass his driving test? – I can't be sure. The thing is, you see, he's a very nervous sort of person.
7. Are you really thinking of leaving the firm? – I'm not sure. It depends partly on whether they offer me higher wages.
8. Are you and Maria going to get married. – Well, I've asked her twice, but she hasn't said "yes" yet.

§ 233

5 Express the sentences in a different way, using if-clauses with the past perfect. If you can see two possibilities, write them both down.

Example: Alex is usually willing to help. But you didn't ask him.
Alex would probably have helped if you'd asked him.
If you'd asked Alex, he might have helped.

1. I've been so busy recently. That's why I haven't written to you before this.
2. Mr Fowler didn't realize how wet the roads were. That's why the accident happened.
3. Diana can't go to the concert. She got to the box-office too late. There were no more tickets.
4. When Carol and Wayne got to the tennis court, it suddenly started to rain. So they went to the cinema instead.
5. When the Conservatives won the election in 1979, Mrs Margaret Thatcher became Britain's first female Prime Minister.
6. Wayne walked home last night, because he missed the last bus.
7. The management didn't give the workers the full facts. Perhaps that's why the strike wasn't prevented.
8. Jane almost got the job she applied for. But one of the directors thought it was a job for a man.
9. Victoria didn't try very hard. Perhaps that's the reason she lost the match.
10. Mrs Davies liked the shoes, but the shop didn't have her size. So she didn't buy a pair.

§ 234

•6 Finish the sentences about the text, using "if" with the past perfect.

In May 1983 Christine Hines saw a programme on TV about Tom Sneva, the American racing driver. She hadn't heard of Sneva before, but the next day she was able to impress her boy-friend with her new knowledge.

"It's an amazing story, Marty," she told him. "In 1975 he was really lucky. He managed to escape death when his car crashed during the famous race at Indianapolis."

"The Indianapolis 500?"

"That's right. The car was on fire as it flew through the air and broke into pieces."

"It sounds awful," Marty said.

"It was," Christine agreed, "and it changed his life. After the accident he started to work for an organization teaching ordinary car drivers how to drive more safely. And religion became more important to him, too. But he didn't lose his interest in racing. In fact, in 1977 he took part in the 'Indy 500' again and came second."

"Who won?" Marty asked.

"A man called A.J.Foyt. Sneva drove a really fast race, but he didn't drive fast enough to overtake Foyt, who drove the 500 miles in a new record time of 3 hours 5 minutes and 59 seconds."

"And you always say you can never remember figures!"

"I can't usually," Christine admitted, "but I wrote this down, because I was so impressed. That's three hours of driving at an average speed of almost 260 kilometres per hour. I worked it out."

"Why did they show the film about Sneva last night? Any special reason?"

"Well, yes. It was really a film about this year's race, you see, the 1983 Indy 500, which Sneva has just won."

"Did they say anything about his car?"

"Yes, it was a March, I think."

"Oh, I know somebody who worked for March a few years ago. They're designed and built in England, you know."

"No, I didn't know that. I don't think they mentioned that in the film. But they said how much his prize money was. 350,000 dollars."

"I don't believe it!" Marty said. "For winning one race?"

"The Indy 500 isn't just any ordinary race," Christine said.

1. Christine ...wouldn't have known... anything about Tom Sneva ... a programme about him on TV. (not know; not see)
2. If she ... the film, ... with her knowledge. (not see; not be able to + impress)
3. Sneva ... death in 1975 ... lucky. (not escape; not be)
4. If Sneva's car ... the air, ... into pieces. (not fly; not break)
5. Sneva ... for an organization teaching ordinary car drivers how to drive more safely ... during the big race – and religion ... more important to him, either. (not start + work; not crash; not become)
6. If he ... in racing, ... the Indy 500 in 1977. (lose; not take part in)
7. Sneva ... Foyt in 1977 ... just a little faster. (may + overtake; drive)
8. If Sneva ... Foyt in that race ... the Indy 500 in a new record time. (manage + overtake; win)
9. Christine ... the average speed ... . (not know; not work out)
10. They ... the film that night ... the 1983 race. (not show; not win)

§ 234

7 Finish the translations.

1. Wenn das Pfund gegenüber dem Dollar stark geblieben wäre, hätte die kleine Export-Firma letztes Jahr viel verdient.
   If ... strong against the dollar, the little export company ... last year.
2. Die Firma hätte keine Arbeiter entlassen, wenn sie einen Gewinn erzielt hätte.
   ... a profit.
3. Barbara wäre nicht entlassen worden, wenn die Firma nicht in Schwierigkeiten gekommen wäre.
   Barbara ... into trouble.
4. Wenn sie ihren Arbeitsplatz nicht verloren hätte, hätte sie sich nicht so schlecht gefühlt.
   If she ... her job, she ... bad.
5. Wenn Barbara sich nicht so schlecht gefühlt hätte, hätte sie besser auf den Verkehr aufgepaßt.
   If ..., ... more attention to the traffic.
6. Hätte sie auf den Verkehr aufgepaßt, so hätte sie keinen Unfall verursacht.
   If she ... to the traffic, ... an accident.
7. Wenn sie keinen Unfall verursacht hätte, wäre sie nicht zu spät zum Interview erschienen.
   If ... for the interview.
8. Sie hätte möglicherweise eine neue Stelle bekommen, wenn sie nicht zu spät zum Interview erschienen wäre.
   She ... a new job ... . § 234

8 The results of the British general election in 1983:

Party	Total vote	% of votes	Number of MPs	% of MPs
Conservative	13,100,782	42.4	397	61.1
Labour	8,456,504	27.6	209	32.2
Liberal	4,211,007	13.7	17	2.6
SDP	3,570,757	11.6	6	0.9
Scottish Nationalists	331,975	1.1	2	0.3
Welsh Nationalists	125,309	0.4	2	0.3
Others	935,932	3.0	17	2.6

Now put the verbs in the right tense.

After the election Roy Steele, who is a member of one of the smaller parties, talked to his local MP about the results. "In Germany," he said, "they use a system of proportional representation (= Verhältniswahlrecht). Shall I tell you what ..would have happened.. if an election in Germany ... (1. end) like this, with these results?"

"If this election ... (2. take place) in Germany," he explained, "the Conservatives ... (3. not be able to) form a strong government. If they ... (4. win) only 42.4 % of the votes, they'd have only had about 42.4 % of the MPs, i.e. 276 – not 397. If a party had got 27.6 % of the votes, like the Labour Party, only about 179 of their candidates ... (5. become) MPs, not 209. And look at the Liberals. Under the German system they ... (6. be given) about 13.7 % of the seats in Parliament, i.e. 89 – not just 17 – if they'd won 13.7 % of the country's votes."

"I think we ought to change our system in future," Roy went on. "If we did that, the smaller parties ... (7. win) more seats, which ... (8. be) fairer."

Roy's MP, who is a member of one of the two big parties, said, "I don't really want to change things. But, if a lot more people should tell me they share your views, Mr Steele, I ... (9. think about) the question again, of course."

"Well, if I ... (10. be) the Prime Minister," Roy said, "I ... (11. introduce) proportional representation before the next election. Then, if the new voting figures at the next election ... (12. be) similar to the 1983 results, it ... (13. be) impossible for one party to form the government on its own. You see, if no party ... (14. have) over 50% of the MPs, there ... (15. have to) be a coalition between two or more parties – as in Germany or in Italy – which I am sure ... (16. be) better for the country.

§§ 232 a/b; 233; 234

Defining relative clauses

9 Give a short definition of each of the following words, putting in a noun or pronoun followed by a relative clause introduced by "who", "that" or "which".

Example: a filling station:
...*A filling station is a place that (which) sells petrol*....

1.	a ferry	6.	customs duty	11.	a link	16.	a musician
2.	a foreigner	7.	a cheerleader	12.	a trade union	17.	beef
3.	apartheid	8.	a deaf person	13.	a target	18.	a hairdresser
4.	a commuter	9.	a limerick	14.	a pension	19.	a cheque
5.	a Greyhound	10.	a lecturer	15.	rent	20.	a pessimist

§ 238 b

10 Finish the replies, so that each comment consists of a main clause followed by a relative clause introduced by "that" or "whose".

Example: Charles won't marry Judy, you know. He can't stand her parents.
– No, I wouldn't marry a ...*woman whose parents I*......
...*couldn't stand*... (whose)

1. Nobody has given more support to our association than Dieter. – I agree, I can't think of ... greater than his. (whose)
2. Here are the documents. You said you wanted to see them. – No, no. These aren't ... to see. (that)
3. Liz won't marry Humphrey. His likes and dislikes aren't at all similar to hers. – I can understand her point of view. I mean, honestly, it doesn't make much sense ... . (whose)
4. Why is the speaker whispering? Why doesn't he speak up? – It isn't his fault, Uncle Bob. It's the microphone ... properly. (that)
5. Here's the list of guests to be invited. Have I left anybody out? – Let me see. Yes, I can think of at least ... forgotten. (whose)
6. I'd like to buy a colour TV for my caravan, to be used both in England and abroad. – I see, sir. In other words, you want a ... programmes transmitted by both the PAL and the SECAM systems? (that)

§ 238 b/c/e

11 Put in a suitable relative pronoun. In some cases more than one answer is possible. Write down all the answers you think are possible.

These days most boats and planes carry a special piece of radio equipment . . . (1) can be used in an emergency. Called a radio beacon, this equipment can transmit a "bleep" or SOS signal . . . (2) can be received many miles away. In fact, such signals can even be received by some of the powerful new satellites . . . (3) are in orbit around the Earth, . . . (4) has led the U.S. and Soviet governments to agree to co-ordinate any information . . . (5) comes to them in such cases.

Before the introduction of this latest generation of satellites, it wasn't possible for the traditional emergency services to be sure of the exact position from . . . (6) a "bleep" was coming. All . . . (7) they were able to say for sure was that it was coming from an area with a 500-kilometre radius. This was an enormous area (over 700,000 km^2) within . . . (8) to search for a plane . . . (9) had crashed or a ship . . . (10) was sinking, particularly if the radio beacon stopped signalling after a short time, . . . (11) meant that help often came too late.

According to an expert . . . (12) works for NASA, somebody . . . (13) is in a plane crash has got a 50 % chance of being saved from death if help arrives within 8 hours – but only a 10 % chance if help arrives after 48 hours. This is why the new "ear-in-the-sky" satellites are so useful. By defining the position of the damaged plane or ship within an area of about 300 km^2, they reduce the time taken by the search enormously, . . . (14) improves the chances of a successful operation.

NASA's Goddard Space Flight Centre in Greenbelt, Md, has been developing new equipment with the help of the Canadians and the French, and their first ear-in-the-sky was on board a weather satellite . . . (15) was launched in 1983. However, it's the Soviet COSPAS satellites . . . (16) have been in the news headlines most often, particularly the two specially designed satellites . . . (17) can transmit messages to stations on the ground in the U.S.A., Canada and France. Within seven months of their launching in 1982 they had already been responsible for sending life-saving help to the scene of 28 separate emergencies.

In September 1982, for example, during a snowstorm, there was nothing . . . (18) the Canadian pilot of a light aircraft could do to prevent his plane from crashing in a wild mountain area of northern British Columbia. All three men . . . (19) had been on board were injured, but they needn't have worried. They were spotted by a satellite . . . (20) was orbiting 600 miles above them. It heard the emergency signal . . . (21) they were transmitting and quickly sent a message to Earth via an antenna near Ottawa. Within hours the three injured men had been found.

A funnier – though in some ways perhaps more worrying – event took place in the middle of a Wednesday night in June 1983, when a COSPAS satellite picked up an emergency "bleep" . . . (22) seemed to be coming from the River Clyde in Scotland. After a five-hour operation . . . (23) had involved the local police, an RAF helicopter, several ships on the Clyde and the nuclear submarine centre at Faslane, Mrs Marilyn Brown und her husband were woken up by a number of police and RAF officers at the door of their home. It was about 6 am.

Mrs Brown told them that she and her husband owned a small fishing-boat . . . (24) was being repaired. They'd been afraid to leave anything . . . (25) was valuable on board, so they'd brought almost everything . . . (26) had been on the boat into their house. Among the items was an emergency beacon. This had been switched off and put on the top of a wardrobe in their spare bedroom.

How on earth were they to know that the beacon on their wardrobe had gone wrong – in spite of being switched off – was sending signals ... (27) were being received in space? “We're terribly sorry about all the trouble,” Mrs Brown stressed, “but at least we've now seen how well the system works, ... (28) is good to know.”

A few days later the police published a statement in ... (29) a man called Brown was accused of stealing a radio beacon from a North Sea oil-rig on ... (30) he had once been employed.

§§ 237; 238 b/c/d/e

12 It will soon be the birthdays of twelve of Mrs Barrington's relatives, and she's asked them what presents they'd each like to be given. Can you finish the sentences, putting in the following items linked by either “he/she” or “that”?

a pair of gloves		can receive all the new channels.
a machine		will keep his hands warm in winter.
some spices		can wear when she appears in court.
a racket		is powerful enough to let him study Neptune.
a sleeping-bag		can beat all his opponents with.
a record	she/he/that	will answer the phone automatically.
a telescope		could put in to try and make it fly.
a TV set		heard on the radio recently.
an engine		has never tried in a recipe before.
a map		is small enough to fit in her rucksack.
an algebra book		shows details of the waters around Corsica.
some clothes		read about in an educational magazine.

Put in the right present for each of Mrs Barrington's relatives.

1. Her father, who's over 70 now, hopes to get ...a pair of gloves that... .
2. Her mother, who loves cooking, hopes to be given ... .
3. Her husband, who runs a small business from home, hopes to get ... .
4. Her son, whose hobby is space, would like ... .
5. Her daughter, who's just become a lawyer, would love to have ... .
6. Her aunt, who's a maths lecturer at Birmingham University, would be delighted if she got ... .
7. Her uncle, who keeps a small yacht in the south of France, wouldn't mind getting ... .
8. Her cousin Betsy, who's planning a camping holiday in Scotland next summer, would like ... .
9. Her sister, who's handicapped and is fairly dependent on home entertainment, hopes to be given a contribution towards ... .
10. Her brother, whose favourite sport is tennis, would like ... .
11. Her sister-in-law, who loves pop music, would be grateful for ... .
12. Her brother-in-law, Marcus, who's just spent six months building a model plane, would like to get ... .

§§ 238 b/c/d; 239

•13 Contact clauses

Make a comment, using a contact clause and putting in "not ... either" or "too".

Example: Monica doesn't like working for the new personnel manager. She says it's impossible to discuss things with him.
– I can understand how she feels. I mean, I wouldn't like working for a boss I couldn't discuss things with, either.

1. Mrs Finch doesn't want to share an office with Mr Jenkins. She says she just can't get along with him.
– I can understand her point of view. I wouldn't ... .
2. Fred finds it hard to get over the loss of his dog. He really loved it, you know.
– Yes, well, I'm sure I ..., too.
3. Listen, Linda won't support what's been planned. She says she just isn't in favour of the plan.
– Well, you know, to be honest, I ... .
4. Helen will be really sorry she can't go on the trip. She's been looking forward to it.
– Of course. I can understand that. Believe me, I ... .
5. The boss intends to buy our raw materials from a different source. He says you just can't depend on Hutchings & Brown.
– You can't blame him. After all, I wouldn't ..., would you?
6. Frank is going to turn down that work he's been offered. He doesn't think he can cope with it.
– It's only sensible. I mean, I ... .

§§ 238 d; 239

14 Adverbial clauses

Choose the correct form for each gap in the text. If you think two of the forms are equally possible, write them both down.

Dear Helmut,

I'm really looking forward to your visit next month and can hardly wait till you ... (1. 'll get/get/'re getting) here. I'll save most of my news till then. But I must answer your question about the new public telephones that have just been introduced here. I'm convinced you'll be as impressed as I am when you ... (2. 'll see/'re seeing/see) them.
Things are changing. You won't need to look for the right coins when you ... (3. use/'ll use/'re using) one of Britain's public boxes in future. In fact, you won't need any coins at all, ... (4. before/since/while) the latest machines – called Cardphones – only accept plastic cards, which look rather like credit cards, they don't accept coins. The telephone company, British Telecom, expects them to be a big success. Obviously, foreign tourists will find it easy to make international calls

. . . (5. as/as if/even if) they . . . (6. 'll be/'re being/'re) unwilling to walk around with their pockets full of coins. What's more, . . . (7. though/since/because) the special plastic cards are made using a new high-technology "holographic" technique, based on special patterns of light, it won't be easy for crooks to make their own versions of the cards and cheat the system . . . (8. even if/though/however) hard they might try.

Let me try and describe what happens when you use a Cardphone. At the moment there are two cards you can buy, . . . (9. while/because/though) they're both exactly the same size. One costs £2 and is worth 40 units (= Telefoneinheiten). The other is worth 200 units and costs £10. . . . (10. As/While/Since) you won't have a card of your own when you . . . (11. 'll arrive/'re arriving/arrive), I'll lend you my card for your first phone call home.

As soon as you . . . (12. 'll be/'re/'ll come) in the phone box, you'll see a narrow hole at the bottom of the Cardphone. As it's rather like the hole you put a multi-journey ticket into when you travel by bus or Underground in Germany, you . . . (13. 'll feel/'re feeling/feel) at home with it at once! Well, as soon as you . . . (14. 'll push/'ve pushed/'ll have pushed) my card into this hole, you'll see a number between 0 and 200 in a little "window" near the top of the machine. That will tell you how much my card is still worth, i.e. how many units I haven't used . . . (15. as/because/since) I bought the card.

Right, well, as soon as you . . . (16. 'll do/'ve done/'re doing) that, you'll be able to dial home. But again you'll find it a bit different from the phones you used . . . (17. as/when/since) you last visited me. For example, you'll be able to speak to your parents as soon as your call . . . (18. is/has been/will be) put through to them. You won't have to wait until you . . . (19. 'll hear/hear/'re hearing) a series of rapid pips – the old "pay tone", if you remember.

When your call . . . (20. will be/has/is) ended, you'll be able to take the card out of the hole again. If you want to buy your own card to use . . . (21. as/while/because) you're here, you'll be able to obtain one . . . (22. whoever/wherever/whereas) you see the Cardphone sign, e.g. at post offices, newspaper shops, stations and airports.

It's simple, isn't it? Even if your parents would probably prefer to get a picture postcard instead!

Best wishes,

David

§§ 243; 244; 245; 246